Decluttering

D1091997

by Jane Stoller

for dummies®
A Wiley Brand

Decluttering For Dummies®

Published by: **John Wiley & Sons, Inc.,** 111 River Street, Hoboken, NJ 07030-5774, www.wiley.com

Copyright © 2020 by John Wiley & Sons, Inc., Hoboken, New Jersey

Published simultaneously in Canada

For general information on our other products and services, please contact our Customer Care Department within the U.S. at 877-762-2974, outside the U.S. at 317-572-3993, or fax 317-572-4002. For technical support, please visit https://hub.wiley.com/community/support/dummies.

Wiley publishes in a variety of print and electronic formats and by print-on-demand. Some material included with standard print versions of this book may not be included in e-books or in print-on-demand. If this book refers to media such as a CD or DVD that is not included in the version you purchased, you may download this material at http://booksupport.wiley.com. For more information about Wiley products, visit www.wiley.com.

Library of Congress Control Number: 2019952817

ISBN 978-1-119-61704-4 (pbk); ISBN 978-1-119-61708-2 (ebk); ISBN 978-1-119-61707-5 (ebk)

Manufactured in the United States of America

V10015977_120419

Contents at a Glance

Table of Contents

Introduction

I am passionate about helping people reach their goals and create the lives they dream of. From experience, I know that decluttering your entire life will help you achieve what you desire. I also know that decluttering is more than simply clearing your physical clutter, although this will definitely help you feel less stressed and more productive. Decluttering requires a complete shift in mindset to ensure that your entire life is in alignment with your goals. This means clearing not only physical "stuff" but also your mental and digital spaces.

Clutter comes in many forms, physical items being the most obvious, but mental and digital clutter also takes up valuable real estate in our brains and online life. This is why I focus on the entire decluttering approach and relate it to your goals. I get deep into the reasons why physical, mental, and digital decluttering is crucial to your success, especially in our increasingly distracted world.

My goal is to get you excited to start decluttering and continue decluttering. Your decluttering strategies will change as your life changes, and they are meant to be adapted. I want to motivate you by explaining the benefits of decluttering followed by practical tips on how to get started and stay decluttered. Often the hardest part is getting motivated to actually begin. I hope this book is the exact motivation you need to get started right now and change your life for the better.

About This Book

Using my passion to motivate you to start and stay decluttered, I have organized this book so that you can quickly reference the areas where you need decluttering help immediately. You can also read the entire book cover to cover to get decluttering motivation, discover more about the benefits of living clutter-free, or figure out where to start.

This book is organized into four main parts:

>> Decluttering your mind

>> Decluttering your home spaces

» Decluttering your workspace and digital life

» Getting helpful tips in the Part of Tens

I tried to be as comprehensive as possible, and the final part of the book includes anything that I may have missed. It also gives practical quick tips for places to bring your decluttered items, how to label your items, and how to organize what is left.

I encourage everyone to read Part 1, which is dedicated to decluttering your mind. I'm a firm believer that this is one of the most important aspects of decluttering, but is often overlooked. If your mind is cluttered, it will affect your entire life — including your health. This is why I put a big emphasis on it, making mental decluttering the first chapter. I put so much time and research into detailing the benefits of decluttering and the negative implications if you don't make this part of your routine.

Part 2 focuses on physical spaces in your home, from closets to kitchens to garages. For these chapters, you can use the sections that pertain to you. Read the entire chapters, or use them as a reference. Sometimes I also discuss categories that could be in a different spot in your home. For example, when decluttering the bedroom you may also need to refer to the closet chapter and storage for books if you have lots of these items in your bedroom.

Part 3 is focused on your workspace, which includes the very important digital decluttering, which today has become one of the biggest decluttering challenges. Because our digital items have storage limits, it's important to get clear on what you need and what you don't. If you make digital decluttering a habit, you won't have to deal with limited storage space on your phone or laptop. This section also includes photo decluttering, which has become one of the hottest decluttering topics due to the prevalence of photo-sharing apps, like Instagram and Facebook.

The final part, Part 4, gives you inspiration to keep up the good work of decluttering, practical ideas on where to actually take clutter, how to organize your remaining items, and of course, how to label items to prevent clutter buildup in the first place.

Foolish Assumptions

As I was writing this book, I made some assumptions about who would be reading it. This book is for you, if

>> You want to achieve your life goals.

>> You want more time and freedom in your life.

>> You want to be able to walk through your entire home and know where everything is without being frustrated looking for things.

>> You want a streamlined closet where you waste no time choosing clothes or searching for anything.

>> You want everything in your home to add value to your life, not just collect dust.

>> You want to be as efficient as possible in your home and work life.

>> You have more digital photos than you need and want to be able to create an organized system once and for all.

>> You want to give back to your community where you can.

>> You are very frustrated with your digital space and often run out of space or can't find files.

>> You want simple ideas to help you feel free of clutter in all areas of your life.

Icons Used in This Book

Throughout the book, I use a handful of icons to point out various types of information and highlight certain points. Here's what they are and what they mean:

AUTHOR SAYS

The Author Says icon is where perhaps I present lots of information beforehand, but I want to put my own spin on it. This is also where I bring up anything that is relevant to my technique or what I consider my signature advice.

REMEMBER

The Remember icon is like a little Post-it note, labeling anything in the book that's key to remember. After reading a chapter, I recommend that you go through it again and test yourself to see how well you remember this information.

TIP

The Tip icon indicates a quick way to remember important material or perform a task. Use these tips to help you save time and frustration.

WARNING

The Warning icon helps you steer around common mistakes. It also gives you a heads-up when a task may be extra challenging or there may be some sensitivity around it.

Beyond the Book

After reading this book cover to cover or taking excerpts of what you need, I recommend that you continue to use the strategies and tips to update and adapt your decluttering habits as your life changes.

Decluttering is not a one-time event; it must be a regular part of your life. I provide a useful Cheat Sheet online that can be your quick resource when you need decluttering motivation or are about to embark on a decluttering mission. This Cheat Sheet provides a few sections around what to ask yourself when decluttering, keeping it realistic, and condensing the most practical tips from the book into a few short bullet points to be your constant declutter reminder. To access this Cheat Sheet, go to www.dummies.com and search for "Decluttering For Dummies Cheat Sheet."

Where to Go from Here

This book is designed to start with Part 1, as I know that decluttering your mind is one of the most important aspects of decluttering, but often is often overlooked or even forgotten. If you're like me, you may want to start with "stuff" rather than your mind because it's easier to see a tangible result. In this case, you are free to jump to any chapter you want depending on your needs. I know that wherever you start in this book, you will find motivation and practical advice to start decluttering right away.

If you're not quite sure about decluttering yet, Chapter 1 gives a brief overview of the concepts and topics covered in the book. Plus, it will likely get you the most excited to start and give you ideas regarding which of the following chapters you want to read next.

On the other hand, if you feel like you are already living a minimalist life and declutter daily, you may want to review the sections about mental and digital decluttering first.

You may be ready to tackle a specific area of your home, and Part 2 includes most areas in most homes. If you can't find a specific area or category, don't worry, as many of the tips and processes for decluttering can actually be adapted easily from a garage to a linen closet to the bathroom. You will find that there is repetitive advice as the same strategies do apply, and if it gets too repetitive and you're well versed in the processes, you can skip to another section. After you implement a few decluttering strategies, you will notice that you now have more time and are automatically using these techniques.

This last piece of advice should be easy to follow: Don't read what you don't need. If you don't have a garage, then you likely won't need to read about garage decluttering. However, since the strategies and principles apply to many spaces, I would read the most relevant chapter for your current needs. Maybe one day you will have a garage, and then you can read that chapter!

When you make it to Part 4, you're ready to employ the techniques discovered and also deal with any remaining clutter tips, such as how to store what you have left. My goal is that you will have reduced stress and increased happiness.

Happy decluttering!

1

Decluttering Starts in Your Mind

Grasp the basics of decluttering, including a complete overview of the process, clutter styles, and the psychology behind decluttering.

Find out about relating decluttering to your goals and shifting your mindset.

Form a decluttering plan once and for all, including getting clutter under control and holding yourself and family accountable.

Chapter **1**

The Basics of Decluttering

The goal of this book isn't to simply inspire you to declutter one or more of your spaces or show you how to go about it. The goal of decluttering is to be able to live your life the way you want to live it by determining your goals, figuring out where there are blockages, and figuring out what's holding you back from achieving what you desire. Then you clear the clutter to help you create the life you deserve.

This book helps you identify which items in your home are truly clutter and what is taking up mental space unnecessarily, which is often overlooked. When you're always hunting for your keys that you lost (again) or searching for your favorite blouse, you will become stressed and distracted, which keeps you from making progress toward your goals. Clutter can be difficult to identify, which is likely why you picked up this book in the first place. Clutter can range from obvious trash to very expensive, large things. To make the issue even more complicated, clutter is different for every person. One person's clutter is another person's joy. Thus, decluttering needs to be an individual quest. Each person will have a different approach to decluttering depending on their lifestyle, and this book will help you determine a method that works for you. The first step is to determine your personal cluttering style.

Determining Your Current Cluttering Style

Decluttering doesn't mean you only need to keep one item of clothing or furniture, or that you have to commit to a minimalist lifestyle.

Some of us can easily declutter and get rid of everything we don't need immediately without giving it a second thought. But for most of us, decluttering is not that easy and goes much deeper into our emotional need for stuff due to our consumerist society. According to the *Huffington Post*, there are more storage facilities than McDonald's restaurants in America. At the end of 2014, there were 48,500 self-storage facilities in America compared to 14,350 McDonald's. This further proves that getting rid of items is so difficult for us that we'd rather pay to store them! People who have excessive clutter stashes can also become hoarders, and approximately 19 million Americans fall into this category. The American Psychiatric Association defines hoarders as people who "excessively save items that others may view as worthless. They have persistent difficulty parting with possessions, leading to clutter that disrupts their ability to use their living or work spaces."

I'm not saying that hoarding, which is considered a disease similar to OCD, is anything remotely close to being a clutterbug. I am using the term clutterbug to describe someone who lets clutter build up over time and hangs onto items for reasons that are more emotional than practical. However, holding onto clutter could eventually lead to hoarding, which is why you should take decluttering seriously and commit to it regularly. Whether you are detail-oriented or a big-picture thinker, you should know your clutter style like you know your blood type to gain a better understanding of yourself and how you can maximize your life.

Answer these questions honestly to start thinking about your clutter style:

>> Do you constantly hunt for things you've misplaced in your home?

>> Do you put things into stacks or piles?

>> When you look at your flat surfaces, such as your desk or kitchen counters, are their piles of things on them?

>> Do you end up buying a second or third item for use in your home because you can't find the one you already own?

>> Do you use shopping as retail therapy rather than shopping only when you really need something?

>> Do you not have room to put away some of the stuff you own?

>> Are there clothes lying on the floor?

>> When you reach for a pen, do you have 50 to choose from but sometimes end up with one that doesn't work?

>> Do you keep every single Christmas card you've been given?

>> Do you keep every plastic food container you accumulate but find that matching lids are missing when you need them?

>> Does your home make you feel stressed out because of all the stuff in there?

If you answered more than half the questions with a yes, you are most likely a clutterbug or on your way there. If you are feeling overwhelmed by clutter right now and you answered yes to several of the preceding questions, you may have some habits that are causing you to head down a self-sabotaging path. Houses with too much stuff in them can be physically, emotionally, and spiritually draining, and that takes away your peace of mind and joy of heart. Don't worry; there's always room for improvement. The first step is recognizing that a problem exists in order to take steps to create your best, decluttered life.

REMEMBER

Don't get discouraged or angry with yourself for your clutter habits — life can be busy and hectic. Setting up a decluttering mindset takes work and dedication. You're not alone.

The next step is to tackle the mental and emotional aspects of being a clutterbug so you can begin to create and maintain new habits that will help you experience clutter-free joy.

There are several different types of so-called clutterbugs. You may fall into one category, all categories, or none of them, and that's okay. I added the clutterbug types in hopes that you may see yourself in the different categories and begin to envision a plan of how you can overcome your own barriers to decluttering. These visions will help move you forward on your quest to declutter.

WARNING

Whatever your clutter personality, many people say, "I will deal with this tomorrow, next week, next month, next year," and we see how this pattern can escalate. No matter what type of clutterbug your personality reveals, you cannot put off decluttering any longer. If you defer this task, it only gets bigger, making you even less likely to deal with it. From paper to tech gadgets to piles of clothing, the task will only get bigger daily. I often also say that people who defer this task are also the ones who end up being the most stressed about clutter.

The emotional clutterbug

The *emotional clutterbug* is the most common type and is characterized by emotional attachment to items that have sentimental value. The emotional clutterbug prioritizes feelings over practicality. It's difficult for this clutterbug to get rid of things, and she often purchases items to fill a void or out of pure boredom.

This clutterbug may also be someone who saves sentimental items due to the powerful emotions they evoke. Most people have sentimental items, and that's okay! They bring joy and serve as reminders of happy memories. You don't need to get rid of all your sentimental items; however, you have to set a limit. If you don't have a limit on sentimental items, it's easy for the amount to get out of control, causing clutter in your mental and physical space.

Here are a few strategies to help get you started dealing with sentimental items:

>> **Commit to regularly evaluating your sentimental items.** If you own a box of concert shirts that are tucked away but you never look at them, why keep them? After committing to regularly evaluate your sentimental items, you may be ready to part with them.

>> **Repurpose sentimental items.** For example, you can frame your favorite concert shirts to make them visible all the time, and then you can discard the rest. Doing so can bring you more joy and less clutter. Plus, having your favorite items on display can help bring more positivity into your life.

>> **Keep only a small dedicated space for sentimental items.** Have a space in your home that is precious real estate and dedicate this space to your sentimental items. This will help you be more conscious of what resides there.

>> **Envision the joy of being able to actually enjoy the true sentimental items you do keep.** When you surround yourself with items that bring you joy and positivity, they are no longer clutter. Ensure that you can make use of every item and get rid of the rest. Trust me, you'll feel so much lighter once you know that every item you own has a purpose — even if that purpose is simply to bring you happiness!

I discuss emotional attachment to stuff in most chapters of this book, so you can get ideas on how to handle sentimental items associated with the chapters in which they're addressed. What's important is that you set limits because you want to be able to enjoy your sentimental items, and finding them quickly is key for that. Keep them in a labeled box (see Figure 1-1) or on display so they can be viewed, not stored away in an attic where you will forget about them.

The just-in-case clutterbug

Just-in-case clutterbugs keep things they may need "someday" or to ensure they have them "just in case." This clutterbug is the type of person who keeps the box a microwave came in just in case he has to return it in ten years. Whether the item is a blouse, a kitchen utensil, or an extra lawn mower, this clutterbug operates from a scarcity mindset and a lack of trust or awareness around items he already has.

Image courtesy of author (photo credit: @avalonmohns)

**AUTHOR
SAYS**

I know many of us fall into this category, and I definitely do. I used to save every button from every skirt, jacket, and blouse just in case I needed it, when in reality I had a button jar so big it mimicked an old-school cookie jar. Plus, I take everything that needs work done to the tailor, and tailors have buttons. This example may seem trivial; you may think, "How can buttons become stressful clutter?" The truth is that clutter is not restricted to size, value, or even whether or not it's tangible. Clutter is defined by anything you own in excess that is no longer practical. Keep this in mind throughout the book and remember not to get discouraged — my goal is to make you excited to declutter. The benefits of decluttering outweigh putting it off any longer.

The "I'm not a clutterbug" clutterbug

We've all been in denial at some point of our lives, and the *"I'm not a clutterbug" clutterbug* is familiar with this feeling. This person may be stressed and overwhelmed but has difficulty determining the cause, even though on some level she knows she has too much stuff. This causes the clutterbug to accumulate even more clutter because she isn't even conscious of her actions. Many people who aren't aware that they're a clutterbug carry subconscious stress and don't know where their anxiety is stemming from. I've seen many people become less stressed and anxious once they admit that they own too much because they can then create actionable steps toward a decluttered and happier life.

Maybe you secretly know you're a clutterbug but don't want to admit it because you are a perfectionist, and you plan to spend the entire next month organizing and decluttering perfectly. Perfectionists can be perfect at some types of jobs and tasks, but they usually have an all-or-nothing philosophy. If you're one of them, be careful — you may never be able to get started because the task is so overwhelming. You don't need to be 100 percent decluttered instantly, and I know for a perfectionist that may be hard to hear. Take the pressure off and start small. Remember that progress is better than perfection.

The "I'll do it later" clutterbug

Along the same lines as denial, the *"I'll do it later"* clutterbug procrastinates decluttering. It's easy to do because often we don't equate decluttering to being fun. I find this clutterbug to be one of the most common types. Luckily, the techniques in this book can not only motivate you to get started but also show you practical solutions on how to go about it.

Constantly putting off decluttering results in the clutter becoming too overwhelming to deal with, and that's why you probably haven't started or just say, "I'll do it later."

Let's face it: We are all very busy and only have a certain amount of time and energy to spend each day. Starting the decluttering process can be emotionally challenging, which makes it even harder to find the time to start. I recommend choosing to spend just 10 to 15 minutes per day decluttering, as this will bring you one step closer to getting things done. Remember that freeing up clutter frees up more time in the long run, since you'll no longer waste time taking care of things that you don't use or looking for things that are buried among clutter.

The "I can't decide" clutterbug

Here's a fun fact: We are actually wired to acquire clutter, which makes it even harder to decide what is clutter and what isn't! Our instincts say that we should store resources for times of scarcity. Have you ever watched a squirrel gather food for winter? This is exactly that mindset, and they're so focused on it that they don't even think about deciding what to keep. Couple this instinct with our insatiable need to consume and buy new things — because shopping splurges produce dopamine, giving us a happy rush — and it's even more difficult to decide what to declutter. You may often feel sad, stressed, or overwhelmed thinking about what to declutter, and it may feel easier to not decide altogether. However, the inability to decide can cause greater stress in the long run, and it's always best to get out of this mindset and create a plan.

The decision about what to toss can be stressful, and that's why it's a good idea to give yourself timelines and tricks to help minimize the painful decision process. For example, if you really can't decide on which frilly shirts to donate, turn the hangers the opposite way. If after a season you haven't worn them, make a commitment to get rid of these items. Or perhaps you don't have room for the books you have read but you want to remember them. You can take a photo instead and discard the physical book. Ideas like these can help make tough decisions that you may not make otherwise less stressful. There is always room for compromise and adaptability when it comes to decluttering, and it may take some trial and error to figure out what works for you.

The "techie" clutterbug

Techie clutterbugs have so many cables, cords, and tech gadgets they don't even know where to start decluttering, what works, or what goes with each device. This is not an uncommon type of clutterbug, and with today's fast-moving technological changes, it's easy to fall into this category. I am a victim of keeping my old phones just in case, even though they are so old they probably wouldn't even turn on. I also keep wires for that DSL modem plug-in just in case the Wi-Fi goes down, and that frayed charger just in case I lose the new one. We are so intimately connected to our tech gadgets that we naturally keep their accessories because we can't imagine not being able to operate without them.

Think of tech gadgets as the worst type of clutter to hold onto because with the speed of advancements, tech gadgets become useless faster than most other physical stuff. Plus, tech gadgets are more widely available, and new versions are always ready for sale. Just as with all types of clutter, there is no need to hold onto what is no longer practical. Pay attention to what you no longer use and have the courage to part with these items to create more physical and mental space in your life. Once you've sorted the gadgets you don't need any more from those you do use, organize the keepers in an easily accessible fashion, as shown in Figure 1-2.

The knowledge clutterbug

Today, limitless knowledge resources are at your fingertips, and what you keep for your knowledge database should be a decision you make based on practical and future reasons. For example, if you purchase the newest edition of a textbook, the previous version should be recycled. Start small if you fall into this category.

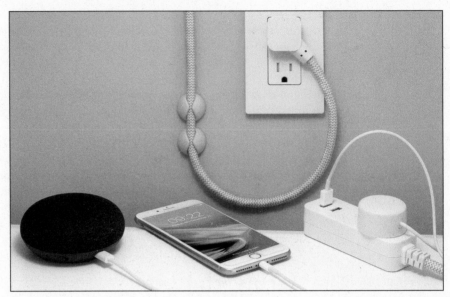

FIGURE 1-2:
Organized
tech cords.

Thomas Kolnowski / Unsplash

**AUTHOR
SAYS**

Knowledge is clutter until and unless it is properly organized in a way that makes that knowledge accessible. My parents have every single *National Geographic* dating back to 1969. After I had a surgery with two weeks' downtime, I took the time to organize every single one by year and put them into slipcovers. The joy that this brought my parents was unbelievable — their memories of reading them, the knowledge they brought them, and the beautiful pictures that are still astounding today. These magazines are filled with knowledge you could find today on the Internet; however, their sentimental value made them extra special. Now that the issues are properly organized, my parents often read editions from past years.

If you have stacks and stacks of reports/papers and have no clue where a specific one is, that's clutter. If they are organized so you can reference them, they can be useful and are no longer clutter. To put it simply, get rid of anything you don't use, or declutter properly so that the items are usable.

WARNING

Important digital, mental, or printed knowledge needs to be dealt with properly. Sensitive information should be destroyed or shredded. Perhaps some knowledge needs to be passed on to the next generation or teams. Important documents should be housed in several locations to avoid losing them. Before getting rid of any knowledge, make sure you evaluate it first and determine appropriate steps. For example, I always back up my digital items as well as store them in a digital cloud.

I go into detail for knowledge clutterbugs in Part 3, which revolves around workspace and digital organization. Digital clutter is clutter too! And also very important is Chapter 11, related to decluttering your books. (I'm assuming you like books since you're reading one right now!)

A WORD ON KNOWLEDGE HOARDING

"Knowledge is power" is a common phrase. People have a tendency to want to be the smartest person in the room, so they may hoard knowledge, both in their minds and in the stuff that contains the knowledge they acquire.

Knowledge hoarding refers to both physical objects and mental knowledge that you should be sharing to help others in your organization or even customers or other stakeholders. For example, this could be documents that you benefit other employees, such as training documents or customer data (or knowledge on them) or relevant information for your customers on future purchases or issues. If you are holding onto data for your own selfish reasons (being it to keep your job or to make more money from sales), that knowledge should be shared with the appropriate parties involved. Sometimes it's unintentional, but it can still be discouraging to those around you.

Being a knowledge hoarder and intentionally guarding information for preservation and or future use can be seen as one of the worst types of hoarding and can also have a negative impact on your organization and/or your business. Make it a point to share your knowledge with those who would be empowered by it, either through your words or physical documents.

The collector clutterbug

I'm pretty sure all of us have collected something sometime in our lives, from stamps to dolls to watches to baseball cards. Anything that can be collected and cherished can also lead to clutter. Remember the days when you used to collect CDs? Well, now most people don't even have CD players. For those folks, CDs are no longer usable and are therefore considered clutter.

TIP

The key is to really understand whether you're a collector, hoarder, or clutterbug. Hoarders are not able to let go, and this is a serious issue that is repeatedly brought up in this book. Collectors take pride in what they have collected, whether it is worth something or not. The collection becomes clutter when it becomes bothersome and inconvenient to manage. It turns from collection to clutter when embarrassment, shame, or secrecy surround keeping the collection. Clutter is the result of accumulating items that you don't have the time and energy to deal with. Knowing how and when your collections reach this point is an important but difficult task and should always be monitored by you and your friends or family to help with the process.

The "I can use it someday" clutterbug

My grandma was the perfect example of an *"I can use it someday" clutterbug*, which speaks to how society has shifted and how the era you grew up in makes a big difference. My grandmother lived through the Depression and still had that scarcity mindset of rationing. She did not grow up in today's consumerist society with the ability to have one-day shipping. So, her affinity for her stuff was different and almost natural. That said, the era you live does not dictate how much of a clutterbug you become. The "I can use it someday" clutterbug of any age or generation can think like this.

I believe this type of clutter is a real problem because it can lead to hoarding. All the clutterbug types can become hoarders, but this one seems the most likely to. Hoarding can be rooted in deep-seated insecurities, whether financial or emotional. Deep down, hoarders feel like they will never have enough resources, and they fear letting go of anything because they believe that they truly will use that item one day. Even if items are useless, worn, or broken, this type of clutterbug hangs onto any and all items.

WHY DECLUTTERING HASN'T WORKED FOR YOU YET

If you don't understand your clutterbug style, you won't know where to begin. Maybe in the past, you approached decluttering in a way that didn't fit your lifestyle (maybe you like an all-or-nothing approach, or maybe you like breaking it down into bits). All of us have different working styles, from the detail-oriented engineer to the big-picture MBA, and our personality style has a lot to do with our decluttering style.

Someone with no emotional attachment to an item can easily criticize you for not simply getting rid of clutter and moving on. While we know that trash is the most obvious clutter, everyone's definition of what is trash can also be different. As the saying goes, "One's man's junk is another man's treasure."

When you look critically at the items in your home, don't automatically overlook something because it cost you a lot of money or it was a gift that cost a lot of money. Even the most expensive item in your home can be clutter. Think about the garage, as this is one area where many big-kid toys reside. These can be the most expensive clutter or non-clutter items, depending on the value and they bring to their owner and how often they're used.

You may be afraid to call antiques or family heirlooms clutter because you don't want to make anyone feel bad. Maybe these items were expensive or have become valuable, but it doesn't matter. Clutter can be cheap, old, new, or very used. Clutter is in the eye of the beholder.

TIP

Depending on how severe your "I can use it someday" tendency is, a good start is to mentally reassure yourself that you will be able to find this item again if and when you need it. You can either buy, borrow, or repurpose the item. You have to give yourself the security that more egg cartons will be produced, more Old Navy black sweaters will be knit, and more magazines will be printed. Resources are and will continue to be available.

Understanding the Psychology behind Clutter

I don't have a psychology degree, but I've done enough research on this topic to inspire others to get motivated. You get peace and satisfaction from being in a decluttered space, both physically and mentally. I could end here, but I want to keep going with this point. You can also empathize with the idea of feeling defeated and overwhelmed by the amount of clutter that exists. When clutter exists, your energy is affected physically, mentally, and emotionally.

Clutter always reveals your mindset. If you operate with low self-esteem, you may own more expensive clothing than necessary because you use retail therapy as a means to feel happy. If you are worried about money, you may keep items that you don't necessarily need. If you've dealt with loss and grief, you may be more attached to sentimental items than someone who has not gone through similar experiences. The bottom line is that clutter is a symptom of deeper things going on in your psyche, and when you deal with clutter, you can transform into the person you are meant to be.

REMEMBER

Go back to a time when you were surrounded by clutter and think about how it made you feel. It could be a cluttered desk, a stuffed attic, or your mind full of so many tasks you didn't know where to start. You don't need a psychology degree to understand that when you think back to these times you get a bit stressed — or in medical terms, your cortisol levels rise.

The negative effects of clutter

Here is where I can get really real on the psychological effects of clutter. The biggest effects are stress and increased cortisol levels. A study done by UCLA observed 32 middle-class LA families and found that all of the moms' stress hormones spiked during the time they spent dealing with their belongings.

Clutter can harm relationships, and studies have shown that where the word "clutter" is used to describe couples' current households, a higher percentage of divorces ensue. Clutter can often be the root of disagreements that can lead to larger problems. Whatever you're living situation is — whether you're living with a roommate, significant other, family, stranger, or dog — those you live with define clutter differently, and that, of course, affects your living situation and your daily moods. Here are some tips:

>> **Listen to your partner's feelings about the clutter each of you leaves in the house.** Make sure you share decluttering habits with your partner. Share your reasons for wanting to declutter and your strategies. For example, you might show your partner the new boxes you labeled "Donate," "Recycle," "Trash," "Sentimental," and so on. Remember, your partner may get worried upon hearing that you're decluttering and fear that you are going to get rid of everything. Be willing to listen to your partner's concerns, voice your reasons for wanting to declutter, and ask for support throughout the process. You can even shed light on the negative effects of clutter to help your partner understand how getting rid of excess stuff can and will improve both of your lives.

>> **Get rid of what you don't need to improve your emotional well-being.** I bet you're thinking that today's consumerist society and keeping up with the Joneses mean that we have to have a lot of stuff and keep buying more stuff to put in our bigger houses and so forth. However, if you see your stuff spreading to a level that you can't organize or keep clean, this can cause stress, especially if you take pride in having a tidy home. Therefore, having a cluttered environment can result in feelings of low self-worth and even depression in some cases!

>> **Improve your focus.** I talk about this at length when I get to workstation decluttering, but I also think it needs to be discussed in terms of life in general. I think that you know that clutter is and always will be distracting. This is not rocket science or anything new. Clutter can compete for your brain's focus, thereby not allow you to give your full focus to what is important. It takes more energy to actively avoid and ignore clutter than it does to actually deal with it.

>> **Change your behavior.** A large part of your energy can be attributed to your surroundings. Waking up to an efficient home with things you use daily versus waking up to a big pile of junk makes a difference. This can also influence the behavior of your kids, friends, and even fur babies. Clutter can cause a chaotic environment not only for you but also for those who are surrounded by you. For example, entering a doctor's waiting room that's so busy you can barely sit and fill out forms affects your mood differently than entering a sterile, clutter-free environment. Never discount the powerful effect of clutter on your mental and emotional well-being.

Why decluttering lets you do more and stress less

Research has proved the positive effects of decluttering and being organized. However, in a fast-paced life, it's impossible to avoid all stress. You're stimulated by stuff and people all wanting your attention. While avoiding all stress may not be a real option, how you deal with your stuff can help manage one aspect of your stress. The more stuff you have, both physical and mental, the more your stress is triggered.

Therefore, if you want to feel less stress, decluttering your life is a good start so you can focus more on the other areas of your life. The process can even be therapeutic once you start eliminating other stresses!

Here are a few strategies to help relieve decluttering stress:

>> **Stop making impulse buys.** This only leads to more stuff.

>> **Clean and tidy up your bedroom.** Where you wake up has a big impact on how your day is affected.

>> **Go through your closet.** You don't want to be stressed wondering what to wear or waste time in your closet.

>> **Clean out your car.** It's amazing how great a clean car can feel during an otherwise stressful drive.

>> **Remove unwanted apps on your phone.** If you're like most people, you phone is with you all day every day and you spend hours staring at the screen. Delete what you don't need.

>> **Unsubscribe to emails.** The less spam mail you get, the less stress you feel. Unsubscribe to what you don't need.

TIP

I juggle many things in my life, and I know you do as well. From personal and business obligations to family and friendships, the time struggle is real with ever-increasing obligations. How you juggle so many things can heavily depend on the clutter you have lingering in your home, workspace, and mind. To really reduce stress and be more focused and productive, start relating clutter to stress and slowly reduce it. Tackle one day or category at a time and be consistent.

If You Don't Use It, Toss It

You've probably heard it said before: "If you don't use it, toss it." This is easy to say. However, I want to give you some quick tips on how to implement this advice. It requires a mindset change. You need to program your mind to say no a lot more. I don't mean to party invites or customer inquiries; I mean to stuff.

Say no when you want to buy something simply because it's your favorite color or it's on sale for half price. The common sale purchase only works if you would actually have paid full price for the item in the first place; otherwise, it will likely end up being clutter.

Before investing in potentially more clutter, always ask yourself these questions: Why do I need this? Do I already have this? Will it serve a purpose?

REMEMBER

Decluttering does *not* mean going without. Losing clutter should be a relief, not something to be scared about. I know when you picked up this book you were already worried you might have to give up too much stuff or be asked to live so minimally that you'd only have one fork and two knives. That is completely not the case.

Removing clutter all around should make you feel more comfortable in your home, office, car, mind, or wherever you spend your time. If the act of decluttering makes you scared, don't give up. You simply need to change your mindset, and you're probably decluttering in a way that doesn't fit your clutterbug type or your lifestyle.

So why not practice getting better at identifying what needs to go? Start by dividing your belongings into categories according to how often you use them: Daily, Weekly, Sporadically, Rarely, and Never. By putting the items into these categories, you can visually see which ones you don't use. It helps calm the process and makes it easier and totally visual. You can use bins, boxes, or bags to organize these items.

You will likely keep the items in the first two categories, so find a permanent place for them. The key to decluttering is not only to get rid of things you don't use but also to make sure you have a spot for the things you do use.

I advise getting rid of the last two categories of items. You'll have to make a tough choice as to whether the sporadic bin is worth keeping. If the items are not practical, get rid of them!

REMEMBER

Stay positive and take mental breaks if needed, but keep decluttering.

When you let go of something, keep track of how much it cost originally. Don't do it to justify keeping anything. (Keep in mind that decluttering doesn't focus on how much an item costs, but rather whether or not it's useful.) This trick is simply to help give you perspective and prevent you from buying things you don't need.

Discovering how much money you're actually now donating or throwing in the trash may be depressing, but this exercise will help you save money in the future! You've already paid for the items, so the money is gone anyway. Use this tip to help keep you motivated to buy less and live better. I call the money you realize is gone the "sunk costs" of decluttering. You have to move on and do it swiftly. The trick is not to make the same mistake again.

Why minimalism works

In short, minimalism means less of everything. Less stuff, fewer bills, smaller dwellings — you get the point. And first and foremost, minimalism can save money and free up your financial resources. When you choose to live simply, you can be more productive and get an automatic financial benefit.

Minimalism does not mean you have to get rid of everything or that you have to live in a sterile, all-white home with one expensive couch in the middle. That may be what you've been trained to believe, but minimalism in this book simply means thinking about getting rid of what you don't need. And then you can enjoy what you have more! It also means that you can give more value to certain material things by buying less and focusing on quality rather than quantity. Figure 1-3 shows the minimalism example some people envision, but it certainly does not have to be the norm.

Aside from the money savings that come along with minimalism, the time savings can be of even greater value, given that time may well be your greatest asset. You can spend less time dealing with all the extra things in your life and focus your time on the things you need.

In conjunction with more time and money, you'll have more energy as your refocused time can be available for other activities. The reduction of a highly materialist lifestyle can prove to be healthier and give you better results. Last but not least, you'll increase your efficiency. Less stuff, more time, more energy, and more productivity. It really is a no-brainer.

I want to reiterate that you don't have to keep only one pair of shoes or one book to adopt this lifestyle. The great thing about minimalism is that the choices are yours to make, and you can do what works for you. You can choose what and how you want to downsize, and there's no right or wrong way to go about it. Once you start on this journey, you may find that you want to embrace it even more after seeing the benefits.

FIGURE 1-3: What most people see when they think of minimalism.

Pexels / Pixabay

You don't have to figure it all out right away; the process can take some trial and error.

Knowing how much is too much

Many people ask me for some concrete rules to help them figure out whether they have too much stuff. Although this differs for everyone, I have some guidelines:

>> **Constantly misplacing things?** When you are wasting time looking for items from keys to blouses to wrenches, this could be a sign you have too much clutter.

>> **Do you have piles of stuff?** Clothing may be the most obvious thing to think about, but the concept applies to stuff in general.

>> **Are you replacing stuff you have lost and can't find?** This is a clear sign of having too much clutter.

>> **Are you purchasing items and then realizing you already had them?** When you start to have doubles and even triples of most things, chances are you have too much stuff. Two copies of the same book? Five pairs of similar shoes? Twenty boxes of crackers?

>> **Are you always worrying about stuff?** For example, do you stress about having people over because they have to walk through your overstuffed, cluttered entranceway?

>> **Do you have a difficult time knowing where to start?** Are you so overwhelmed with the clutter in many areas of your life that you can't even choose one spot to start?

>> **Do you feel overwhelmed even thinking about decluttering?** Similar to not knowing where to start, do you feel overwhelmed about the entire process?

>> **Are you always late paying bills and arriving at appointments?** This is another clear sign of clutter buildup.

>> **Can you not use places in your house?** For example, can you not park your car in the garage?

>> **Do you want to just start over because of clutter?** Maybe you're tempted to say "Forget it, I'm moving to Indonesia."

>> **Are you renting a storage unit that you never get items from?** Clutter starts before you even rent the locker — if you're considering renting a locker, you have too much stuff. When you have a storage unit, you accumulate even more, and the longer you keep the unit, the more stuff accumulates. When you'd rather pay for a place to store your stuff miles away than let it go, you've reached a turning point. This also often leads to a waste of time and money.

>> **Do your kids have so many toys they never know what to play with?** If you're overwhelmed by clutter, chances are your kids may be as well. Having too many toy choices is also known to hamper creativity, especially in the earlier years.

>> **Do you find you never eat all your food because you over-shop and food goes bad?** This is easily done, especially in North America where we have massive fridges. Europeans, on the other hand, still shop daily and have less food storage space available, which automatically cuts down on food waste.

>> **Do you have to move things to sit down?** This is an obvious sign that you have too much stuff.

>> **Do you have more than one junk drawer?** I forbid junk drawers. I say having an essential drawer for rubber bands and matchboxes that you use is okay, but junk just accumulates, much like clutter.

Too much of anything can be considered clutter. If you start to accumulate too many shoes, for example, they may become an overwhelming pile of clutter that you never use. Similarly, a collection intended to bring you joy can turn into clutter if you're not careful. You may have to do some serious soul-searching to figure out how much is too much.

Taking stock of anything in your home that you have a large selection of is usually a good way to start identifying what may be clutter. What is the right amount you should have? That needs to be determined by your lifestyle.

Determining the right amount for your lifestyle

Items that used to be functional can turn into clutter, and this is where you need to get realistic about what you use. You need to be brutal with your real lifestyle — not the one you think you have or want to have. If you love camping and have every item possible but have not camped in ten years, it's probably not part of your lifestyle and you don't need those items. Having a fantasy about the lifestyle you want and keeping items "just in case" is a common downfall. Chapter 10, which covers decluttering your garage, can give you more insight, as previous "lifestyles" usually end up in the garage.

A personal example is that I gave up my cheerleading shoes ten years after I graduated and stopped cheerleading. For ten years I wanted to hold onto the fact that I was a cheerleader, but in fact, I was a "retired" cheerleader and those shoes were taking up space in my garage — plus, I was limiting the shoes' ability to be used by someone who was actually cheerleading! I ended up donating them to my local high school, and they were used for many more games and competitions. This makes me happier than if they were collecting dust in my garage. Get realistic with your current lifestyle, not your past, fantasy, or future lifestyle.

You can always repurchase something next year or ten years from now — for example, if you decide you want to start camping again.

Your lifestyle changes, and that's normal. When you have kids, you may no longer need your rock climbing or motorcycle gear due to time constraints, but if you do start again, there will likely be even better technology for you to get when that time comes.

Lifestyle changes happen to everyone, even those who are self-described minimalists. This is also completely normal as your life circumstances are always changing, and therefore your needs also change. If something was once useful and now you see it collecting dust in the corner, it's clutter. The thing about clutter is that what may have been useful or brought you extreme happiness in the past can now be clutter, making it even more confusing.

It's important to be diligent when decluttering, make it an ongoing process, and adapt to your lifestyle changes. You have to question items every time you use them, look at them, or pick them up. Be honest about whether you'll ever use your expensive motorcycle jacket if you sold your bike and don't ever really have a desire to ride again. As I'm writing this, I'm thinking I finally need to declutter my big box of motorcycle accessories that I haven't used since my motorcycle accident in 2009. I knew that I would not want to get on a motorcycle again, yet I've held onto my riding clothes for ten years! (Excuse me while I take a writing break to declutter.)

Another factor that affects your lifestyle is where you live. You own different items depending on whether you live in a city or the countryside, and how much time you spend in your home.

You obviously have too much stuff if you don't have room for it in your current dwelling. Even if you know or think someday you'll get a bigger place, if what you have doesn't fit in your current space, then you need to declutter today. Live in the present, because chances are if you save items in anticipation of having a bigger space, they may have turned into clutter by then. This can be a really tough challenge, especially when you're downsizing to a smaller space. It doesn't seem fair that some of your belongings can't join you in your new smaller space. However, it's a blessing in disguise as it forces you to make tough decisions regarding what to keep. You also have to really assess your storage space in your new place and make sure that whatever you're storing isn't clutter and doesn't take up space for other important items. The bottom line is that your space does matter, and often the smaller the space, the more likely you are to be forced to declutter naturally.

TIP

If something doesn't bring you happiness or you don't use it, then it's clutter and it has to go. Whatever method you see fit for determining this is up to you, and the remainder of this chapter focuses on giving practical advice to help you tackle that very question.

Places in Your Life That Probably Need Decluttering

When most people hear the word decluttering, they automatically think about "stuff" and places where they have too much of it. Common areas are the closet, attic, office, and garage. While those may be the most obvious spaces, in the following sections I give you an overview of the four major categories I associate with clutter — the first and foremost one being your mind.

Your mind

The problem with clutter is that it's usually referred to as physical stuff — things you can use, feel, touch, buy, donate, or sell. Lots of options exist for getting rid of physical clutter. However, the real problem is that clutter is also in our minds, taking up very valuable space in our precious brains! You only have so much real estate in your home for the things you love, and the same goes for your precious mental space. Just as you spend time taking care of your body by exercising and eating nutritious food, so must you also remember to declutter your mind to make it the most effective. So how do you know if your mind is cluttered?

Do you sometimes feel like your brain is in overdrive and you can't keep track of things, projects, or life in general? There is absolutely no correlation between mental clutter and how much personal responsibility or work a person has. The busiest person with a decluttered mind can seem more in check with his mental space than someone with significantly fewer responsibilities. The amount you have on your plate is not the problem; it's how it is organized! If your mental space is a chaotic mess, then you should probably declutter your mind. And don't get discouraged or skip over this part because it may seem stressful or "airy-fairy." All of us are victims to having a decluttered mind at some point; the key is to recognize it. Just like your cabinets and cupboards, your mind can also benefit from tidying and decluttering from time to time!

A big tip that I firmly stand beside is adding a focus to your time and giving the task at hand priority instead of working on multiple cluttering tasks at once. I believe so much in this that I sell "time cubes" on my website. Their sole purpose is to decrease the amount of time you spend multitasking. You may feel that you're a great multitasker or that life often demands multitasking. However, just because you're good at multitasking doesn't necessarily mean it's the most productive use of your time. Multitasking occasionally may be necessary, but it increases stress and creates more clutter. Trust me on this: Multitasking keeps your brain in clutter mode.

Try to keep on a single task as much as possible. Always have a focused to-do list that is centered around your high-priority goals, and don't have more than seven items on that list. Otherwise, you'll be overwhelmed, and the temptation to multitask and clutter your brain will be even greater. Keeping this to-do list not only helps to keep the tasks you can accomplish in a day realistic but it also prevents you from starting your day being cluttered, as a cluttered to-do list can already set you on the path to stress.

REMEMBER

Less outside information coming in means fewer distractions when it comes to making important decisions.

If the preceding points don't convince you to declutter your mind, this one should: The media can totally consume your life and also have a negative impact on your health and mind. Plus, just as it makes sense that the more stuff you bring into your home the less room you have, the same is true with your brain: The more stuff you let in, the less room you have. You can spend hours online reading blogs, watching YouTube videos, perusing social media, and catching up on the news, and this information can cause stress and clog up your mind! Of course, lots of this information can be useful when needed, and you can use it to be constantly learning and increasing your self-development. But it's important to limit the amount of information you consume and get the other stuff from the media that's not useful or negative out of your mind. Tim Ferriss, a productivity guru, suggests taking media detoxes. He says if something that is happening in the world comes up in a conversation and you don't know about it, ask about it then. (The amount of time wasted on media was his reason for his media detoxes.)

So, you're probably thinking this is impossible, but it's not. Set limits on how much time you spend on social and other media. Today there are even apps to monitor your screen time. Having a set amount of time keeps you hyper-focused during that time to make the most of it instead of clicking on a cute kitty video that pops up. And you're allowed to be selective about the content you consume. Just as you can choose what to feed your body, you can choose what to feed your mind. Avoid negative content, follow reputable sources, and organize your email and notifications so that nothing can sneak past to add clutter to your brain.

Take time to unwind, disconnect, and be creative. Maintaining a focused and decluttered mind doesn't mean that you don't need mental breaks and what I call "creative time." I have the best times when I can simply reflect or my calendar is free for a few hours. Yes, I do have lots of spaces in my calendar. Although I believe in being planned and focused, free time is where my creativity blossoms. Chapter 2 provides more practical strategies and resources for how to declutter your mind and how it relates to your lifetime goals.

Your home

Often the problem is that we are busy, and when we come home, we are too tired or overwhelmed to even begin to think about decluttering. I hope to change that mindset gradually and not only show you that decluttering is fun but that you can also incorporate it into your daily routine naturally. This section takes a look at some practical solutions to get you motivated to start decluttering your home. Part 2 provides several chapters on tackling specific areas of your home, including closets, bathrooms, kitchens, laundry rooms, kids' rooms, garages, and storage spaces. You may have other rooms I don't touch upon, but you can use many of the same principles and tools I provide throughout the chapters.

Here are a few benefits of decluttering your home, no matter what area you declutter:

>> **Knowing where everything is.** This not only helps you save time but disallows more clutter because you don't buy duplicates or more than you need.

>> **Setting the mood for the day.** I don't have to tell you your home and/or where you start your day can have a drastic impact on the rest of your day — and your life! That old saying that says make your bed to accomplish the first task of the day is spot on and relates directly to decluttering.

Your workspace

You have invested time in your mind and home to declutter, and I suggest tackling the workspace as well. The next section takes a look at digital organization, but this section focuses on the workspace itself. Problems arise when you are not holistically decluttered. I think you know that a messy workspace is less efficient than an organized one, but what you may not know is that it not only makes you less efficient but it can also frustrate your co-workers and limit your chances of getting that next promotion. If you've wasted time looking for things, have been chronically late for meetings, or can't find your meeting notes, these are all signs of a cluttered desk.

Start decluttering your workspace and give everything a home similar to the way you would in your own home. Start by getting rid of nonessential items and make organizing your workspace a daily habit before you leave for the day. Put a reminder in your calendar to take ten minutes at the end of each day to organize your space. An office swap is also a great time to do a deep and thorough declutter. If your office is moving to an open concept shared workspace, that's even better for decluttering. Embrace the new age and skip to the digital organization chapter if you're really interested in decluttering your workspace and going digital, a must for many new office shared spaces. Chapter 12 provides an in-depth view of office decluttering.

Here are some benefits to help you get motivated. Workspace decluttering

>> **Helps your productivity:** This should be obvious as you can find things more easily, waste less time looking for things, and increase your overall mental awareness.

>> **Helps your business succeed:** You may think this is a long shot, but the success of your business and career depends on you, and you want to be the best, most efficient business lady or gentleman that you can be. When you're comfortable in your space and are able to focus, you save time and are more productive. It's a no-brainer. I assume that at some point in your work life you have tried to put an important file on your desk and then couldn't find it because of your cluttered workstation. Being comfortable at your work is the most important key to success. Keeping your workspace tidy and clutter-free and your space more open leads to greater productivity. Remember or think

back to how hard it was or is to complete a task when you were in an uncomfortable place, physically or mentally, and then vow to never work like that again. Take action and make it comfortable.

» **Increases the likelihood of you getting that promotion:** Being organized and clutter-free boosts your performance. Yes, you read that correctly: Being clutter-free can really help to boost confidence, which in turn increases your likelihood of being promoted or doing better in your business. So how exactly does this work? A cluttered desk may mean that you have lost something important or wasted precious time at some point. Maybe you needed it to make a sale or your boss requested it. Having files and resources you need when you need them helps boost confidence and credibility and leaves a lasting impression.

» **Makes a better first impression:** First impressions of your workspace are as important as first impressions in interviews. I worked for a decade in the construction industry in operations, and the mentality was that the more stuff you had in your office, the more knowledgeable you were. I would walk into seasoned plant managers' offices with stacks and stacks of books, papers, procedures, and manuals, and they were proud of it. I had worked there so long that I knew and used all of these resources. Yet when I asked them to find the latest safety procedure on cleaning concrete drums, it took them hours to find it.

Having an overload of stuff can truly make some people feel that it affects job security. If you walk into a lawyer's office and see a lot of fancy legal books that he's probably never opened or read since law school, do you assume he is better equipped to take your case? Many professions do require manuals and resources that may only be used once in a career but hold information on a specific case or project. If you're in this type of career, then you need to be aware and try to declutter for yourself and to be ahead of the times. Most jobs/careers don't require you to have thousands of papers sitting behind you to confirm your knowledge.

» **Keeps you healthier:** The more clutter you have, the harder it is to clean your desk, which means more germs are lingering, especially if you have lots of co-workers or customers who stop by. Clear the clutter and use disinfectant wipes (I recommend using the organic ones).

» **Helps you prevent procrastination:** Everyone procrastinates at some things — some people more than others. It's human nature to do the things you love first before you do things that you don't like doing. Lingering clutter can add to your procrastination, and at some point you've probably even procrastinated decluttering your workplace. Don't worry; that's okay. I've done it many times, and I bet you have too. The first step is admitting it. However, learning to avoid procrastination without being forced to do so is important. If you're forced, you may miss an important detail, feel stressed the entire time, or have to give up another task to complete it. Many people say that procrastination has its benefits because they work better under pressure, but it can also mean you don't get anything done.

>> **Builds time management skills:** Today time management skill is needed for practically every job, business, or career. You see it listed on every job posting, and customers demand it. Time is your greatest asset, and how you manage it is completely up to you. Even if someone else manages your calendar or schedule, you still need to make the rules. So how does decluttering benefit time management? Clearing the clutter helps you clear your mind to more effectively plan for achieving your priority tasks. Starting to declutter may seem like a daunting task that takes lots of time, but it will save you lots of time in the future.

If, after reading the preceding benefits, you want to declutter your workspace, here are some steps to get started right now:

1. Remove everything from your workspace/office.

For a complete workspace overhaul, or if you are forced to leave your huge cushy office for the shared workspace concept, begin by removing everything from the room. And I mean everything: desk drawers, stuff in cupboards, and so on. If your office is moving, you have to do this anyway, but do it even if you're staying put. Trust me: What you put back in will be valuable, because taking everything out of a room and then putting it back in is a lot of work.

TIP

Once the room is empty, take advantage of the chance to clean it. Vacuum, dust, scrub the walls — anything you can do to get that room in the best possible condition. You don't often take things completely out of your space, so when you do, take the time to clean as well.

2. Evaluate the stuff you moved out.

This may sound easy, but where do you start? Consider everything to be on a level playing field; all the stuff is equal. This makes you see everything as potential clutter — furniture, files, pens, wall art. Everything is in the same category, whether potential clutter or necessity.

3. Choose practical necessities.

This is the tough part because you'll want to put everything you like or sometimes use back into your workspace. You need to be tough — brutal even — with your things. Only bring items you use daily back into your office.

4. Place things in their new place.

Once you've made some brutal decluttering decisions, find a special place for the items you're moving back in. You need to think carefully about where to put things and give each item a special place to not only maximize space but also to help you continually declutter. Anything that doesn't have a spot should not stay in your office. If you're doing a total workspace overhaul, furniture makes the biggest difference in getting to that clutter-less space. Make sure your furniture is functional and is in the best spot to maximize efficiency.

This step is extremely important and should not be overlooked, as decluttering is more than just throwing things away — it's getting to your optimal efficiency level.

5. **Make a commitment to regularly declutter.**

You will see this advice pop up in practically ever chapter and section of this book. Decluttering is not a one-time occurrence but should be done all the time. We all know that clutter will seep back into our lives, and workspaces are no exception. Make a commitment to continually evaluate and update your space and efficiency, and you will leave a lasting impression on customers, co-workers, and everyone who looks up to you. Figure 1-4 is an example of a decluttered workspace that can be a reality with regular decluttering.

FIGURE 1-4:
A clear
workspace.

Thomas Q / Unsplash

Your digital life

Digital life is complicated, as we do so many things online! I have dedicated Chapter 13 to digital organizing, and as our society moves more away from paper, I suspect that digital organization will become more important. For example, we have work files, games, movies, songs, emails, tweets, Facebook posts, pins, webinars, photos, blogs, recipes, Skype calls, and the list goes on. I know sometimes I even save or document something that I would never keep if it were in paper form, and I would never print it. But yet I allow it to take up valuable real estate on my computer, and what's more disturbing is that it could cause me to lose time while sorting through files and documents I no longer need.

When email was invented back in the day, I created my very first Hotmail account. Yes, I am dating myself, but I still use that account from 1996 sometimes; I just can't get rid of it. I may need to take my own advice about email declutter and let go of this email sometime soon!

Think back to when you first got email. I know I used to print them all. I was scared that if I didn't, they would be gone forever. I mean, how could a computer or the Internet be smart enough to store my emails?

Fast forward to today, when you should not be printing emails. However, in my work with corporate offices and small businesses to improve business processes, I still come across this practice, even in 2019, when email and cloud services are very secure. I see VPs, admin assistants, controllers, event planners, and plant managers with printed emails in their office. When I ask them about it, the response is usually, "Oh, I really needed to make sure I follow up on that email," or "It is very important," or "I file it under that person's name"! Those answers are mind-boggling to me.

The problem remains that we have so many digital things to save on our computer. And to be honest, most of our business and life is now digital, but we really don't spend any time dealing with the digital files we have created. What's even worse is that sometimes we have files saved in multiple places in our computers without even knowing it. Chapter 12 tackles this topic in further detail, and Figure 1–5 shows a digitally organized computer screen that will be the result of digital decluttering.

Now, I am not a technical genius at all and there is much that I don't know about computers and technical gadgets, so my digital decluttering may be basic. But what I do know is that you don't need to be technically inclined to have a thriving business online or to clutter your computer. I also know that regular digital decluttering can improve productivity and good work. I am a firm believer in decluttering regularly rather than waiting until you get that dreaded note on your computer stating that you've run out of space.

FIGURE 1-5:
Clear computer
screen.

Image courtesy of author (photo credit@lohmmedia)

Following are a few tips on digital decluttering:

>> Set up your digital decluttering strategy before it is too late. Create an easy-to-manage system, such as organized folders for invoices and receipts.

>> Name things properly so that you can find everything quickly in your digital world.

>> Don't get overwhelmed by spam; deal with it immediately.

>> Unsubscribe to anything that causes you stress.

Chapter **2**

Creating Your Decluttering Mindset

When you think of decluttering I know that you think of "stuff," but I hope that after reading this chapter you can also relate decluttering to achieving your goals. In order for this to happen, you need to incorporate and sometimes change your mindset around decluttering.

In this chapter, I dig deeper into this concept. I ask you to trust me about relating your goals to your clutter personalities and see the linkage to how clutter is blocking your from your goals.

Determining Your Decluttering Mindset Goals

I want you to accomplish all your life goals, including your goals around decluttering. You've probably never actually written down any goals about decluttering. Or maybe you have, and that's why you bought this book in the first place.

One goal I want you to set right now is that this is the year you will finally be free of clutter and not accumulate more. Make decluttering a part of your lifestyle.

This is the year that you will do it, and I promise it will make all aspects of your life lighter, less stressed, and hopefully more fun.

If you skimmed through Chapter 1 or didn't read it all, go back and read about your potential clutter personality. In order to maintain a clutter-free home, you need to get to the root of why things pile up in the first place. In Chapter 1, I go through several cluttering styles, the most common ones being "too busy," "don't know where to start," "must save everything," and "I will do it later." The first step is identifying the style that you can relate to and understanding that many people are with you in this same challenge! By identifying what kind of clutterbug you are, you can identify your weak spots, which you can use to achieve your goals.

Now is the time when you are going to get real and relate decluttering to all your life goals! I think 90-day goal planning is great not only for business and personal goals but also for decluttering goals. Figure 2-1 is a goal sheet I encourage you to fill out to relate your goals to decluttering in the following time frames:

>> 90 days

>> One year

>> Five years

Then write down a few decluttering goals you have, whether they relate to physical spaces, processes, or your mental state.

Think about the spaces that you are constantly surrounded by in your home, and your processes or your routines. Use the attached template to start with your large goals and then work your way to the decluttering goals, and you will see how they fit together at the end of the exercise.

REMEMBER

Being able to see how decluttering can help you achieve your tangible life goals will further motivate you and allow you to see the benefits as you achieve your goals. I am a huge believer in goal setting, and I am often amazed at how my written-down goals actually happen. The power of writing them down seems to firm the commitment and allow your mindset and the universe to take note.

Evaluating your lifestyle

After you've spent some time reviewing your goals and seeing how decluttering fits, the next step is to make sure they align with your current lifestyle and your future projections.

90-Day Goals	Date

1-Year Goals	Date

5-Year Goals	Date

How is clutter (both physical and mental) blocking any of these goals?

Areas in my home/office that I will work on to declutter:

FIGURE 2-1:
Use this
exercise to
determine
your life and
decluttering
goals.

The main area/room I want focus on as a priority:

A bad decluttering habit I am going to break:

Form courtesy of author

For example, if your goal in the next year is to move to the city for the new company you're starting but you currently have a 4,000-square-foot home full of stuff, you can bet you will need to start decluttering. Perhaps this stress is already on your mind and maybe even holding you back from starting sooner! Don't wait until moving day to declutter. Start today and you'll achieve your goal faster, easier, and likely with reduced stress. Every time you get rid of an item, make a mental note that doing so is going to help you achieve your dream goal.

Maybe your goals are more financially related, and you're hoping to save a certain amount of money this year. Decluttering totally fits into this goal because you want to be saving money instead of buying stuff you don't need. Or you could even be selling to help exceed that financial goal!

The previous exercise has you think about the future in 90 days, one year, and the next five years. Whenever I do this exercise with clients, I am amazed at the similar results. Usually everyone is excited or wants more freedom in her life. Sometimes the word freedom doesn't show up in words but in the goals themselves. Often clients want to have a more flexible life, be able to travel more often, move to a different place, or have more money and freedom. And decluttering can help with all of these goals. It is amazing how freeing yourself from "stuff" and clutter can give you room to make your other goals fall perfectly into place.

I am going to ask you now to review and evaluate your current lifestyle. Are your items for your lifestyle now or for your future? How can they align?

Ask yourself questions as you go through the areas of your life that entail a lot of stuff. Is it clutter? Could it actually be holding you back from achieving your long-term goals?

When you first look at your lifestyle items, do you immediately think "I need these" or "I really should give this to someone who can use it"? You need to examine the stuff and really evaluate whether it fits with your current lifestyle. If your first response is "I really need to keep that camping tent" even though you haven't used it in ten years, think hard before you move on to the next lifestyle item. Ignoring the truth and not obeying this rule will truly keep you overstuffed in all facets of your life and probably have a negative effect on the very goals you're trying to achieve.

To help you with this, ask yourself what you want in your life. Freedom? Space? Happiness? Peace? These are the usual responses that most people I have worked with give. Clutter keeps us from achieving those very goals! And we spend hundreds of thousands of dollars buying larger homes when what we should be doing is evaluating our lifestyles and goals first. Precious real estate in our homes and our minds is much more valuable when it is clear and free rather than cluttered.

Keep this in mind as you continue on your lifestyle decluttering mission. Walk through the rooms and your workspace, and focus on items and how they fit into your current lifestyle. Ask yourself: Do you use it? Do you adore it? Can someone else be using it?

Here are some tips on how to break free from clutter:

>> **Declutter, declutter, and keep decluttering consistently.** Decide what to keep and swiftly get rid of the rest.

>> **Realize you are not what you own.** We often worry that getting rid of our stuff is like getting rid of a piece of ourselves. However, you are not stuff, and your memories, dreams, goals, and ambitions are not contained in objects; they are inside of you already! Your "stuff" is simply getting in th way of you achieving your dreams.

>> **Don't bring in more items without extensive questioning.** Another constant theme in this book is to make sure you buy consciously. The following are all good questions to ask before making a purchase: "Do I really need this?" "Will this add value to my life?" "Is this item worth the space I am going to give it??"

>> **Eliminate distractions.** If you can get rid of excess stuff, you can find the real freedom to dive into your life goals, deepen your relationships (with people, not items) and discover the life you want.

Mapping your processes

As much as I love goal setting, I also like processes, as they allow me to really see where improvements can be made. I don't think they should be limited to the business world. I also incorporate them into my personal life, and they have helped me achieve my goals as I was able to identify what was holding me back — or the "bottlenecks" as I often refer to them, but it is similar to a blockage. This may sound daunting or like you need to hire consultants to help you, but trust me, you don't. It can be really simple to map out what is not working and find ways to improve. This step can save not only time but also really put things into perspective about where and what needs to be improved.

As with any problem, there is usually a bottleneck that keeps you from fulling achieving your highest potential and may also be the reason you are not decluttering. Clutter is likely part of the issue.

See Figure 2-2 for a super-quick exercise on mapping out your process goals. I have broken it down into Personal, Work, Social, Financial, and Personal Development (which could be education) categories, but feel free to make your own sections.

For example, say under "Social" your goal is to host dinner parties monthly but you know one of the reasons you can't is that your dining room is not properly organized. Could clutter be one of the reasons for this?

If your goal is to apply for a course on personal branding but you can't find the time, what is keeping your time cluttered? Can you free up 30 minutes per day by removing a task, outsourcing, or increasing your efficiency?

TIP

When you're looking at ways to achieve your goals via processes, keep in mind that those processes don't have to be big or revolutionary to be effective. The simpler the better. For example, maybe you want to own your dream rental vacation home in five years in the Caribbean. When you look at the goal, you see that the processes holding you back are saving money for it and finding the time you need to actually research and visit the options. Therefore, you can circle or identify these two blockers. Decluttering can give you more financial freedom to save more, and you can dedicate your decluttering time to tackling those areas that are holding your time back now. Is there a way you can free up more time immediately without sacrificing your financial goals? Can you try outsourcing some tasks so you can work remotely on others, giving you freedom plus more income?

Relating processes to decluttering may seem far-fetched, but freeing up your mind to focus on this is a great exercise and can help you look at your clutter — both physical and mental — from a different perspective.

WHAT AREA OF CLUTTER IS HOLDING YOU BACK
With your top priority in mind map out your process and circle improvement areas.

Example below:

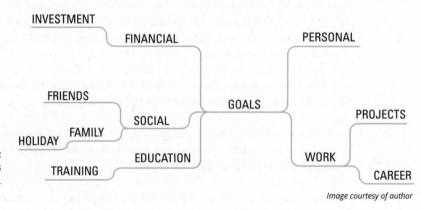

FIGURE 2-2: Simple process map.

Image courtesy of author

Determining what isn't working

Figuring out what's not working in your life to achieve your goals is tough. However, you have already done the hard work to determine the answer. Look to your mapped-out process circle to see what isn't working — maybe you already have it circled. Start at this part of the process that is keeping you stuck or holding you back in some way.

Again, it doesn't have to be revolutionary; simply understanding where you need to improve can be the simplest thing. It could be spending a dedicated 15 minutes a day on your social media for your company to achieve the influencer status you are hoping to get for next year's goal, as right now you don't have time or don't schedule that time. Or it could be spending 30 minutes at the end of each week organizing your accounting so that you aren't overwhelmed when taxes are due.

Sometimes your goal is a physical item, which is okay! Remember, if you use it and it adds value to your life, then it is not clutter! If your dream car is your five-year goal, perhaps decluttering your current car or big-kid garage toys is on the horizon to help you save or make space for it!

Determining areas in which you're seeking improvement

Finding where you need to improve may seem very similar to the preceding advice of looking at your process map to determine what's not working, but now I want you to focus on *areas* of your life. This should be a general theme that can drastically help you improve your life and keep decluttering toward that goal.

Is the main area your finances, your space, your lack of flexibility, or lack of creative outlets? What area is holding you back? It could even be as simple as your closet because you never feel great about what you're wearing and waste so much time daily in your closet to still not feel confident.

REMEMBER

One of my mantras in life is a laser-focused closet will also ensure that you are on the way to a structured, system-driven office space. Wasting even ten minutes a day in your closet due to clutter adds up to 2.5 days a year — over 60 hours! And I know you can use that time to work on your goals or spend the time doing what you love. Chapter 4 goes into detail about closet organizing. A simple time-waster of ten minutes a day can really add up. If you do this in other areas, such as the garage, kitchen, and bedroom, your time wasting because of clutter adds up even more.

Getting Clear on What You Need

Getting clear on what you need goes to the heart of decluttering. I am not going to tell you what items you should put in the trash or what is practical, as I can't physically reach out of this book and help you move items or give you support. I would have no emotional attachment to your items, so it would be easier for me to declutter. But I want to really help you get clear on what you need. Up until this point, maybe you've had problems with letting go of things, even after reading about changing your mindset and determining what clutterbug category you fit into.

Try something new to help you get really clear on what you need:

1. Identify all your clutter that is stealing your energy.

This is the time to get real. Look at each space in your home and workspaces and dig deep. They may look okay on the surface, but I want you to really acknowledge where disasters lie. Hidden drawers, piled magazines from three years ago, or antique furniture you can't get rid of and haven't used since 1999 but that definitely steals your energy each time you have to dust its intricate details. Get real with yourself and allow the energy you feel when you enter rooms and go toward each item to help you. I know it may sound airy-fairy, and no, I am not asking you to write a letter to each item you own as other gurus have been to known to recommend. I suggest simply going on your energy scales.

2. Plan a time to go through all the things you really need.

Yes, this advice you will see over and over again in my book, and I stick to it because I love planning everything, and decluttering is no exception.

3. Plan time for decluttering sessions.

Use a time cube and spend no more than 60 minutes. Give yourself a treat after, or some type of reward for your hard work. Swiss chocolate can work wonders for this, especially if you want to enlist family support.

4. Gather your supplies.

No, don't go and buy more supplies or boxes. Find two boxes you already have and label one "In" and the other "Out."

5. Move your items.

Pick up an item you have in your cluttered area and put it into a box. Don't think too much about it; just do it. Then do it repeatedly until your time-cube goes off.

Logically, you keep the stuff in the "in" box. The "out" box goes away immediately. Schedule a pickup from your local thrift shop if you think you may keep it longer than needed.

I have a very hard time telling you what is practical, what's emotional, and what is trash because these are personal decisions, but the following sections offer some tips. I encourage you to be honest with yourself in making these decisions.

Is it practical?

Ask yourself the following questions to determine if your items are practical:

>> Do you use this item on a regular basis?

>> Does it provide value to your life?

>> Can someone else use it?

Remember you don't need to get rid of all your sentimental items, but determine whether or not you're hanging onto something that no longer provides value.

If you're an emotional clutterbug, you need to be even more honest about your items and determining how they fit into these categories.

Is it emotional?

Dealing with emotional items is often the most challenging part of decluttering, and I struggle with this myself. Getting rid of stuff is difficult for most people but especially for those who treasure memories connected with possessions. The possessions contain different memories for different people, and while some see them as trash, others revel in the memories those possessions provide them. I spend lots of time talking about how you can still keep your sentimental items and also give advice on how to determine what is sentimental and what isn't. For now I want you to acknowledge that emotions will arise during the decluttering process and that sometimes you are going to need to accept that you no longer need many of the objects you are keeping. Your memories will stay forever, but your stuff does not have to.

REMEMBER

Be gentle with yourself during this process and acknowledge all the feelings that arise.

Mentally preparing yourself for decluttering is important, and the first step is to realize that emotional attachment you have to certain items and be able to deal with it swiftly using many of the principles and tools provided in this book.

TIP

You have many options for getting rid of clutter, which also may help with some of the guilt of getting rid of things. Donating or giving away is a great way to declutter.

Is it trash?

Time to dive into deciding whether or not an item really is trash. I got this tip from an article I read years ago, in which they called it the ten-minute declutter exercise. You can easily use your smartphone to set a timer for ten minutes or go to my website, www.organizedjane.com, and buy one of my time cubes, though it may not be as instant as reaching for your smartphone at this very moment.

Figure 2-3 shows the time cube being used for various trash challenges that you could do to get started or even to keep decluttering. This challenge is great for doing quick decluttering, which avoids the overthinking and thoughts of "maybe I can use this someday." This is best if you get a trash and recycling bin and set the time cube timer to 15 minutes and only declutter the area until the timer goes off. The short amount of time and using a timer will make it feel like a race and increase focus.

FIGURE 2-3:
Use the time cube for trash challenges.

Images courtesy of author (photo credit: @avalonmohns @visualsbyamber)

AUTHOR SAYS

I use a time cube instead of my phone because it prevents me from being tempted to check my phone and lose focus on decluttering.

Get two trash bags and set your timer for 10 minutes, 15 if you're really feeling this exercise. In the first bag you're going to put trash, and in the second bag you're going to put things you can donate or pass along. From books to clothes to kitchen supplies to garage items, go through as many rooms as you can and stick to the timer. If you continue to do this super-fun (well, at least in my mind) exercise daily, you will certainly start to declutter faster, but the first time you do this exercise, notice what you can immediately discard. Those are items that don't fit your current lifestyle and/or goals, and you can probably keep going on similar, related items. The same goes for the donation bag, which contains items in better shape or of more value that you want someone else to enjoy.

Stop Cheating Yourself

Yes, we cheat on diets and sometimes on the speed limit and maybe in various other places in our lives. I want to you to stop cheating on clutter. Do your exercises, remember the clutterbug types, and when you fall back into one of your old habits, recognize it and keep moving forward.

What to look for when decluttering

To begin the decluttering process, it's important to circle back to the exercises you've completed.

- ❯❯ Go back to your goals and determine your bottlenecks.
- ❯❯ Start with these bottlenecks and move onward.
- ❯❯ Prioritize tasks instead of doing everything at once. This will also make your decluttering process more sustainable.

TIP

You may have trouble deciding which items you actually use or may use in the future. Here is a simple trick that works especially well for gadgets. Empty all your drawer contents into cardboard boxes. Keep these boxes out for one month. I know this is already making some people feel crazy, but just trust me. For one month, put items that you use back into the drawers. For example, if you start with the kitchen, after you use a utensil or gadget, wash and store it back in its spot. When the month is up, it's pretty safe to say that it what's left in the box is clutter and you don't need it. Donate it to someone who can use it.

Checking for hidden clutter traps

I could make a super-long list of potential clutter traps, and they would be different for everyone. Here, I list the most common ones to get you thinking about your clutter habits.

Entryways and mudrooms

Entryways and mudrooms can be major clutter traps that we always seem to forget about. The entryway is usually the spot where we first enter the house and typically leave items, sometimes never giving them a home. It's an easy place to stow-and-go when you're in a hurry and racing to the next meeting or appointment. The key to keeping your entryway and mudroom clutter-free is to ensure that everything and everyone has a designated space. What I mean by "everyone" is not that you have to have a place for a human to reside, but rather a spot for everyone's essential entryway stuff, such as hooks for backpacks and jackets, dishes for keys, bins for hats, and so on. Determine what everyone needs and then create specific spots for those items.

Paper

Manage your paper trails, as this can often become one of the biggest clutter traps! First of all I try to go digital, but then this advice would be to manage your digital trail.

If you have lots of paper and you're too busy to deal with it at a certain time, make sure you have some kind of drawer or basket to put it in. Then when you're ready, deal with it swiftly at once. Get rid of flyers and junk mail first and fast. Tear out pieces of things you want to read or catalogue items if you need them to avoid keeping what you don't need. Deal with bills, time-sensitive items, correspondence, invitations, and so on immediately and then discard them.

TIP

If you want to get digitally organized, take photos of invites and add them to your electronic calendar.

Try to focus on the bills first, as you want to maintain good relationships with providers and you want services like electricity to continue. When you're done sorting and dealing with the important items, you can go to the leisure catalogues and items you put aside. But the more catalogues you get, the more stuff you want to get. Same goes for certain types of magazines that are known to make us want to consume the latest gadgets and trends. Alas, I enjoy reading about my passions just as much as you do. Just be aware of the potential clutter traps in paper — and today, digital stuff.

Junk drawers

You're going to hear me talk about junk drawers a lot, as I do believe in what I call an "essentials drawer" for the items that you really need. But simply calling it a junk drawer is something I don't agree with because then you are more likely to fill it with junk. Get rid of your junk drawer.

Anything that can't close

If your closet drawer is too full and it can't close, this is a pretty clear sign that it's a clutter trap and you need to deal with it. If you can't close your desk drawer because it's overflowing, that's an area that needs attention too. If your closet door is starting to look like the one in Figure 2-4, start decluttering now!

FIGURE 2-4: The closet is in serious need of decluttering.

Daniel Day / Getty Images

Boxes that aren't see-through

It is important to label any boxes that are not see-through. I love see-through boxes because you can see exactly what is inside them. Labels are the next best thing, though, and they allow you to easily identify the contents inside. I go into details about labeling in Chapter 17, and Figure 2-5 shows various labels and tags you could use with boxes.

Anything behind closed doors

As noted earlier, if you can't close a door, you know there is too much clutter. However, anything behind even doors that close properly may be clutter.

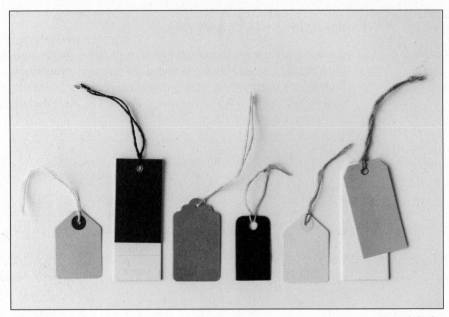

FIGURE 2-5:
Labeling boxes
is essential
when you can't
see what's
inside.

Rawpixel / Pixabay

Carefully consider unnecessary memory clutter. I can't stress this enough in this book, but your home is not a museum, and therefore it is not meant to display or house everything that once had a memory for you. We even keep some things we don't like or use because someone gave them to us, or we feel guilty letting something go because it cost so much or is rare. But what good is it doing by taking up valuable real estate in your home? And if something really is valuable, then you can donate or sell it and make someone else happy!

Items from our life that don't have value for others are sometimes hard to part with. For example, the key card from the first vacation with your now husband has no meaning to anyone else. But the rule of thumb should be that if it serves no purpose, it should go.

Chapter **3**

Forming a Decluttering Game Plan

After going over the effects that clutter has on your mind, wallet, family, life goals, and overall well-being, I hope you're ready to really start a decluttering plan. You may only have a few boxes of items lying around, or you may be ready to apply for the next episode of *Hoarders*. All of you have different life goals, and therefore different decluttering goals, to help you free up space, time, and stress.

I think you know I am not expecting total minimalism; I never said you had to fit your entire life into a backpack or have only one fork. My goal is that by the end of this chapter you will be ready to move on to the spaces in your home and office that need decluttering support, and you will have the tools and resources to start and make decluttering part of your everyday life. You will be ready to toss, donate, gift, repurpose, and basically get rid of things that do not serve a purpose in your life and are simply taking up precious space in your surroundings and mind.

Whether you want to downsize or upsize your surroundings, your decluttering strategy should relate to you getting back to the things you love and having more time to focus on your goals.

Effectively Dealing with Clutter

In the previous chapter I talk about your goals and lifestyle, and now it's time to really make those practices a reality. The quicker you are at dealing with clutter, the less likely it is to build up. I have found that once you are over the emotional hurdle of clutter, it becomes much easier to deal with. The next big hurdle is the sunk costs associated with the clutter. The value it once had is gone, and in some cases, can be recuperated when you sell that item, but the lesson should be to be more wary of future clutter that may make its way into your home and know how to deal with that.

REMEMBER

Everything should have a place in your space. If you found a plate in the bedroom, you would immediately return it to its home without a second thought because you know it's not where it belongs. That should be the case with all of your belongings. If you have trouble deciding where something goes, it may be clutter that you need to let go of — and do it fast.

Being proactive versus reactive

You've probably heard the term "proactive" in business settings and about your health or your studies. By dealing with things proactively, you can achieve higher results than by simply waiting to react when things come to you. This concept relates directly to decluttering as well.

Being proactive instead of reactive means that instead of waiting to let clutter build up or until everything is a mess, you take constant steps toward decluttering, especially the bottleneck areas that you identify in Chapter 2.

I am a big fan of the Franklin Covey group and the late author Dr. Stephen Covey who wrote 7 *Habits of Highly Effective People.* The number-one habit is being proactive. As the book states, "Reactive people believe they are not responsible for what they say and do — they have no choice. Instead of reacting to or worrying about conditions over which they have little or no control, proactive people focus their time and energy on things they can control." And I know that we are responsible for controlling our own clutter.

Keeping a proactive mindset and creating a routine and systems can make decluttering an automatic part of your life.

Creating a system that you stick to

I talk about systems a lot, and you're probably already thinking about how you can work decluttering into your current routine. And if you're not thinking about this, then I have not done my job right up until now. Creating systems and routines that are an organic part of your life makes decluttering not only sustainable but also something you don't have to think about because it's just an organic part of your routine.

And there is a reason you picked up this book. I don't want to get philosophical, but I suggest you start implementing the things you are discovering in this book right now rather than reacting to it as clutter builds. If you're in an emergency situation or having trouble dealing with clutter, have a look at Figure 3-1 to help you get started. Take a photo of the card and keep it on your phone or print and it post it somewhere visible. These simple questions can help you stick to your decluttering goals, and you will soon be asking them of yourself without even looking at the card!

<table>
<tr><td colspan="1" align="center">DANGER
Clutter Card</td></tr>
<tr><td>
• How long since this has been used?
• Does it work properly?
• Does it add value to your life?
• Do you love it?
• Do you have something similar?
• Is it easily replaceable? Can I find the information somewhere else?
• Is it taking up valuable space for something else?
• Does the space cause me stress?
</td></tr>
</table>

Image courtesy of author

FIGURE 3-1: Clutter danger card.

Maximizing efficiency

Regardless of how much you have to declutter, you want to be as efficient as possible when dealing with it. You want to feel in control of the process as much as the result. Here are a few tips to maximize your decluttering efficiency:

>> **Start with one area.** This is advice that I give everyone who starts on any organizing challenge, especially since at the beginning you will not find decluttering pleasant. You may even find it stressful; therefore, you should start small. Start with one area. It should be your highest priority or the area that causes you the most stress or is the least efficient area of your home or workplace.

>> **Give yourself a timeline.** As with any goal, you need to have an attainable date to finish so you don't get frustrated and give up.

>> **Plan time.** In addition to completion dates, you need to plan the time you will declutter. Shorter time spans can actually increase your chances of tackling the project. It's amazing what you can accomplish in a set 15-minute declutter challenge. It will also feel more like a game or challenge, and all of us usually have a bit of a competitive edge, even when decluttering. Experiment with different amounts of time that work for you and then stay consistent!

>> **Use time cubes to keep you on track.** Maximizing your time is so important that I sell time cubes on my website to promote efficiency. And I use them every day. Today we are so distracted by social media, emails, Netflix, kids, and so forth. Our lives are fast and busy, and distractions are always lingering.

Figure 3-2 is an image of this simple time cube gadget that can help keep you on track for many tasks, including decluttering. The time cube is a very straightforward tool to keep you on task and better than a phone time as you won't be distracted with texts, emails, or other notifications coming through. The primary task of the time cube is to countdown the time. The cube has the numbers 15, 30, 45, and 60 on it, and when you place the number side up it starts to count down and blink red. For some reason, when this timer is blinking at you it keeps your mind focused. Like I said, it can take less than 15 minutes a day to declutter. Use a timer to keep focused on only decluttering efficiently, and don't leave the room or area during that time until the timer goes off. You will be amazed at the results!

FIGURE 3-2:
Time cube in
action.

Image courtesy of the author (photo credit: @avalonmohns)

>> **Have your Donate, Sell, Toss, and Repurpose boxes ready.** I talk about these boxes a lot, especially in the next chapter, which deals with closet decluttering. Trust me, I want you to buy or repurpose boxes with these labels on them. Yes, I am telling you to get some stuff; these boxes will continually remind you to Donate, Sell, Toss, and Repurpose. They will also aid in creating a decluttering sorting system that you can keep going. See Figure 3-3 for boxes are that are beautiful and could remain even in the smallest of dwellings for decluttering purposes. You may think you need big, ugly boxes to sit in your living room to declutter, but I am here to debunk that myth! (These boxes are available for purchase on my website organized-jane.com.)

>> **Get rid of clutter.** Do this immediately, because the longer clutter stays in your house, the more it may just work its way back into your home and never leave. Arrange a pickup from a local charity if you're worried you won't be able to actually get rid of the items. Remember, getting rid of stuff is difficult for everyone, and you can keep the memories without keeping the stuff.

Avoiding the all-or-nothing approach

The all-or-nothing decluttering approach can be intimidating, overwhelming, and may even make you bitter. Here's how:

Intimidating

Choose a point of attack and then start with one item when you enter a room and decide on it as quickly as possible. Then move onto the next item. I know that many of us, myself included, are sometimes intimidated when we even hear the word "decluttering," and that is what I want to avoid. If you truly think of it in terms of "I have to do it all today," then yes, decluttering will be intimidating. To avoid this, be kind to yourself and those around you and start small in sections or categories.

Overwhelming

Along with being intimidated, feeling overwhelmed is probably the most well-known emotion when we hear the word "decluttering." And that feeling of being overwhelmed — in many things in life, not only decluttering — is what causes us to not start something. We are overwhelmed with the amount of work it takes to start our own business, so we don't do it. We are overwhelmed with how hard the newest boot camp exercise class is, so we simply don't go. And we are overwhelmed just thinking about where to start decluttering, so we don't. All of these examples are proof that something great could come if you started and were not held back by being overwhelmed. So, again, you don't have to declutter your life in one day, just as you don't have to start a business or start with the craziest exercise routines right off the bat. Ease into decluttering the same way you would any of these tasks. Schedule daily and/or weekly decluttering into your calendar to hold yourself accountable and beat the overwhelming feelings.

FIGURE 3-3:
Labeled decluttering boxes.

Image courtesy of author; photo credit @lohnmedia

Getting sick of it and feeling bitter

I promise you that if you stick to decluttering, you will get better at it, just like you will get in better shape once you start exercising. I always say start small and stick to it, and before you know it you will be decluttering without even thinking about it.

And back to the old saying, "Rome was not built in a day." You can't lose 20 pounds in one day, and the same is true of decluttering. Small steps and lifestyle adaptions and changes will bring you to your goal.

The all-or-nothing approach is not sustainable for most people because it doesn't actually foster new habits.

Busting through the "I might" syndrome

Going back to the decluttering mindset, operating with scarcity beliefs not only holds you back from getting rid of clutter, but it also produces lingering stress because it makes you think of what *could* happen. If you don't know whether you are this type of clutterbug, refer to the clutter personalities in Chapter 1 to see if you can relate to the personalities. You may be one or several, or in an odd case, you may be none and not need any help decluttering. Then maybe you're reading this book to validate everything you're already doing — or you probably have ideas of your own to add!

Regardless of your clutter personality, *you need* to bust through the "I might use it someday" belief today — this very second — because if you have this mentality forever, you will be holding onto unnecessary clutter.

I am not going to lie; this is the hardest problem that most of us have when it comes to clutter; hence, why I keep bringing it up. And it is often linked with emotional reasons. For example, if you grew up not having a lot of money, perhaps you were conditioned to keep everything. Therefore, you hold onto things that may one day come in handy, even though they never do. No matter how much money you have or don't have, if you're not going to use an item in your current lifestyle, then discard it swiftly.

Much of this stuff may be unusable anyway: unidentifiable cords, manuals, gadgets that you don't know what they are for. There is no use holding onto these.

Having random items also is touché for this syndrome. Maybe you look at that laminated hand painting an artist got you and think, "I can never buy it again, and what if someday I want to frame it and hang it in my house?" Chances are if you haven't hung it up yet, you won't.

And that's not to mention sentimental items, which are also tough as you really may never *need* them, but you *want* them to hold on to memories. But think hard about those broken eyeglasses your grandmother wore that bring you memories. Are they are worth keeping, or can you look at old photos of the two of you together where she is wearing the glasses instead?

So, bust through this and get rid of clutter. Have you used it in a year? Do you have an actual recent memory of the item that brings you so much joy that you want to permanently put the item on display in your home? Ask yourself the difficult questions and then make some decisions.

Moms usually are known for having a "someday stash." If you're a mom reading this, now is the perfect time to make the change. If you're looking to help your mom declutter, then use the techniques in this book to ease her into the idea and help her get over the "I might need it someday" syndrome.

Less clutter, less stress.

Choosing a Method for Future Purchases

I promise this chapter is getting more into the practical side of how to declutter and stay decluttered. I've said a lot about styles, reasons to declutter, and the benefits associated with decluttering, but now I want to give you some practical advice. One of the best pieces of advice I have ever received — that I am excited to pass along — is about methods for not even letting clutter come into your home!

I can't bring back the costs you incurred for all the stuff you bought, but I can help you understand the concept of the sunk costs and give you ideas and tools to make more rational decisions in the future about what to keep, toss, and bring into your space in the first place.

And lucky you, today more than ever we can use technology to our advantage to help prevent clutter from building up in the first place.

Adding existing items to an app

Apps are my friends. I only have apps on my phone that I use at least weekly, as I don't want a cluttered phone. If you prefer lists or notebooks or Excel, that's okay as well; however, keeping up items entails more of a maintenance issue. For some people, it is still therapeutic to write in notebooks and make physical lists, and I am in no way saying that is wrong. I just like apps.

Depending on the bottlenecks or blockages you identified in your goal-setting exercise (see Chapter 2), is there an area in which you are purchasing too much or that's causing you the most stress? I am in no way saying put every single item of everything you own into an app, as you wouldn't be able to have a life or job for a year if you did this. I am asking what your high-priority areas are. Where are you buying too much? Buying doubles? Stressed about having too much stuff? Start with this area.

For example, maybe your bathroom is always cluttered and causing fights between you and your partner or causing you to lose money because you can't find items before they expire. Can you never find anything in your closet so you keep buying to replace what you probably already have? If the closet is a big issue, I recommend skipping ahead to Chapter 4 to review the best apps for keeping track of your closet inventory.

For mostly everything else, I recommend the Snupps app. Snupps keeps track of what you own on a visual organizer platform. You can make shelves for anything from clothes to collectibles. It has social sharing features so you can share with your communities.

With Snupps you can make shelves for all your items! But like I said, don't go overboard. Choose an area in which you always need to know what you have so when you're out shopping, or even home online shopping, you can quickly glance at the app and say, "Oh yes, I already have four of those pale yellow vases, and I don't need a fifth."

This tip has really helped me save money and time in my bathroom when it comes to skincare and makeup. I was a self-diagnosed makeup junkie and skincare whore, and I loved to have everything and keep it way past its due date, until a skincare outbreak due to expired products changed my viewpoint on how I needed to keep my bathroom decluttered.

In addition to keeping unsafe expired products, I was throwing away hundreds of dollars monthly because I didn't have a handle on the products that I had already and was just plain buying too much. Figure 3-4 is an example of my products in the Snupps app.

Having this app with me at all times saves me money, time, and my health, so I know it's a no-brainer. The initial investment of my time to input the makeup has been far exceeded by the benefits.

Switching from items such as makeup to something more digital, I want to discuss files. I go into serious detail about digital organizing in Part 3, but I want to highlight a few points regarding having your files at your fingertips.

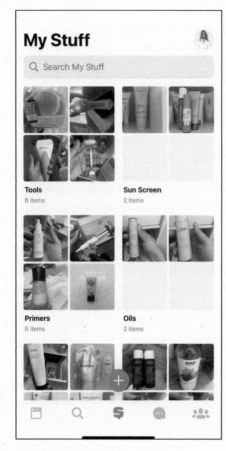

FIGURE 3-4: I love to use the Snupps app.

Source: Snupps.com

Gone are the days when we need to print everything. Heck, gone are the days when we need to email ourselves stuff or carry around USB sticks. Digital files should be seamless from your computer to your phone, whether you are an Apple and IOS user or a Microsoft Android user, or a combination of both. I am average tech savvy and I figured it out, and today I know what files I have on my decluttered computer and I can bring them up on my phone/tablet when needed.

This is kind of like carrying around an app with all your items or a briefcase with everything you might need; however, it is much more efficient.

Searching for digital files and then trying to send them somewhere can be a major time waster. Make it a point to get your digital files organized and seamlessly available. More on this in Part 3.

Scheduling shopping trips

We all shop. Some of us love it; some of us hate it. Being the latter does not mean that you buy less. Maybe you buy more to avoid shopping again.

Whatever love/hate relationship you have with shopping, the key is to make it intentional, whether you're shopping for food, clothes, cars, or vacations.

Have in mind what you need, what you already have, and of course your budget and purpose. If you're shopping aimlessly for a new blouse but don't really need it and can't remember what you already have, you're likely to buy more than you really need.

Schedule your trips based on your needs, and as simply as that, you will be a lot less likely to buy on impulse and overbuy what you already have. Be intentional with all your purchases from this day forward.

Shopping online the right way

I love online shopping, and it has definitely made me more efficient. Who doesn't love shopping without leaving your house? Yes, some people have argued the cost of shipping, but when I factor in gas prices, the wear on my car, and my time, I always prefer paying the shipping and having it delivered right to my door. Plus, today there are many ways to acquire free shipping, although some of them are triggers for buying more, so be careful.

Scheduling your online shopping

Just as I advise scheduling your physical shopping trips, I suggest you schedule your online shopping.

Scheduling allows you to think ahead, plan what you actually *need*, and avoid making random purchases. Since we schedule everything else in life, why don't we do the same with online shopping as well?

The best way I have found to schedule online shopping is to physically put it in your calendar. If you're using a digital calendar already, that is a bonus: You can enter the websites you plan to buy from in the notes, so when a window pops up for your 30 minutes of online shopping, you already know where to go.

Perhaps you need to do some research before you buy, which is wonderful, but set time limits. You can get lost in analysis paralysis and end up wasting time and being more confused than when you started. Before you research, know your needs and budget, and then set the timeline to decide.

Now, many of you are probably thinking, "Well, when I saw the Instagram pop-up for the teeth whitening solution, I just bought it in literally ten seconds and it saved me so much time." Yes, perhaps, but did you really need that teeth whitener, of which you already have ten that are not used? If you're planning a trip to L.A., for example, and want to whiten your teeth, it's probably best to schedule a shopping trip either online or in the store to buy this product so you will be ready to use it when it actually arrives! The moral of that story is that today we are inundated with products coming to us, and with the web basically watching our every move on the Internet, we are targeted with hundreds of ads weekly that are usually curated to our style and taste. And I am sure this trend will keep going; marketers having access to our wants and needs is making it easier and faster to sell things to us. I have no problem with this concept, as when I truly need something, I love it when it shows up and I can easily buy it. But it is the want that we need to be disciplined about with this type of targeted marketing approach.

Therefore, schedule your online shopping because it's easy to go from being super-productive on your computer to shopping online for a useless gadget you don't need but are now consumed with reading hundreds of reviews about. Don't go down that hole; stop yourself. And never randomly shop online when you're bored, tired, or stressed. The 3 a.m. purchases I have made are the worst clutter I have accumulated.

While I stress that shopping trips should be scheduled, today it is overly easy to just hop onto a site and start shopping. And having the extra convenience of all your credit cards and PayPal info saved can be a great time-saver but also can be extremely costly with regards to accumulating more clutter.

We all have our payment methods linked to everything! Of course, this makes sense for recurring purchases as a time-saver and ensuring we stay on track; however, try to not do this for anything online shopping–related.

Unlinking all your payment methods

Unlink your payment methods now, or the next time you're online shopping, you may be buying too much! Figure 3-5 provides a clear visual of how easy it is today to buy online with your linked credit cards.

This is one of the best tips to help you minimize your online shopping sprees. If you need something, you're likely to be ready and you can use your wallet to input your credit card info. If you are just shopping on the fly and the prompt asks you for a credit card but you're not willing to get up or during the time you walk to get your wallet you change your mind, you probably didn't need the item in the first place.

FIGURE 3-5:
Online
shopping
can be a little
too easy.

Mediamodifier / Pixabay

I do want to stress that online shopping can be more efficient as today stores don't even carry items or sizes you may need, so they actually suggest buying them online. It is very annoying when you physically take your time to visit a store only to be sent home to buy it online. Avoid this by starting online.

WARNING

There are times when you need to physically visit a store, and that's okay too. Sometimes, you have to see how the item works, compare it to another model, or try it on for size. Whatever the reason, just make sure the trip is scheduled.

Holding Yourself Accountable

With all this great advice, you may be wondering how you actually follow it. You are probably thinking, "Yes, I will never make another unscheduled shopping trip again!" But then, alas, you do. So how do you stop yourself?

Listing your items

List what you need. Simple as that. Make a list in your notebook. On your computer. In your agenda. Just do it. I love lists!

Finding an accountability partner

Ask someone to help you as with anything else in life! We need a person to help us along the way just like we need tutors, personal trainers, mentors, teachers — whatever it is, we just sometimes need to talk to someone or get advice. And decluttering is no different.

Find a friend, family member, co-worker, neighbor — whomever you can share your decluttering goal with — and ask that person to help you along the way. Trust me, people love to do this and will likely also get motivated themselves to declutter. If you were to tell your neighbor that you want to declutter your garage this summer and ask him to help keep you accountable, I am sure he would oblige.

You can ask your accountability partner to be on the lookout for you getting too much new stuff or to help you declutter what you have. You can even ask for help reviewing what you have when you're planning to buy something new.

I guarantee by the end of your decluttering challenge your accountability partner will be right there with you decluttering her life, and then maybe you can keep it going with other areas.

Make sure to keep them related to your lifestyle goals.

Using the emotional versus practical checklist

Is it practical?

» Do you use this item on a regular basis?

» Does it provide value to your life?

» Can someone else use it?

Is it emotional?

» Are you keeping this because of a memory?

» Do you have similar items attached to this memory?

» Is the item a gift from someone special but something you don't use or like?

» Would your friends or family see the value in this item?

Making Decluttering Fun

The reason we procrastinate in our life is usually because we don't like doing the task at hand. And sadly, decluttering has gotten a bad rap for not being fun. There are lots of ways to change this, including starting today and reflecting on the positive benefits that will hopefully motivate you to continue decluttering in a sustainable, organic way. If the benefits are not enough to help make this fun, check out the following ideas.

Turn up the tunes

Turn up the tunes, put on your favorite podcast or show, grab a glass of champagne, do whatever to make the process more fun. Plus, realize that with each item you remove physically or from your mind, you are one step closer to reaching your goals.

Enlist a friend

Guaranteed you have a friend, co-worker, or neighbor who has also been putting off decluttering. Figure 3-6 shows the smiling faces of friends helping friends declutter. Ask for help and give help in return. This is especially important for emotional clutterbugs because friends don't have the same attachment to your things as you do.

FIGURE 3-6: Friends decluttering.

Wavebreakmedia / Shutterstock

Celebrate your success

Recognize your progress, celebrate milestones, and don't get discouraged. Keep on going! Every little bit of decluttering will save you time.

And with that I leave you one of my favorite quotes. "For every minute spent planning, an hour is earned." – Benjamin Franklin.

2

Getting Rid of Clutter in Your Home

» **Making the most of your closet space**

» **Organizing accessories**

» **Taking seasons into consideration**

Chapter **4**
Decluttering Your Closet

M ost people laugh when I say that I love organizing and decluttering closets in my spare time. From the time I was a small child, my closet was always the focal point of my bedroom. Growing up in rural Canada, our shopping options were very limited, so for me it was less about what was in the closet and more about how it was set up, my organizing strategy, and of course, it was always clutter-free.

As my love for fashion grew and I was able to move to a larger city for college, I started to shop a lot. This was when I knew I needed to have a constant decluttering closet strategy to not only keep my closet organized but to keep my shopping habits in check (a girl could only have so many Forever 21 tube tops). I used to spend Saturday nights decluttering and reorganizing my closet instead of joining the clubbing festivities. Friends would constantly be in awe of my closet and would garner my advice and tricks at any chance they got. This is where I developed my signature tips, tricks, and closet organizing processes, which have since become a profitable business.

Your closet is one of the first things you see in the morning, and it's also the hidden time waster that, once refined, can increase your overall confidence and save you time and energy. Creating a decluttered, streamlined closet can help you stay focused, productive, and efficient — starting first thing in the morning. Closet decluttering also frees up space and helps you save time getting ready every day. Finally, it can also benefit others when you donate pieces you haven't worn in years. Follow the steps in this chapter to change your closet habits, optimize your space, and refine your style to save money and fit your lifestyle.

Creating a Closet Decluttering Strategy

Recent studies show that when people hear the word "declutter," 50 percent of the population think of their closets, which often triggers emotions regarding purchase regrets or even financial concerns of overspending on items (some closets could have funded a down payment on a house or been used to help pay a child's college tuition). Decluttering can also be difficult for people who haven't determined their signature style, as it often leads to hanging onto extra items they "might" need one day.

My advice to get started is simple: Push your resistance to the side, dive in, and determine ways to keep your decluttering momentum.

Diving into the decluttering process won't magically make everyone better or smarter consumers when it comes to closets. That "high" associated with getting new clothing is hard to forget, and this makes it even harder to start because you also have to change your ongoing habits to sustain the process.

WARNING

Decluttering involves being brutally honest with yourself about more important things than which shirt to keep. Going back to developing the decluttering mindset, the closet relates to bigger-picture topics including finances, consumer habits, and breaking the cycle of binge-shopping and then purging.

Here are a few strategies to help get you started:

>> **Commit to regularly evaluating and tossing things as needed as opposed to only doing yearly decluttering clean-outs.** Your commitment to constant decluttering versus one-time binges will also drastically help with keeping track of new purchases, taking inventory of what you already have, and avoiding overbuying.

>> **Determine a strategy for how to make closet decluttering a habit.** For example, schedule quarterly decluttering sessions on your calendar to stay on track.

>> **Compartmentalize categories to start with rather than your entire closet.** For example, start with your shoes, then your handbags, then your work attire. This process helps you avoid that panic of feeling like you have nothing to wear if you declutter your entire closet at once. Tackling categories can also help give you a sense of accomplishment when you complete each category.

>> **Avoid immediately replacing items due to the potential "empty closet syndrome."** Decluttering your closet can make you feel lighter and more organized, but it won't immediately change your purchasing habits. Make sure

you stay mindful in your decluttering habits to avoid impulsive purchases post–closet overhaul.

>> **Envision the rewards of not only how much time you will save in your closet but how much better you will feel with the carefully selected pieces that remain.** Having a carefully curated closet helps you feel appreciative of the items you own. Knowing exactly what you have will also encourage you to take better care of your clothes.

Executing Your Closet Decluttering Strategy

Once you've determined whether you're doing a complete closet overhaul, a quarterly decluttering session, or tackling your closet categorically, the next step in the closet decluttering process is creating a strategy to help you feel lighter and save time and energy. Your strategy can help you feel successful and focused in both your work and personal life.

REMEMBER

For example, when you're assigned that next travel assignment for work, you'll feel confident accepting it as you won't have to think twice about packing. Knowing exactly what you're going to wear every morning will help you better tackle business meetings, boss mindsets, and networking events. You will notice immediately how much less effort it takes to not only show up to work but perform better. Your newly decluttered wardrobe will give way to time-saving and confidence-boosting routines.

For personal trips, you will also enjoy not only the packing process, but the unpacking process as you will not have excess clutter left over in your suitcases or in your closet.

Your day-to-day life will also feel more focused, and when company comes over, you will proudly be able to display your closet and share your decluttering closet secrets.

I place a lot of emphasis on planning, which I think is important for decluttering any space from both physical and mental standpoints. But then you actually have to dive in and declutter, and the closet is sometimes the most overwhelming. To give you extra motivation, start with the following exercise to help you further commit to getting started.

Trying the time-wasting closet exercise

TIP

You want to be as efficient as possible, so it's important to determine how clutter is affecting your time. Most often, closet clutter is the reason that people are chronically late, struggling to figure out what to wear in the morning, or even wasting time and energy during the day worrying about what to wear.

The best way to figure out how much time you're actually wasting in the closet due to clutter is to track this time for a week. You don't have to track everything you do in the closet, but simply track your daily closet habits regarding decluttering. Here are some tips to get started:

1. **Make notes on your phone about how much time in the morning you waste.** Are you spending time rifling through drawers trying to find an item you lost?

2. **Record the actual time on specific categories of clothing.** This step will help prioritize which items are the biggest decluttering time wasters. See Figure 4-1 for a shot of my recent time-wasting analysis.

3. **Analyze which areas of the closet cause you the most stress.** You'll likely find you're spending the most time on the areas that are most cluttered.

DAY	Wondering what to wear	Looking for a specific item	Re-ironing/ re-washing	Changing outfits	Travel packing
Day 1	10	20	0	0	0
Day 2	0	0	10	0	0
Day 3	20	0	0	0	0
Day 4	0	10	0	0	0
Day 5	20	0	0	5	25
Day 6	5	5	5	0	0
Day 7	0	0	0	10	0
TOTAL	55	35	15	15	25
Grand total = 145 minutes					

FIGURE 4-1: The results of my time-wasting exercise.

Image courtesy of author

Now is the time to jump in and start the decluttering process. As with my advice in previous chapters, you can start small, making it a daily ten-minute task, or choose one category to start with and do a complete overhaul. If you are choosing the latter, ensure you have blocked enough time in your calendar to jump in with no distractions.

Finding the happy clothing balance

Getting your clothing balance correct can often require years of trial and error. What I mean by clothing balance is having the right amount and type of clothes that you use daily for your lifestyle. The amount of time needed to find this balance is an individual exercise, and there is no specific time frame that can be prescribed. Finding a balance between what you should or want to be wearing and what you actually *do* wear is difficult. Breaking these actions into the following steps can be helpful:

1. **Review your lifestyle.**

   Accounting for both your work and personal life, what do you wear the most? Is it work suits, jeans, or activewear? Is there something that you should be wearing more for work or personal purposes?

2. **Determine your needs.**

   Once you categorize your needs and what you're actually wearing, do you find you have too much of one clothing item that you don't need or should not be wearing? Are there any key items you want or need that are missing? Categorize clothing as work or personal and then determine the amount of time spent in each. In some cases 80 percent of your clothes may be for office-type work, and hopefully they're a bit versatile to also wear for personal outings.

3. **Circle back to what you currently wear.**

   Hopefully it fits into your work and personal lives. If not, determine what you need, and be realistic!

Optimizing Your Closet Space

You are probably thinking that a small closet is easier to declutter, but this is not necessarily the case. Larger spaces let you see more of the items inside, which can cause less clutter to build up. However, on the flip side, larger closets can also be the reason you accumulate so much stuff and feel the need to fill the space. The moral of this paragraph is that closet space alone is not the reason that clutter builds up.

If you have a small closet, don't get discouraged, as there are plenty of ways to streamline and organize the space to make it seem bigger. The first step when maximizing your closet space is to declutter; then with a few products, installations, and decorating tips, tiny closets can be the perfect size.

Taking inventory

Without knowing your inventory of closet items, it is inevitable that you will acquire more clutter or "stuff" than you need. Taking inventory of what's currently in your closet will automatically help you declutter! Assess each piece. If it's not even worth keeping track of, it's not worth keeping at all.

Here are a few top ways to take inventory in your closet:

» **Get an app.** There are tons of closet apps on the market. It may seem tedious, but trust me, it is a game changer. Not only will you have your entire closet with you when you shop, but it also makes trip planning easier, encourages you to continually declutter, and keeps you conscious of how much you are adding to your closet with every new purchase. To see my favorite apps, please see the nearby sidebar and look at Figure 4-2 for a glimpse of the Closet+ app in action.

» **Take photos.** If technology is not your thing, or if you're too scared to make the commitment to document every piece of clothing, take photos of each section of your closet. Although less detailed, photos can give an overview of what you have and can be used for basic inventory purposes.

» **Make a list.** Old-school methods still work. Using a notebook or an Excel spreadsheet to list your items can be helpful, but it can be a lot of work to sustain and doesn't give you a visual overview.

» **Review quarterly.** I am an advocate of quarterly decluttering regardless, but if all the preceding points don't work for your lifestyle or you aren't ready to fully commit to an inventory tracking system, review your closet inventory quarterly and make the best mental notes possible.

Evaluating your space

While you may dream of 500-square-foot closet spaces, adding closet space is not necessarily the best approach to decluttering. Less space naturally forces you to be more conscious of what you are putting into that space. I recommend evaluating the space to make sure it fits the clothes you want to keep and that your existing clothes have a well-designed home. You want your space to reflect your needs and optimize your efficiency. Evaluate whether you need to add or change the space to make it easier to grab items, or add another section if there is not enough room.

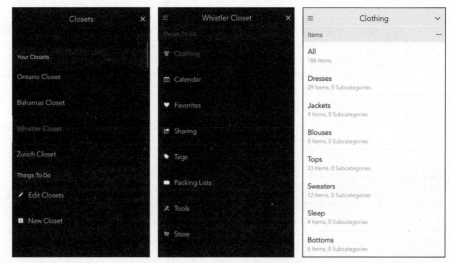

FIGURE 4-2:
The Closet+
app in action.

Source: Closet+ (closetapp.com)

MY RECOMMENDED CLOSET APPS

There is a difference between simple closet inventory apps and fashion apps. I focus solely on apps that you can use to keep track of your items to help with the decluttering process. Then you will know what you have instead of buying more. Here are my favorites:

Closet+: A simple closet app where you can either upload a photo of your items or take a picture. Main features include multiple closet options, categories, outfit planning, cost-per-wear calculator, and tags. https://closetapp.com

Purse and Shoe Cache: Stores detailed information on your shoes and handbags, including purchase details, notes, and photos. http://www.mypursecache.com; http://myshoecache.com

Snupps: Keeps track of what you own on a visual organizer platform. You can make shelves for anything from clothes to collectibles. It has social sharing features so you can share with your communities. www.snupps.com

There are plenty of fashion apps that help pick out your outfits, show when you last wore an item, and offer many more functionalities. Although these apps can be useful for decluttering in terms of selecting combinations and seeing what you haven't worn in months, you may not be ready for or need all these fashion-savvy functions to get started.

REMEMBER

There are no guidelines for how much closet space a person typically needs. A small New York city dwelling might have the tiniest closet space, but the person living in it might work in fashion and have more clothing needs than someone living in a larger house with less clothing needs or interests. (However, given that my mom is an architect, I know a few important closet dimensions that can be considered "typical," which I discuss in the following sections.)

To properly utilize your space, you may need to create either more hanging or shelving space depending on what is needed for your items. Closet organization is a big business with do-it-yourself packages available at home improvement stores or Ikea and professional consultants and custom builders available to those with a bigger closet budget. Whichever way you go, there are some basic closet organization ideas you can apply to your situation.

Organizing a walk-in closet

Walk-in closets can vary in shape and size depending on your home's layout. If you do have the chance to design your closet, it's a great time to work in your specific lifestyle clothing choices and build around them. This way you will have the appropriate rods and shelves versus too much shelving, which then prompts you to buy more if the shelves look empty. Typical walk-in closet shapes are square, rectangular, and L-shaped. Figure 4-3 shows your basic rectangular walk-in closet space.

FIGURE 4-3:
A walk-in closet with custom organization.

Irainero / Pixabay

The key is to design a solution around your already decluttered items that fits your current needs and lifestyle. I have seen many large walk-in closets that are clutter-free, and it usually stems from the owner doing thorough planning and also making the space part of their home — something that they are proud to show off with no fear of guests seeing a cluttered mess.

Organizing a reach-in closet

Reach-in closets (see Figure 4-4) are typically found in smaller bedrooms and apartments. They are usually rectangular and approximately 8 feet long. They are perfect for single users, and with decluttering strategies, I have seen these closets fit most people's needs. The key to organizing a reach-in closet is to be sure to plan for seasonality, if it applies, as sometimes modifications or extra storage space may be needed for seasonal items. Your goal with the reach-in closet is also to make it part of the home and not be afraid to open it when guests arrive. This is a sign of a peaceful and clutter-free space.

FIGURE 4-4:
A reach-in closet with an organization solution added.

Jose Soriano / Unsplash

Determining what to hang and fold

Don't underestimate the importance of deciding what to hang and what to fold! If you have four shelves full of folded pants, it may be time to reevaluate whether you need them all. If you have no room for your hanging blouses because your pants are taking up all the hanging space, this is another opportunity to reevaluate what to hang and fold. Keep in mind the type of clothes you own and what takes up the most space. Do most of your clothes hang or need to be folded? If you mostly wear sweaters and t-shirts, you need a lot of shelving. If you mostly wear a lot of collared blouses and dresses, you need plenty of hanging space.

I don't want to go into details of what to hang or fold since this book is dedicated to decluttering rather than organizing. So I suggest you declutter first and then make sure you are properly hanging and folding what is needed. Following are my guidelines to help you get started.

What to hang:

>> Pants with a crease (pants without can be folded)

>> Blouses made of any material (iron and button top, middle, and bottom buttons)

>> Jackets

>> Blazers

>> Slippery silks and satins

>> Clothes made of delicate fabric

>> Most dresses

>> Camisoles

What to fold:

>> Sweaters

>> Knitwear

>> T-shirts

>> Jeans

>> Sweats

>> Lingerie

>> Special dresses (things that are heavily beaded, or dresses similar to a Hervé Léger bandage dress)

Donate, Repurpose, Tailor, Sell, or Toss?

TIP

During the inventory process, I recommend labeling a few boxes "Donate," "Repurpose," "Tailor," "Sell," and "Toss." I sell these boxes on my website to help you have a seamless decluttering process. Once you have your boxes, you can place your items in the appropriate box as you go through them and accomplish multiple steps at once.

» **Donate:** As Chapter 1 discusses in detail, donating should be at the heart of your decluttering mindset. Being able to donate your items to benefit others not only helps your closet but also helps you improve other people's lives. In our consumerist society, you need to be aware of not only how much you are buying but how you can further your belongings' sustainability. Donating does not just mean giving away items to your local thrift shop; it can also mean giving items to neighbors, friends, and family. I often schedule friends' dates where we swap clothing — over champagne, of course! As long as your items are in wearable condition, someone should be wearing them!

» **Repurpose:** An often-forgotten part of decluttering is that a multitude of closet items can be repurposed. Clothing can be cropped, cut, changed, added to, or even used for cleaning rags once it's unwearable or stained to the point of no return. Jewelry can be melted into other shapes and sizes, scarves can be used for decorations, and leather boots can be used for repair patches or made into smaller leather goods.

» **Tailor:** Tailoring can mean so much more than getting your jeans hemmed. I'm guessing you won't wear clothes if they don't fit properly. Even if you love that special blazer, you won't wear it if it hangs weirdly or looks boxy. Find a good tailor and bring in items that you're not ready to part with but never wear. Trust me, a good tailor can work wonders for your decluttering habits, especially since many brands fit similarly.

» **Sell:** This advice may sound contradictory to my first point of giving clothing to others who may benefit, but this point is also still very valid. I suggest you resell valuable, lightly worn items. This approach is a great way for fashionistas to keep wearing the top trends and be able to frequently switch styles. There are many apps, online consignment stores, and retail stores that sell lightly used items. Strike up a relationship with a consignment store if you have many items or start your own online store on apps like DePop. Remember, pre-loved items are a great way to still capture a piece of your money back if you want to always be on top of trends but not have a closet full of never worn items.

» **Toss:** At some point, closet items will no longer be usable. They may be too stained, ripped beyond repair, or just plain overworn such that you cannot sell, donate, tailor, or even repurpose them. At this point, you can toss these items.

TIP

The best way to stay on track with decluttering via this box method is to keep the boxes in your closet as a daily, constant reminder to continue decluttering. For year, I've suggested to clients, friends, and family that they label a few boxes in their home to make decluttering part of their daily routine. But let's be honest: Who wants a ratty cardboard box, or worse, a plastic garbage bag lying around in their closet? I've designed pretty labeled declutter boxes to help you stay on track and help you make decluttering a sustainable habit and for you to stay fully committed. These look very cute in closets and check out my website to get them.

Again, decluttering will happen naturally once you make this process a habit. An hour of closet updates every quarter will keep you on track and hold you accountable. At the very least, it will be a reminder once it pops up.

Another key to staying on track is to recount how you feel when you actually declutter. Especially with donations, it's important to realize that your decluttering is benefiting others. If you journal, take notes of how your feel after a closet declutter; likely, these small actions will help keep you motivated to stay on track. Here are a few more ideas to hold yourself accountable:

>> **Schedule weekly calendar pop-ups.** A weekly reminder, even if only five minutes, titled "Closet Declutter" will keep you on track in your decluttering mission.

>> **Create quarterly friend dinners and decluttering sessions.** Sharing your task with friends adds a fun, team aspect to decluttering.

>> **Have pre-scheduled pickups for your donation items.** This ensures that your items actually get donated instead of sitting in the garage for weeks.

>> **Get your family or school involved by arranging donation drives.** Having a support system makes the decluttering process much easier. Schedule in a few donation drives so that you're held accountable to your goals.

Decluttering Accessories

Accessories can often make up the remaining clutter that causes the most stress, so don't skip this important step! The small things can cause more clutter than larger items, and having perfectly organized boxes for all your accessories is useless if you never use them or forget you even have them and end up buying more.

The following sections walk you through the ins and outs of decluttering your different types of accessories.

Sorting your seasonal shoes and boots

Most of my organizing advice centers around creating systems that work for your lifestyle, and shoe and boot storage is no exception. I always suggest sorting through your shoes as the starting point for decluttering accessories. I recommend categorizing the process as follows:

» **Sort by type or occasion.** My advice usually centers around sorting by similar types, colors, and usage. Shoes and boots can easily be sorted into type and/ or occasion. For example, you can organize by exercise shoes, daily work shoes, and special occasion shoes. Boots can also be further broken down into height, warmth, and function.

» **Sort by usage:** Seeing all your boots and shoes lined up by how much you use them makes you more aware of which shoes and boots you actually use and which ones to declutter. Sorting by usage also makes you aware of which shoes are overworn and helps you keep a rotational system going to evenly wear your footwear. As shown in Figure 4-5, I encourage you to look inside every shoe box to really figure out what what you currently have.

FIGURE 4-5: Shoe decluttering requires knowing what's in those shoeboxes.

Image courtesy of author (photo credit: @avalonmohns)

REMEMBER

Once you have your boots and shoes sorted, it will be easier to declutter more efficiently. As with most of my other advice, make shoe decluttering a habit by doing it quarterly or seasonally.

Decluttering your handbags

Handbags are my true passion. (Full disclosure: I cringe when I have to declutter handbags.) It is perfectly fine to have one handbag for all occasions and many others based on your style or needs. My advice is to update and evaluate your handbags to make sure they are efficient, fit your current lifestyle, and add ease and purpose to outfits.

Note: For men, this section may seem useless, but there are many "man bags," such as briefcases, travel backpacks, and duffel bags. Therefore, handbags in this book are unisex.

Decluttering handbags should involve thorough analysis of what you need for staples, what you currently have, and whether you're in the handbag game strictly for purpose or for investment and fashion. The differing approaches to handbags will eventually determine your decluttering style.

Which of the following handbag users are you?

>> **Purposeful handbag user:** Someone who solely has handbags for purpose versus style will have a very streamlined collection, and decluttering is usually a simpler process. Keep that which is functional and you use 80 percent of the time. You still may have a few staples; however, your primary concern is function and that the style and color fit with most of your outfits.

>> **Fashion handbag user:** If you collect a variety of different handbags based on fashion trends, decluttering is very important; otherwise, you will end up with a handbag wasteland.

>> **Investment handbag user:** Classic handbags can become not only wardrobe staples but also investment pieces if cared for properly. Keeping these bags stored properly away from clutter preserves them and ensures you are using them enough. Figure 4-6 shows ideal handbag storage with plexiglass dividers, which can allow for all items to be viewed, accessed, and properly stored.

Decluttering inside your handbag

I am by no means going to attempt to list what you need or don't need in your purse; all of us have different needs, and there is a reason why most magazines and social blogs ask celebrities what's inside their purse on a monthly basis — it's fascinating to know what other women carry in their purses!

FIGURE 4-6:
Handbag
storage.

Image courtesy of author Photocredit
@carlyingramphotographypro

What is also fascinating is the amount of clutter that can end up in your purse and stay there for years. I think purse decluttering is very important for a variety of reasons, including your health, as carrying too much can cause pains in your back, neck, and shoulders and can lead to worse problems. The *Journal of Physical Therapy Science* states that typically we should never carry more than 10 percent of our body weight, meaning a 130-pound woman should never carry a purse heavier than 13 pounds. If you get close to exceeding this rule of thumb, consider a second, roller bag for larger or heavier items such as computers, or declutter more!

I want to help make sure your purse stays clutter-free and practical; you don't want your purse to resemble a junk pit or time-wasting item because you can never find anything.

A purse is something that usually you never leave the house without, and I am just as passionate about what is inside my handbag as I am about the beautiful designs and colors they come in on the outside.

From my experience, you are either one of two types of handbag users: You have multiple handbags in different sizes, shapes, colors, and textures for different occasions. (Of course, you have decluttered your handbags to make sure the ones you have are actually used, but you enjoy switching handbags for special occasions or even daily.) Or, you have one handbag you use every day for all occasions.

You may also fall somewhere in between and switch your handbags sometimes or rarely, but I find that most people fall into one of the two preceding categories.

If you are like me and switch your handbags for occasions, this does not mean you're off the hook. You still need to practice some handbag decluttering tips. Typically, if you are switching handbags constantly, they are naturally more decluttered because you physically have to move items from one handbag to the next on a regular basis, and this in itself helps to prevent clutter. However, when moving items between purses, don't just move them. Check to make sure you're moving things you actually use!

If you carry only one bag consistently, you need to make an even more conscious effort to do a thorough edit of what's in your handbag.

Here are some suggestions to help lighten your purses:

- >> **Go through your handbags quarterly.** This is especially important if you don't switch handbags. A quarterly declutter session should be the minimum frequency you declutter your handbags. The more often you declutter, the less stuff you accumulate!

- >> **Go digital.** As much as possible, avoid carrying too many coins or cards. Keep store membership numbers in your phone, and avoid carrying too much cash.

- >> **Use see-through pouches.** If you like to carry essentials with you in your purse, instead of having them loose, consider a see through-pouch. This way, you will be reminded of what is in it, making it easier to declutter. I sell these pouches on www.organizedjane.com.

- >> **Consider a handbag organizer.** If you switch your purses often, consider investing in an organizer that you can transfer from one to the next. However, this still means you need to be mindful to declutter the organizers.

- >> **Spend a few minutes daily organizing.** Since our purses are so important and I practically panic when I lose sight of my purse even for a second, I encourage you to spend a few minutes at the end of your day to check the inside of your purse.

Figure 4-7 offers a peek inside my decluttered handbag, complete with see-through pouch so I can easily see what's inside.

Storing your scarves

Another big accessory that seems to be daunting on the decluttering front is scarves. From winter to summer, scarves are an understated fashion and practical accessory that have challenged organizing gurus for years! I keep my larger scarves on scarf hangers, and I fold my smaller silk scarves (see Figure 4-8).

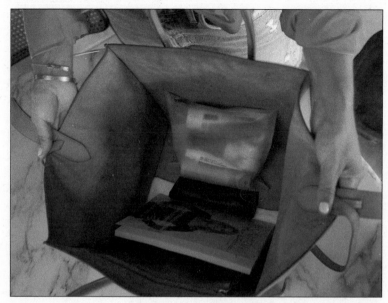

FIGURE 4-7:
A sneak-peek
inside my
handbag.

Image courtesy of author; Photocredit @lohmmedia

Here are my top tips for scarf decluttering:

>> **Take inventory.** Similar to inventorying clothes, find a way to do this for scarves. An app, photos, or lists are helpful. Physically taking inventory of them helps you sort which ones you want to donate, repurpose, tailor, sell or toss.

>> **Be brutal.** The number of scarves you own can sneak up on you. Try them on and ask yourself whether you wear them or not. If it helps, take photos of yourself wearing the scarves and ask your friends for advice.

>> **Determine what's sentimental.** If you have sentimental scarves passed down from friends or family members, make a special box for them and store them in a safe place. I recommend putting a see-through lid on the box or a photo on the outside so that you can keep track of what is inside.

>> **Consider what's real-estate worthy.** If you have expensive scarfs that you never wear, consider selling them or putting them on display by framing them and making them part of your home décor.

Decluttering jewelry

Jewelry is an interesting and often overlooked part of the decluttering process. It's easy to forget about because it doesn't take up much physical space. Jewelry can be highly sentimental, valuable, and often has hidden meanings.

First things first, you need to fully commit to a jewelry declutter because it's important not to have things hidden in boxes or drawers that you don't wear or even remember that you had.

One major step for jewelry decluttering goes back to finding a style balance and how much you accessorize. Some people love to change accessories daily and have pounds of jewelry for every occasion. I refer to this jewelry as costume jewelry, not because you are wearing it for a costume, but because it helps to distinguish between more expensive jewelry that is usually purchased from a designer or reputable jeweler versus jewelry from a store selling many accessories. It is not a bad thing to wear many different accessories, and this is completely a style choice.

Whether you are constantly changing your jewelry to match your outfits or you stick to your staples, decluttering strategies are necessary. Consider the following factors:

>> **Frequency of use:** I talk about this term a lot because it applies to your whole house. Sorting by frequency of use automatically helps you declutter your jewelry. Determine what your staples are and what you wear once in a while, and declutter accordingly.

>> **Repurposing potential:** I mentioned this advice for clothes, and the same thing can be said for jewelry. If you don't wear a certain piece, make it into something else, give it to a friend, or sell it.

>> **Storage possibilities:** How you store your jewelry effectively determines how you can continue to declutter. Jewelry stored in boxes tucked away at the back of your closet will continue to be clutter, and you will likely get more. Have your jewelry visible and easy to access. If you need to keep your jewelry stored in a safe because of its value, then perhaps having it visible will not be an option, but keep valuable safe real estate free and clear of lingering clutter.

Belts

I added this section about belts because I am always amazed by how this accessory is often forgotten. We seem to have more belts than we need or than even fit. Go through each and every one of your belts and resist the urge to keep the ones that "might fit" someday or that you "might" wear with certain pants that you don't own.

Everything else

We have lots of other items that make their way into our closets. Stick to all the tips I have given you so far, the biggest being that if you don't use it or wear it, it is clutter. Evaluate and move on.

Planning Seasonally

Effectively planning for each season ensures that you're ready and excited for the next season.

My motto is quite simple: If you haven't worn something this season, will you wear it the next? Many factors likely come into consideration: emotional, practical, financial, and fashion. If after two seasons it still has not been worn, then maybe some stronger questions need to be asked. I am not saying to get rid of your classic cashmere coat that you didn't wear for two seasons as chances are you might wear it again, but the pink puffy jacket you haven't worn for two seasons is likely a different case.

Seasonal items fall into the following categories:

>> **Day-to-day wear:** What are your staple items? This clothing should be assessed quarterly, and if you move to a different seasonal climate, make sure you declutter for that season.

>> **Sporting attire:** Some sports are seasonal, and related clothing, such as ski attire, should be stored when it can't be used. If you didn't use it, evaluate it before you store it.

>> **Vacation staples:** These items may be part of your seasonal routine if you vacation at the same time and place annually, or if you have certain staples you always take on vacation. However, when you return from trips, make sure to note what you did not use or wear and declutter immediately.

Chapter **5**
Decluttering Your Bathroom

Bathroom clutter is often forgotten behind closed cabinets or drawers, and products are often expired or no longer needed when you finally deal with it. I wish I could see a show of hands of who is reading this right now and thinking about their overflowing bathroom cabinets. Consumer research shows that bathroom cabinets are now filled with over 140 million products! Cosmetic trends also have our bathroom cabinets filled to the brim. And to make matters worse, I bet you have multiples of the same product in your bathroom, which is not only clutter but could be a dangerous mess if left too long.

Decluttering Your Products

I love decluttering bathrooms, mine and other people's. Call me crazy but bathrooms usually are the smallest rooms in most homes and they can be the messiest, so decluttering them brings me intense joy. I am also a recovering makeup junkie. I used to spend hours poring over the latest *Seventeen* magazines when I was a teenager to learn new techniques and read about the best new beauty products. After getting my first job busing tables at the ripe age of 12, I began spending my hard-earned cash at the local drugstores and department store makeup counters, endlessly chatting with the staff and trying every new product that ever existed. When Sephora came to NYC in 1998, it was like a dream, and

I wasted so much money on countless products that I didn't need or had similar if not the exact same items already. To sum it up, my addiction was real, and it was only when I became an organizing expert that I realized I had a serious problem and completely changed my makeup and skincare shopping habits.

The point of this story is that your bathroom shopping habits have a lot to do with how cluttered your bathroom is. It is quite similar to the garage in the sense that your habits and hobbies have a lot to do with the amount of clutter you accumulate. You may not think of skincare and makeup as a hobby, but tell that to the countless makeup YouTubers making seven figures on their delightful monthly favorites and product reviews. I don't allow myself this guilty pleasure anymore because it only leads to more products.

WARNING

As you may have already realized, bathroom decluttering goes deep into your bathroom cabinets as well as your habits around grooming and lifestyle. Yes, it is sometimes a sensitive subject. From pill poppers to makeup junkies like my former self, this decluttering subject may make you deal with some of your inner bad habits that can be worse than the junk drawer syndrome that I discuss in the kitchen chapter.

However, I am here to help you work through this. You may not have any bad habits, in which case this will be a straightforward chapter. Maybe your only bathroom possessions are your toothbrush and a comb and, in that case, you can skip this chapter altogether. Alas, for the rest of us, don't get discouraged and declutter on. I am confident that the dreaded bathroom cabinets will soon emit a clutter-free, zenlike serenity that the entire bathroom should reflect, as seen in Figure 5-1.

Here are a few strategies to help get you started:

>> **Avoid storing multiples.** I think being prepared for anything is important, from earthquakes to having spare toothpaste so you don't have to run to the store at midnight. However, I don't agree with storing multiples of all your bathroom products and certainly not more than one extra of each. If you're at Costco and you see your exact moisturizer on sale in a set of 20, think twice. Will they expire before you're even ready to use them? Will you switch moisturizers next month? Will your skin type change? Are you willing to give up your precious real estate in the bathroom for these to sit for possibly years?

>> **Let your bathroom real estate guide you.** Often, I caution against space — just because you have a 1,000-square-foot attic doesn't mean you have to fill it! The bathroom is usually the only room in the house where I say that space should help you determine how much stuff you can physically keep. And more often than not, especially with newer modern bathrooms, there is actually less storage space. So, let this be the first sign to declutter.

FIGURE 5-1:
A zenlike
bathroom.

Rene Asmussen / Pexels

» **Your bathroom is not Sephora.** This was a hard one for me to grasp. I loved
to have every lip color, collagen treatment, and newest face massaging gadget
in my bathroom. But you don't need endless numbers of products that
essentially do the same job or are the newest trends. As I mention earlier,
you can have a spare of your essentials, but that is it. Do an inventory of how
much you have and how much it cost you, and you will soon realize how much
money you are wasting on bathroom products! The bathroom can be a
serious money pit!

» **Let go of the past.** I talk a lot about this concept, especially when dealing with
sentimental items, and bathroom products are no different. You don't need to
keep the prescribed throat spray for that strep throat you had five years ago.
That special shade of eyeshadow you wore at your wedding ten years ago
and haven't worn since? You likely won't wear it again, and neither will your
daughter. Ditto the overpriced beard oil you bought two years ago but always
forget to use. Bathroom decluttering applies to both genders. Even dogs
somehow have more shampoo selections than I did when I was a kid.

Determining your essentials

Now that I got through the tough stuff, I want to focus on what really is essential, and I mean *really* essential. I want you to remember that bathroom items are easy to replace, find, and source. The pharmaceutical and cosmetic industries are two of the largest industries in North America; therefore, you can replace anything. Plus, they continue to innovate. This is one area of decluttering that you can freely declutter knowing that tomorrow you could buy ten more easily if needed. Keep this in mind as you work through the chapter.

The medicine cabinet is a good place to start.

Medicine cabinet

Now, chances are you have lots of items — not only medicine — in this cabinet, and I challenge you when you're doing this exercise to focus only on medicine.

Go through all your cold remedies, prescriptions, pain relievers, and whatever else you have stored and check expiry dates first and foremost. Then toss what you have not used in the last year. Yes, even the NyQuil. You may say, "But I could get a cold this year." Yes, you could, but you also could not. And chances are your local pharmacy will have an updated cold medication for if you need it.

When it comes to medications, I even get a bit scientific. According to a study at the University of California, many staples that you have in your medicine cabinet, such as nasal sprays, eye drops, and even some lotions, have ingredients that can inhibit mitochondria, which is a bad thing. This can lead to many diseases and even affect fertility. Therefore, you really don't want to keep more products than you need. It's hard to determine which products are harmful from ingredient lists, but any ingredient that ends in "ammonium chloride" is best to stay away from if possible.

WARNING

When medication is prescribed, it's usually for 7–14 days and should be completed, so in theory you shouldn't have any left over to declutter. But I know I have done this, and you may have too — you don't finish it and think you can use it the next time you get sick. This is very dangerous, and using medication without talking to your doctor first, even if you have taken it before, can lead to misuse, development of antibiotic resistance, and susceptibility to other diseases, plus you may not be getting the right treatment for what you actually have.

So what is the best way to quickly declutter your medications? Taking them back to the pharmacy is the best advice, as pharmacies professionally dispose of them. Don't flush them down the toilet as this can contaminate our waterways.

After you have decluttered your medications, determine if your medicine cabinet is actually the best place to store the medications that you are going to keep.

Most medicine should be stored at room temperature — 68 to 77 degrees — and kept away from moisture. My bathroom does see moisture, especially when I shower, and most bathrooms are prone to higher temperatures and humidity, making them poor places to keep drugs. So, after you declutter, consider moving your medication out of the medicine cabinet or your bathroom in general. And whatever you do, keep the label. You want to avoid the cluttered mess of unidentifiable products shown in Figure 5-2.

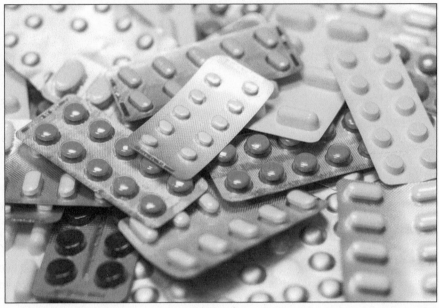

FIGURE 5-2:
Without labels, medication becomes cluttered and hard to identify.

Pexels / Pixabay

Toothbrush and essentials

I strongly advise that you only keep products you use daily in your bathroom. Separate the stuff that you use each and every day — toothbrush, toothpaste, shampoo, and so on — from the stuff you don't use daily, such as antibiotic cream and first-aid supplies unless you're sterilizing cuts and icing bruises daily, in which case you may have bigger problems than a cluttered bathroom.

TIP

And consider keeping your toothbrushes away from anything that splashes or sprays. Instead, put them in a see-through holder that can be easily cleaned (as pictured in Figure 5-3) and set them in a safe place to avoid dirt and buildup.

Superkitina / Unsplash

FIGURE 5-3: Use a clear container to keep your toothbrush protected and your countertop clean.

Setting strict timelines for product lifetimes

After you go through your dangerous medicine cabinet and determine what is truly essential, set timelines for all your products. Coming up are the guidelines I try to follow. These are just my guidelines — you might disagree completely, which is fine. Some expiration dates are actually set by the FDA, hopefully for safety reasons and not to sell more products. If nothing else, seeing these expiry dates may make you think twice before you buy and store too many multiples. The bottom line is that if you don't use something in your bathroom, it is clutter and it should go.

Another thing to keep in mind is that any products that have been compromised by heat or light can actually expire even faster! The more you focus on only essentials, the less you need to worry about extensive expiry lists!

Makeup

Following are my recommendations on how long to keep makeup:

>> **Mascara:** Three months — yes, that is right. I cry sometimes when I think about this. (**Disclaimer:** I keep mine for about six months, but three months is the recommendation.) Otherwise, you can be at risk of an eye infection, and I have one friend to whom this has actually happened!

>> **Liquid eye liner:** One year; again, due to the risk of eye infection.

>> **Eyeshadow:** Powder forms can last up to three years depending on the quality. Liquid eyeshadow has a shelf life of one year, after which it starts to separate.

>> **Lipstick:** Up to three years. Lip gloss may start to separate after one year, especially the thin cones. Lip balms can actually last up to five years.

>> **Blush:** Powders can last up to three years; creams usually one year.

>> **Bronzer:** Up to three years.

>> **Foundation:** This is a tough one as it depends on the type. Oil-free foundations usually last only a year, while ones with oil can last up to two years. Follow the supplier's recommendations.

>> **Concealer:** Liquid forms last up to one year; powder up to two years.

>> **Other powders:** Up to two years.

Everything else

We often forget how long we've had miscellaneous bathroom products. Create a system to help you keep track of when your items are expired. Here are some guidelines to follow:

>> **Moisturizers:** Up to two years; however, check the expiration dates because sometimes products in jars are pretty but not properly packaged, so they expire faster than they should. How manufacturers package moisturizers can make a huge difference in how long they can last. You now see many lotions in darker glass bottles for this very reason.

>> **Sunscreen:** One year (this is actually federally regulated).

>> **Acne products:** Any products containing benzoyl peroxide will only work for three months.

>> **Anti-aging products:** It depends on the ingredients, but anything with vitamin C, retinol, or glycolic acid tends to break down pretty quickly. It's best to stick with six months.

>> **Shampoo:** Unopened shampoo should last for three years; however, remember you don't need to buy a bunch of extras. Once opened, shampoo is good for two years. The same rules apply to conditioners.

>> **Deodorant/anti-perspirant:** Up to three years, but check expiry dates.

>> **Toothpaste:** Check the expiry date, since most toothpastes contain fluoride and this ingredient expires.

>> **Soap:** Usually up to three years; the same applies to body washes.

>> **Shaving products:** Up to two years. It's important to note that depilatory and bleaching creams usually only last for up to six months because of their harsh ingredients.

>> **Nail polish and remover:** Some say that nail polish remover actually never expires, which may be a good thing as it's one of those things we don't usually use daily; however, nail polish usually goes bad in under two years.

WARNING

I tried to be comprehensive with this list; however, I also want to mention that organic or all-natural products, which I totally recommend if you have the option, actually expire much sooner! You really need to watch them, as their ingredients expire very quickly due to the use of less chemicals in their recipes. Even more reason to keep a clutter-free bathroom if you are into organic products!

Minimizing unwanted products

It may seem repetitive to determine your essentials, but now I want you to go a step further, and I am going to help you with four quick questions to help make your bathroom product decluttering easier.

Ask yourself these questions:

>> **Do I use this?** This should be a quick yes or no answer. I did not ask you if you will possibly, maybe use it one day.

>> **Is this a duplicate or extra?** Of course, you can have a spare for your most-needed supplies, emphasis on most needed. But how many extra lotions do you need? Do you really need to keep that sparkling lip gloss? Remember the timeline of beauty products from the previous sections and think hard about whether you need to keep that extra. Perhaps you can donate it or pass it along to a friend who would love it!

>> **Would I buy this right now?** Chances are you're keeping some things because you feel bad about the money you spent on them. Toiletries and beauty supplies can be very expensive. But this question can help you analyze without considering cost. Think hard about your products, the color, the way it works or doesn't work for your skin type, and whether it's as effective as you thought it would be. If you wouldn't buy it again right now, then it is clutter and it's time for it to go.

>> **Is the space worth it?** Are the products taking up precious space? Can you transfer them to a different container or make them smaller, remove the packaging? Or declutter extras? The bathroom is often the smallest space, and therefore real estate is very precious.

The following sections provide some more simple tips.

Cosmetics

Go through all of them, keeping in mind the product expiry noted earlier. Then go through the remaining non-expired items and determine whether you actually use them. I know that you have some beautiful colors that look better in the case than they do on you. Keep only what you use and give the rest away to someone it might look great on!

Makeup brushes

I know that when I buy a complete set, I end up using only one or two brushes. If this is the case for you, discard the remaining ones you don't use. This is also a great time to clean your makeup brushes, as this often isn't done consistently. The less you have, the easier it will be to keep to a regular cleaning schedule.

Hair accessories

Go through these with a fine-tooth comb (don't mind the pun). I know that scrunchies are back in style, and you can tell me that you should have kept the ones you had when you were in eighth grade. But think back — would you really wear that scrunchie from 20 years ago? And chances are the elastic wouldn't work anymore! With many trends we sometimes wish we'd kept something, but trust me, 99 percent of the time, we wouldn't use or wear it. Toss hair accessories you don't use, as giving these away can be tough sometimes (many people can be fussy about hair germs).

Skin care

Be brutal with skin-care products. Many of you will pick up a product and think, "Oh I wish I used that more" or "If only I used this every day, I wouldn't have these fine lines." If you haven't used it consistently, chances are you won't start. Again, check expiry dates and test products to make sure they still smell right.

Nail polish

If stored properly, nail polish can last quite a while, but do you use it? Or do you get your nails professionally done? Check for clumps and proper consistency.

Medication

REMEMBER

I want to reiterate this point: Swiftly get rid of expired or unused medication, and remember that you probably should not be storing it in your bathroom anyway due to temperature fluctuations and steam caused by showers and baths. Don't forget to properly dispose of medications at the pharmacy rather than flush them.

Appliances/gadgets

Sort through your hairdryers, straighteners (do you have two?), shavers, face massagers, nose clippers, or whatever other bathroom gadgets you may have. These are usually items that you hold onto for "someday," but if you haven't used something in the last year, what are the chances that you will? I suggest even treating yourself to a treatment instead of buying the equipment. For example, instead of buying a foot bath you use twice a year, why not get a pedicure for the same price?

Hair brushes/combs

I have a pet peeve about hair and dirt buildup in combs. Sometimes when I see combs that are full of hair or other debris, I get a bit sad. I suggest the less you have, the easier it is to keep these clean. Go through the ones you use and toss the rest, as old hairbrushes are often also not welcome at donation places.

Knickknacks

Decorative items sometimes make their way into your bathroom, but I suggest taking a hard look at these items and determining whether they are taking up valuable space. Could replace a purely decorative item with something more functional instead?

Trial sizes

I fully admit back in my makeup junkie days I was also addicted to trial sizes, especially all the free ones that the makeup counters would give me. I convinced myself I needed to have a stash for my travels, but alas, I never used them. Be honest about what you use. Often you can donate these if they're unopened or give them to friends who run an Airbnb, as they love to have travel sizes for their guests!

Perfume/cologne

Perfumes and colognes are other items that may be better stored outside the bathroom due to temperature fluctuations. I have heard various recommendations on how long you can keep perfume, ranging from one to five years. Review all your bottles and what you actually apply. If you have more than you can use, this is a great item to donate to a friend because everyone loves getting a new scent. Pass along the scent love!

Bath accessories/toys

Often large bathtubs can be real estate for fancy bath mittens, loofahs, bath bombs, and fancy bath bubbles we rarely, if ever, use. Plus, if you have kids, how many bath toys do they have that line the bathtub walls? Check these items for mold, which can easily happen to things that sit on damp surfaces, and then of course discard what you don't use.

First-aid supplies

As I mention earlier, I don't actually recommend storing these supplies in the bathroom unless you're super accident prone and use them daily. Go through your supplies and see what you actually need to restock and what you never use. Chances are you have no Band-Aids but enough alcohol swabs to swab the neighborhood clean. My first career was in the construction industry, and during our monthly safety meetings, we had to check the first-aid stations to make sure they had been restocked. A sign was posted asking everyone to make note of what they took out of the first-aid kit. This made stock easy to replace. The construction industry ingrained safety into my head, and it's a great thing because when an emergency does happen, you want a well-stocked first-aid kit. And one you can find, not lingering behind other clutter!

Other personal stuff

We all have other products we use or think we might use. Go through your entire bathroom and discard as needed, keeping in mind all my tips thus far.

REMEMBER

It's easy to rebuy cosmetics, toiletries, and medications. They are readily available and better to rebuy than hold onto because these products can expire or their chemistry can easily be altered. Why risk it? Declutter now and if you do happen to need a similar item one day, trust me, you can get it.

Determining what you need versus what you think you "might" need

Getting the right products in your bathroom can take trial and error. Just when you think you have a routine, your favorite product is discontinued or you need to change based on your skin's changing needs. It is a balance to find out what works best and what to keep. Figure 5-4 shows a few simple products, which is what most of us could live with, but we have more.

AUTHOR
SAYS

This figure shows coconut oil, which personally I find works wonders as a multiple bath product, hair mask, face cream, foot cream, body lotion, and so on. Coconut oil is one of those super products that we have had all along!

There is no specific formula or time frame that can be prescribed to help find the actual products you might need, as our bodies and lives are always changing. So to help at least find what you need at this current moment and break free from your current clutter, I have put together the following general tips:

>> **Enlist support.** Get a friend or even a professional to help you choose the right products for your skin type. Check in twice a year like you do with the dentist, as your skin can change, resulting in the need for different products.

>> **Buy smaller sizes.** The smaller the bottle, the less chance of expiry and the higher your chance of finishing it.

>> **Research.** You may spend time researching what you eat because food goes into your body. What you put on your skin also enters into your body, and you should know what is in your products. Trust me, the more you research and find out about the hundreds of chemicals in bathroom products, the more likely you'll be to make your list of products much smaller.

FIGURE 5-4:
Decluttered products.

deanna alys / Unsplash

Decluttering Your Towels

I think towels are worth discussing because they're some of the most important items in the bathroom, and we use them multiple times a day! We use towels for bathing, to dry our hands, to remove our makeup, to stand on, to wipe sinks down, and so forth. You may not normally associate towels with clutter because you use them so often and they are a necessity. However, while this may be true, you can also make some thoughtful decisions about your towels, whether you are buying new ones or on a mission to declutter your existing towels.

Many people ask me, "How many towels do I need to keep?" There is no universal answer, but I can give you general advice and factors to consider on this topic. Figure 5-5 is an example of how I fold my guest towels, including a black makeup towel on top to help preserve my other towels.

FIGURE 5-5:
Folded guest
towels.

First things first, take a good, hard look at your towels and see what shape they are in. If they are in bad shape, can you use them as rags instead? Can you donate them if they are still in okay shape? Use them for your furry friends? This is the obvious towel clutter that you should be able to swiftly deal with. The harder towel clutter is related to how many you need.

TIP

To determine how many towels you actually need, I like to limit the number of towels used by myself and guests because I don't want to waste more water washing them all the time. Track how many towels you use in a week, and see if you can challenge yourself to use less. Not only is it more environmentally sustainable to use fewer towels, it also helps you save money due to constantly putting them through the washing machine.

Keep it simple

Each person in the household should have at least two full sets of towels. That can include a large bath towel, hand towel, and face towel. You may want to get a few more face towels for each person because faces are likely washed more frequently. Plus, I keep two additional sets on hand for guests. This is my rule of thumb to keep it simple. This allows for one set to be available while the other one is being washed. Many people, including myself, don't mind using a bath towel more than once before it needs to be washed. Like I've said, this practice can also help to save the environment one towel at a time!

REMEMBER

Hang up wet towels to make sure they dry properly before the next use.

TIP

My biggest keep-it-simple tip is to find a color/brand you like and stick with it. This way, towels are easier to replace, and you don't need to buy 50 of them at once. I prefer all white; they're easy to bleach, replace, and find.

Finding your staples

To further my advice on keeping the quantities simple for everyone in your household, I also believe in keeping the colors consistent.

Here are some things to consider:

>> **How many people live in your house:** As I mention in the preceding section, your rule of thumb should be two full sets of towels per person.

>> **Your laundry frequency schedule:** Whether you do laundry daily or twice a month affects how many towels you need.

>> **How many bathrooms you have in your home:** If you have one bathroom, it's simple. When you have ten, you need multiple hand towels at the very least.

>> **Guest frequency:** If you have guests every weekend, you may need more guest towels than if you have guests every few months.

>> **How much space you have to store towels:** Having more space doesn't mean that you have to keep all your towels, but if you literally have no space in your bathroom, consider decluttering more.

Staying consistent

Consistency is key. If you manage your towel inventory per household capita, it should make your towel decluttering efficient and sustainable.

SHOWER CURTAINS

I prefer built-in walls or doors versus shower curtains, but if you have shower curtains, these can also be clutter if you have too many. Check to make sure your shower curtain is clean and you still like it. You can usually wash them if they are not plastic. A new shower curtain can give your bathroom new life, but then you don't need to keep the old one.

A few other consistency tricks are to find ways to repurpose your old towels so you can declutter them easily. You can demote them to cleaning rags or garage rags, or they can be kept in kids' rooms for spills or art projects. From car cleaning to dusting rags, old towels can always be repurposed.

If your towels are still in good enough shape and maybe they don't match your theme, they are a great item to donate. I love donating because then the item not only physically leaves your home but you are also passing it on to someone who probably needs it more than you do.

If your towels or washcloths are too dirty for you to use yourself, likely they are not able to be donated. But if they have a fray or are just a bit worn out, they can be given to animal shelters, homeless shelters, or thrift stores.

Bathroom Traveling

Don't get confused by this title. I don't mean that you need to travel to different bathrooms, but when you travel, you usually take a few things with you. I find it extremely important to be ready and decluttered for this occasion. Nothing is worse the night before a trip than having to squeeze products into tiny travel containers, or worse, having to check a bag because you're bringing all your lotions, potions, and bathroom supplies.

I challenge you right now to get your travel essentials prepared, even if you don't have a trip planned. This way, when you do travel you will have all your necessary travel items with you. You can basically grab 'em and go. This is where you can use all your travel sizes, but don't go crazy. You tend to use less while traveling, so bring the essentials in small, ready-to-go sizes. Once you're back from your trip, replenish what you used and declutter what you didn't use, as likely you won't use it next time, either. Figure 5-6 shows a simple, see-through, TSA-approved bag in which to carry your toiletries for traveling. The one shown in the picture is available for sale on my website, but any similar bag will do.

Image courtesy of author (photo credit: @avalonmohns)

FIGURE 5-6:
Decluttered travel supplies ready to go!

Chapter **6**

Decluttering Your Kitchen

How often have you visited someone's kitchen and wondered how on earth they keep it looking so perfect and decluttered? This may be extra confusing if this person has a large family or hosts weekly dinner parties.

However, the amount of time you spend in your kitchen or the number of people reaching into your refrigerator should be no indication of how cluttered or uncluttered your kitchen is. If you eat out seven days a week and never set foot in your kitchen, then basically everything in your kitchen is clutter!

Many of us use our kitchen at least three times daily, or at least spend most of our time in our kitchen. Even if you have a big house, the kitchen is the usual spot where families and dinner parties always seem to congregate. Perhaps your kitchen looks perfectly decluttered until you open your drawers, or maybe your kitchen surfaces are jam-packed with appliances, vitamins, and overfilled glass jars of dry condiments.

There are many different kitchen needs, and the kitchen can often be the most challenging and daunting room in the house to declutter. But don't fret! I am here to give practical advice that you can use today. Just remember: Start small. Even ten minutes of daily decluttering adds up to five hours of decluttering every month, which will surely help you get on track and stay on track.

There are two ways to lessen the feeling of clutter in your kitchen: Add more storage or have fewer items. I talk about how to improve your kitchen storage and also encourage you to keep only what you really use.

AUTHOR SAYS

On a personal note, I am not a chef or any kind of great cook. I use my kitchen to make really basic meals. I try to eat healthy, but I am in no way a super foodie. However, the advice I give can pertain to any level of cook or chef. I completely understand that if your passion is cooking, you will have a few more items in the kitchen than perhaps the average cook such as myself, but the principles of clutter remain the same. If you are an avid chef, take this chapter with a grain of salt . . . no pun intended.

The Basics of Kitchen Decluttering

First and foremost, I want you to think about what you're doing in the kitchen the most. Your kitchen should work *for* you, and if you have items you never use in the middle of your counter and your most-used gadget tucked away, you need to reevaluate their placement. I encourage you to make some tough decisions in this chapter. For example, items that don't necessarily look that pretty but are highly functional may need to take a spot front and center in your kitchen.

Before you dive into this chapter, think about what you use every day and what you actually do in the kitchen. Cooking, making tea, whipping up a smoothie, and creating a new baking recipe all require different equipment. This chapter is all about *you* and making sure your kitchen works for your lifestyle.

REMEMBER

The amount of time you spend in your kitchen should not have an impact on how much stuff you have! If you spend hours cooking, it doesn't mean you need to have every new appliance or gadget that is marketed to make cutting onions less sad. Spending more time in the kitchen means you have to consistently spend more time evaluating what you actually use. As with most of my advice, I contend that your kitchen has to fit your lifestyle, and if your lifestyle changes, you have to adapt. As your cooking habits, dietary needs, and family size change, you will be reaching for different tools, appliances, and kitchen essentials. You will need to keep decluttering and add it into your routine. At the beginning of this process, decluttering may feel like a constant challenge. Don't worry — soon it will be an organic process that seamlessly fits into your life.

Here are a few strategies to help get you started:

>> **Don't have endless multiples.** I know you have more plates, mugs, and cups than you need. You may not have enough of one kind or way too many of another. Go through these and sell, toss, donate, or repurpose the extras.

» **Consider functionality versus aesthetics.** You can get carried away making your kitchen look really pretty. Focus again on only what you use and need on a regular basis.

» **Evaluate your storage.** Is your storage and layout space the most efficient? Most of us tend to use what is already in our kitchen, but I encourage you to think about what would make the most sense. Today there are lots of easy ways to update your storage space.

» **Optimize your items' positioning.** Kitchen items should be positioned so that you can see what you have immediately. This is especially important for food because it has an expiry date, and not seeing what you have only adds to food wastage.

» **Be practical.** It's important to think carefully when putting items away. Even if you have a see-through cupboard, that bright bowl you reach for every day should be front and center even if it doesn't match the rest of your décor. This is also important for heavy items or special occasion items.

Evaluating your space

Today many of us live in tiny apartments, condos, or small homes, and they usually come with a small kitchen. Even some larger spaces have smaller kitchens because they were not properly designed or were rebuilt. I want to make sure that whether you have a large or small kitchen, your space is as efficient as possible. The first step is to declutter your kitchen items and get realistic about what you need.

TIP

Try not to accumulate so many kitchen gadgets or devices linked to food fads and trends. If your friends are constantly gifting you items because you're a foodie, perhaps mention you would like more experiences as gifts rather than "stuff." You can let everyone know that you're on a decluttering mission to avoid accumulating more items. For example, foodies may like cooking classes or restaurant gift certificates instead of another set of cutlery.

Dive into some practical ways to evaluate your spaces:

» **Take a look at your cupboards.** If you have so much stuff that your cupboards can't close properly, you are not using your space as efficiently as possible. Try to reduce the amount of stuff you own and then determine how you can optimize storage. Consider installing shelves; reducing packaging; and storing goods in jars, bins, and baskets that take up less space. Beautiful, tall glass jars can look nice and actually take up less space.

» **Be logical.** Are super clunky, barely used gadgets taking up too much space? When evaluating space, you have to be ruthless. Yes, you might use that juicer one day, but have you used it in the last year? In the last six months? Be brutal when evaluating these larger gadgets that we often hang onto because they were a gift or we think we might use them one day. The good news is that if they still work, you can likely sell them!

>> **Evaluate your stockpiles and bulk.** Do you have so much food that you don't have space to store it all? It's important to have dried and canned food on hand for emergencies; however, is your space optimized for this? Can you build a higher shelf for these items as you're not reaching for them daily? And even emergency supplies should be decluttered and restocked annually, as your needs may change.

Before you go crazy with your stockpiles, try to buy only what is really necessary. Trips to Costco can leave any kitchen stuffed to the brim with too many of one item and items so large that they don't even fit on your shelves. Don't buy something in bulk just because it is on sale; buy items only because you need them.

AUTHOR SAYS

I don't buy in bulk anymore. When I first moved to Europe, I was wondering where the Costco was because I felt that I needed to always stock up, even though I lived alone. I quickly discovered that shopping in bulk is not the European way; instead, they grocery shop more often, sometimes daily, and only get what they need for that day or the next few days, not the next 50. Europeans have less space and typically smaller dwellings than North Americans, so this could be part of the reason for less bulk. However, it is also a different mindset. The University of Arizona published an article that related more food waste to buying in bulk and contended that the idea that buying in bulk actually helps you save money is a total myth! Next time you feel bad for forgetting to bring your reusable bag to the grocery store, think about how much worse you feel when you can't use the food you bought and it goes to waste.

Following are tips for storing goods more efficiently:

>> **Stock "like" items together.** This may seem like a no-brainer, but it's also the best way to evaluate whether your space is really working for you. If you have so many one of product that it's overflowing and none of another type of food item, why is there an entire shelf devoted to the one with the least amount of stuff?

>> **Stock "related" items together.** Similar to the preceding tip, keep similar, related items together as well. This includes items such as your baking supplies or ingredients for dishes that you are always cooking. Storing related items together instantly makes your space more efficient.

>> **Keep items close to where you need them.** Keep things as close as possible to where you actually use them. For example, keep your spices near your stove if you're always adding spices to your stovetop items, or your knife blocks close to the place where you always chop and dice.

>> **Evaluate the inside of your cupboards.** Don't forget about the amount of space your cupboards have to offer. Installing a few racks can be a simple trick to better utilize empty space.

Many people have asked me how much cupboard space they should have. If you're starting from scratch by building or renovating a new home, seek help from a kitchen designer who is familiar with the newest space-saving kitchen layouts that can make the most sense for your space.

The National Kitchen & Bath Association (NKBA) gives a few rules of thumb about calculating the total frontage for your shelves and drawers.

In the kitchen, the standard measure for storage space is shelf/drawer frontage, which can be calculated by cabinet width multiplied by cabinet depth multiplied by the number of shelves and drawers.

The NKBA recommends a total shelf/drawer frontage of

1,400 inches for small kitchens (less than 150 square feet)

1,700 inches for a medium kitchen (151 to 350 square feet)

2,000 inches for a large kitchen (more than 350 square feet)

Figure 6-1 gives in-depth size recommendations for shelf footage by the NKBA.

	Small	Medium	Large
Wall	300	360	260
Base	520	615	660
Drawer	360	400	525
Pantry	180	230	310
Misc.	40	95	145

FIGURE 6-1: Recommended distribution for shelf/drawer frontage.

*All in inches

Source: NKBA

Determining your needs

Getting clear on what you need is the basis of kitchen decluttering. If you aren't careful, your kitchen can easily turn into a giant storeroom.

The amount of kitchen storage should ideally depend on what and how much you have. The more items in your kitchen, the more items you need to store. In the next section, I go into specific rules of thumb for the proper number of items and how to keep an eye on volume levels. For now, I focus on your kitchen needs.

Every kitchen is as unique as the person, family, or tribe it is supporting. This means that every kitchen has unique uses. The uses of the kitchen can change all the time, which makes consistent kitchen decluttering extremely important. If possible, I suggest decluttering your kitchen quarterly.

Ask yourself these questions to get started:

>> What is the current size of your household?

>> How often do you cook?

>> How often do you entertain guests?

>> What area of your kitchen is the most inefficient?

>> Which kitchen storage area is the most stuffed or overflowing with items?

>> Is your storage efficient? Do you have to walk far to get what you need?

>> Which cabinets and drawers are used most?

>> What other stuff is in your kitchen that is not related to cooking? For example, do you have paperwork, computers, laundry detergent, or mudroom supplies stored inefficiently in your kitchen?

Now pay close attention to how your kitchen is currently organized and make a simple list of what you know could be improved. Use Figure 6-2 to note these improvements.

Next, I always say that you need to take inventory of your entire kitchen before you can fully measure its improvements. You've already thought about what you do in your kitchen, and now it's time to go through everything thoroughly. Make a checklist if you need to, and take note of the items that you actually have. A check-list can be a great way to quickly review your inventory of stuff, most of which falls into the following categories:

>> Small appliances

>> Food storage

KITCHEN DECLUTTERING IMPROVEMENTS

MOST USED KITCHEN AREAS

-
-
-

Top ways to improve these areas

-
-

-
-
-

Image courtesy of author

>> Preparatory items

>> Utensils

>> Silverware

>> Pots and pans

>> Bakeware

>> Glasses, cups, and drinking items

>> Dishes

>> Serving ware

>> Flatware

>> Linens

>> Storage containers

>> Cleaning supplies and tools

>> Bulk storage

>> Management/home office

>> Miscellaneous

Don't worry, this does not have to be exact and can be done in under 15 minutes. It is more of an exercise to get you started on the decluttering process, because as you go through the list and add your own items, it will quickly become clear where there is excess. Another useful exercise is to go through your food in your pantry, fridge, and freezer — I encourage you to do this quarterly. Use the checklists in Figure 6-3 to help you with your food inventory.

KITCHEN INVENTORY
Take note of how many you have

PANTRY	Quantity	Notes

KITCHEN INVENTORY
Take note of how many you have

FRIDGE	Quantity	Notes

FIGURE 6-3: Kitchen food inventory checklists.

KITCHEN INVENTORY
Take note of how many you have

FREEZER	Quantity	Notes

FIGURE 6-3:
(continued)

Image courtesy of author

AUTHOR SAYS

You may have noticed that in the first few chapters, I recommend apps for keeping track of what you have. Personally, I always use paper and pen for my kitchen, but by all means, use whatever works best for you.

I trust the inventory list helped you to declutter a few things as you were going through it. The next section in this chapter gives you some very general guidelines on how many you should have of selected items.

Now, it's time to declutter even more. I don't need to remind you of the benefits of decluttering, as I talk about these in Chapters 1 and 2 quite extensively. I find that kitchen decluttering is especially important because not only does it help with kitchen hygiene and cleanliness, but it can also bring increased energy, creativity, and motivation for staying healthy and cooking healthy meals.

Ask yourself these questions as you go through your items:

>> Do I use this item?

>> Is this an extra?

>> Would I buy this again?

>> Does this help to make my kitchen life more efficient?

Optimizing Your Kitchen for Efficiency

One of the most important ways to optimize your kitchen is to make sure that you have only what you need and that your efficiency and accessibility are dialed in. You want items that you use every day conveniently located, and you want everything to go back to its rightful spot after you use it.

Functional for the win

Your kitchen needs to be as functional as possible. The best way to optimize your kitchen for your functional needs is to categorize the storage areas based on the following examples. Some of these categories may not apply to you, but do your best to use the ones that do:

>> Consumables

>> Non-consumables

>> Cleaning

>> Preparation

>> Cooking

>> Baking

>> Serving

>> Herbs

>> Others

Decluttering the right tools

I don't want to give advice on what you need or should have in your kitchen, but I want to get specific about everyday tools and go through the ones that can lead to clutter:

AUTHOR SAYS

>> **Dish towels:** I know as soon as you read this, you're either thinking you need to purchase more dish towels or that you already have too many. Whichever thought you have, go through all your dish towels and discard ones that are past their due date; if they're torn or ragged, get rid of them. Then, evaluate what you have left and whether you actually use them. See if the ones you're discarding can be repurposed for cleaning rags, donated to thrift stores, or given to animal shelters.

I could write an entire chapter on dish towels, but I think that would only bore you. I love good quality dish towels as they truly can last for years, even with an intense amount of wear and tear. I have found that European dishtowels, especially those from Switzerland, are the best quality dishtowels and surpass any I have found in North America. If you are purchasing dishtowels elsewhere, make sure they are 100 percent Turkish cotton because they are softer and more durable than other styles. I keep two dishtowels in my kitchen at all times; one for drying hands and one for drying dishes.

>> **Mixing bowls:** Go through these and eliminate what you don't use or what you have in excess.

>> **Spices:** Going through your spices can be a messy job, but you have to do it. I bet there are a few that you have never used or have maybe even expired. Try keeping only the spices you actually use, as you can always rebuy a spice if you want it again down the road, or purchase a small amount in a bulk section if you need it for something specific.

>> **Storage containers:** I am not sure why there is a lid monster in every kitchen, but that's just the way it is. Go through all your storage containers and discard any without a lid. The better the quality of your containers, the surprisingly less often the lids go missing. Maybe it is because you take better care of

quality items or you're more careful overall, but investing in good storage containers will help you be more mindful of their uses.

» **Cutlery:** I am sure you have a few stragglers that you don't use, or sets that aren't complete or are missing all the little spoons or a few forks. I suggest donating the cutlery that doesn't match your set so that everything has a streamlined and organized look.

» **Medicine:** Even if you keep medicine in your bathroom, go through all medication and discard what is expired and what you didn't finish when given a prescription. In Chapter 5 about bathroom decluttering, I speak in depth about the dangers of keeping medications. Also, if you do store medication in your kitchen, make sure that it is away from steam from ovens or kettles, and either stored or locked away from anyone who should not be accessing it.

» **Vitamins and supplements:** It took me years to finally develop a consistent vitamin routine, and this not only saves me hundreds of dollars in vitamins I don't need or forget to take, but is also making me a healthier person. If you take supplements or vitamins, make sure you are keeping only what you actually take. Get rid of anything you don't take consistently. I got help from an expert in nutrition to help me figure out my vitamin needs, and I now only buy the ones I need. It is very easy to fall into the latest trends with vitamins and buy things that "promise" to make your hair stronger, reduce your body fat, or instantly clear your skin. I would check with a professional before starting any vitamin regime to keep your clutter at bay and your wallet happier.

» **Cookbooks:** Go through these and keep only what you use. This is tough as you may think you'll need one as a reference someday, but be realistic and remember that the Internet has a recipe for everything.

» **Cleaning supplies:** Whether you store these in your kitchen or not, chances are a few cleaning supplies are always in your kitchen. Don't keep a huge stash of items, or multiples. Make sure that each item is labeled properly and store only what you actually need in the kitchen. Also, move the bathroom cleaners to your bathrooms, and any other specific supplies to their respective places.

» **Bakeware:** I get that you used to love to make muffins in the shape of hearts for your kid's Valentine's Day bake sales, but do you use them anymore? Anything not used should be either tossed, sold, repurposed, or donated.

» **Oven mitts:** Chances are, you have one oven mitt that you have used since you graduated high school. If this is the case, consider upgrading your oven mitt or minimizing the number you have.

» **Aprons:** I believe in using aprons because they help keep your clothes clean and happy. Go through your aprons and only keep the ones you use. I only keep ones that make me look good (I know that's funny, but some aprons have a magical way of making you look slimmer, taller, and more stylish when cooking, while others make you look like your grandmother). I swear you are going to look differently at your aprons after reading this.

>> **Coffee mugs and glassware:** Only keep what you need. Do you use the mugs with your kids' pictures on them from 1998? Maybe these are sentimental items, and if they are, then they should be stored with other sentimental items instead of in the kitchen. Most people have a lot of mugs or glasses, but you only need one or two per person in your house. The next section talks about optimal levels for these items.

>> **Gadgets:** Don't save those impulse-buy kitchen items if you don't already use them. Get over their sunk cost; donate, sell, toss, or repurpose them; and move on. I want you to assess all gadgets, even things like your microwave — if you have only used it once in the last year for popcorn, is it really necessary in your kitchen?

WARNING

Many people ask me about decorative items in the kitchen and whether or not they are clutter. For example, nicely labeled spice jars or glass jars with pasta can be decorative even if they aren't often used. I can't tell you what decorative items you should keep, since how you decide to style your kitchen is a personal choice. I can, however, warn that decorative items may be taking up valuable space for items you actually use. Also, anything decorative needs to be wiped down more often than it would in another location because it gets dustier and could be splashed upon while cooking. Whether you keep or discard decorative items is up to you, but keep these considerations in mind when they're in your kitchen.

Figure 6-4 shows a before-and-after example of decluttered cutlery meant to inspire you to get started. Decluttering cutlery and utensils is a great way to start quickly, won't uproot your kitchen, and will give you a sense of accomplishment.

Selecting optimal numbers of dishes and cutlery

Many people ask me exactly how much of each item they should have in their kitchen. Although this differs for each person, I have some general guidelines I try to follow.

To sum it up, you need enough dishes for a daily meal and a few extras for spares and guests.

This may not seem like a lot, and you may like hanging onto extras in case your items aren't clean or are in the dishwasher. The solution is simple: Clean your dishes or empty the dishwasher. The less you have, the more you will also stay on top of kitchen chores or force others in your family or tribe to help out.

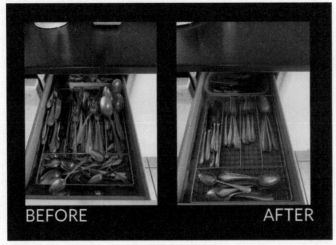

FIGURE 6-4:
Before
and after
decluttering
kitchen cutlery.

Many people hang onto excess items in case they have a party. Ask yourself this: When was the last time you had a party? Last week, last year, or never? If the answer was either of the latter two, you likely don't need to have a mass of spare dishes. You can rent or borrow dishes if you have a party.

Setting volume levels

Now I get down to specific volumes of things and go even deeper into the questions raised earlier.

Knives

The essentials are usually a chef's knife, a paring knife, and a bread knife. You probably have others as well that you use frequently and store close to where you use them. If you have multiples of knives, consider donating them. If they are poor quality or broken, discard them. Quality knives are important for chefs or avid kitchen cooks, so prioritize quality over quantity.

Dishes

I refer to these in sets. There is no golden rule of how many sets of dishes you should keep, but I try to have enough plates and bowls in each set for the number of people who are in my house eating regularly and the number of meals a day that are served. Of course, it depends on the size of plates you use. Maybe you use smaller dishes for breakfast and larger dishes for lunches, but these should all be part of a matching set. Remember, I recommend you clean your dishes after each use so that you don't need excess sets while your dishes are dirty. Whether or not you have a dishwasher may affect the number of sets you have. If you're the mom who is hosting kids all the time, maybe you need more of a certain size plate for the time being. Think about your lifestyle and then be ruthless with the number of sets you actually need.

TIP

A special note about sets. When you buy a full set of, for example, eight dishes but there are only two of you in the house, you don't necessarily have to keep them or store them in your kitchen. You may opt for an alternate storage space and then get more when needed or keep them to replace broken ones.

Holiday stuff

Do you have special Christmas tree plates you use every Christmas? If so, store them with your Christmas decorations instead of in your kitchen. Be mindful of how many holiday accessories you are buying; if you buy new ones every year, they could add up quickly to much more than you need, have room for, or actually use. Plus, I believe less is more when it comes to holiday decorating.

Kids' stuff

I grew up using the same utensils and plates as my parents, but I was born before the huge marketing boom took place for kids' accessories. My parents were also European with very strict manners around food — I was never allowed to make a mess or use my fingers to eat! These days, kid-friendly dishes can come in every cartoon character or animation that has ever been produced. The key is to declutter these as soon as they're no longer needed or when your kid outgrows them. These items are great to pass along to other mommy groups if they are still in good condition. Resist the urge to keep them as sentimental items or for your future grandkids. Just don't go there.

Silverware

Your silverware drawer is likely the most opened drawer in your home. I call it silverwear out of habit, but it may not be silver and it can also be called cutlery. These items can be plastic, gold, stainless steel, or whatever material you happen to have chosen. Since we use silverwear so much, it generally doesn't make sense to totally minimize this (let's be honest — we need more than one fork in our lives). To begin decluttering this drawer, I suggest taking everything out and doing a deep clean at least quarterly. With this being one of the most used drawers in the household, it also accumulates the most dirt and usually has the greatest number of different people's hands always rummaging through it.

Here is a calculation to help you determine how much silverware you need: Multiply the number of people in your house by the number of meals you eat by the number of times your run your dishwasher (skip this step if you don't have a dishwasher). This means that even if you only wash your dishes at night, they will all be ready the next morning.

I won't go into details about specifics such as salad forks, dessert spoons, and butter knives. If you do very formal dining and use fancy silverware daily, then it's fine to keep them. The point is, only keep what you use!

China

Some of you may have special-occasion china. Perhaps it was gifted to you, you collect it, or you simply like it. Again, if you use it, then keep it. But don't hold onto it because it was an expensive gift and you feel bad about getting rid of it.

If it is display china, then it's likely not in your kitchen. I would warn against this: Today's modern men and women do not have time to regularly dust their special China (I know I definitely don't). However, if you keep using it as a decoration you love, that's okay too! We all have different tastes; just remember that decorations and trinkets can become clutter over time and require constant dusting and reevaluating.

Coffee mugs

Coffee mugs are a tough category, and again I give you a calculation rather than a number.

If you never have guests: Multiply the number of people in your household (who use mugs) by the number of mugs they use per day by the number of times you run your dishwasher (skip this step if you don't have a dishwasher).

Here is a couple examples:

> There are two people in your house, you both use two mugs a day, and you run the dishwasher once a day. You should have four mugs.
>
> If you run your dishwasher every three days because there are only two of you, then you likely need 2 x 2 x 3 = 12 mugs.

If you often have guests, add a few mugs and think about how many guests you normally have. Whether you have one couple or several couples staying with you makes a difference in how many you need.

Chances are, you will keep more than the calculation allows, but this is the best practice for decluttering.

If you have collector or sentimental mugs, really think about whether or not they need to be stored in the kitchen. Broken mugs can be repurposed into vases, makeup brush holders, and so on. The bottom line is you don't need 50 mugs for two people unless you consistently entertain a lot of coffee or tea drinkers!

Plastic bags

Yes, it's great to have a few on hand, but you don't need to keep every plastic bag you were ever given. Keep only a handful of that you know you will use in the next six months. Try to bring your own plastic or reusable bags when you shop, as many places charge for plastic bags. While five cents per bag may not seem like much, decluttering those bags once you're home takes up valuable time. Plus, minimizing your use of plastic bags helps saves the environment, which is the biggest reason.

Freezer items

The freezer is often where we put food that we will use "later." From my experience, freezers can be the biggest clutter traps in any kitchen, especially in North America. In Europe, they don't have large freezers and they don't have this clutter problem. Go through your freezer regularly, as I can guarantee some items already have the dreaded "freezer burn" and will have to be tossed. Annual freezer decluttering is a must, but I recommend doing it quarterly.

Utensils

Utensil decluttering depends on what you use. All I can suggest is that they are organized so they're within easy reach, as shown in Figure 6-5.

Pantries

If you have a big walk-in pantry, your friends are likely jealous. They won't be jealous, however, of how much longer it will take you to declutter. In my experience, pantries are clutter havens. Usually, they have high, deep shelves, are not properly lit, and are the perfect place to store clutter.

Do yourself a big favor and get extra lighting, as this really helps you to see what you have in your pantry. Then, trim down your pantry supplies, especially if you're keeping a lot of extra items such as plates, extra wine glasses for those parties you're going to have someday, or picnic supplies for the picnics you never seem to have time for.

Image courtesy of (Wiley image)

A word on outdoor accessories: Reusable plastic wear is great for using outdoors, especially if you have a long summer season and use it regularly. Having multiple spares of plastic wear is probably unnecessary if you only use it sparingly or once a year. Also, take note of how much extra disposable outdoor cutlery and dishes you have that you are saving for the time you "might" go to the park or "might" have that BBQ. These items are great to donate to local events, which are often in need of these supplies. As always, make sure you don't keep more than you need!

Another word about kids and pantries. Before your kids dump their backpacks into your pantry, make sure that they are emptied. It's best if they have a special hook for their backpack. Keep backpacks off the floor if possible, but not too high so that kids can still access them when needed.

Getting rid of junk drawers forever

Many of you may already be thinking that is an impossible feat. I am not saying that you need to get rid of the drawer that you have in your kitchen for essential items that you grab on a weekly, monthly, or annual basis like scissors, tape, and the odd marker to make labels.

On the contrary, I suggest having a drawer like this! Yes, you heard me right! And in your drawer, you need to have blank labels and a marker so you can label and relabel your items as needed.

I want to go back to the word "junk drawer" because it has a bad rap, and rightfully so. Many of you probably remember reaching into your mom's junk drawer and finding buried treasures — Pokémon cards you thought you had lost, that old McDonald's Happy Meal toy you got five years ago, or a pencil that needs sharpening. You probably also remember not being able to close those junk drawers, getting sticky fingers from rifling around in them, and worst of all, not actually finding what you needed! That is why I say get rid of junk drawers forever. And do not call your kitchen drawer with essentials a junk drawer. If you do, your kids, partners, friends, dog walkers, or even guests will put junk in it. Tame the beast once and for all by renaming this drawer the "essentials drawer."

I converted my mom after she actually got rid of her junk drawer only to make the exact same one the following year. I had to label it "essentials drawer" and also give her these tips:

>> **Throw stuff away.** As with any other place in your home, declutter this drawer regularly!

>> **Separate what is left.** If you have similar piles, decide on the best way to keep them separated. Get dividers, small bins, or plastic containers to help keep everything organized. I find that napkin rings work well for really small items, and dividers for the rest. The goal here is not to move items to another spot in your home. If an item does not go back in the essentials drawer, try to be diligent about donating or tossing it.

>> **Evaluate it regularly.** Your household will be inclined to toss all their "junk" into this drawer, especially if they're used to it being a junk drawer. It is estimated that 80 percent of stuff in typical junk drawers is junk; hence, the name. Make sure once you change this drawer's purpose that you don't let junk back in. Keep this new drawer close to the trash so you can easily purge items.

>> **Make it visible.** See-through drawers are not really a thing yet, but to get you started, or if junk starts to build up again, dump all the contents into a see-through container and leave it on your counter. Let your household know it will be in the trash shortly to encourage them to grab any items they want or need. Discard unclaimed items immediately.

>> **Get rid of the physical drawer.** If all else fails, and you have tried everything but the junk drawer cannot be tamed, consider getting rid of it. Keep a see-through caddie or box on your counter or desk for your essential supplies — this way you'll constantly be staring at it as a reminder to declutter. Again, this is the last option I can recommend.

Figure 6-6 is a real-life example of my mother's drawer before and after decluttering. Once called the junk drawer, it's now been renamed the "essentials" drawer.

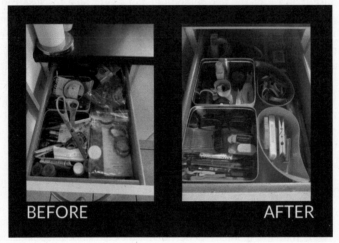

Image courtesy of author

FIGURE 6-6: From junk drawer to "essentials" drawer.

Chapter 7
Decluttering Your Bedroom

I f you have read this book in order, you've already gone through Chapter 4, which is entirely devoted to your closet. I believe that any organizational plan starts with the closet as it is one of the first things you see in the morning, and that is why I devote an entire chapter to decluttering it.

However, another thing you see first thing in the morning — and the very last thing you see before you drift off into a hopefully peaceful sleep — is your bedroom. If you skipped the closet chapter, I suggest revisiting it before diving into this chapter, as I focus only on bedroom items here.

Make sure you also apply the closet concepts to any wardrobes or chest of drawers that you have in your bedrooms. Remember, you are likely wearing only 20 percent of the 80 percent of clothes in both of those places, and it's important to declutter anything that you have not worn in a year.

If you have books in your bedrooms, make sure you take a look at Chapter 11, which addresses book decluttering. If you happen to bring all your bathroom items into the bedroom, you may want to revisit Chapter 5 on bathroom decluttering.

I focus on what clutter most people have and use in the bedroom, and there are, of course, many exceptions. You may have office items, exercise equipment, play rooms, libraries, and many more types of items. You may be living in a studio apartment where you don't technically have walls, but don't let that stop you from decluttering what is immediately around your bed space.

Decluttering for Peaceful Sleep

Your bedroom should be a sanctuary or peaceful retreat. You know that your bedroom is for sleep, relaxation, and maybe a few other adult activities, all of which are meant to take place in a peaceful setting.

Often, our bedrooms become grounds for laundry, unpacked bags, paperwork, and other miscellaneous items. One of the reasons that this happens is that the bedroom is usually tucked away behind a closed door, making it easier for clutter to accumulate. When guests come over unexpectedly, our bedrooms may be an easy place to stash clutter and close the door for later. Also, today we are accustomed to taking work home with us or even working from home, which causes work stuff to seep into our bedrooms.

Whatever the reason clutter may have accumulated, you need to quickly deal with it, as your bedroom is one of the most important rooms in your home. Your future sleep and health depend on it!

When I look at Figure 7-1, I feel as though this is a truly relaxing minimalist bedroom setting. I am not suggesting you have to go to this extreme and get rid of everything, but keep this photo in mind as you work through this chapter. The less bedroom furniture and stuff you have, the more relaxed you will feel and the better you will sleep.

Banishing clutter from bedside tables

Anything that you keep in your bedroom can affect your sleep. Clutter can actually prevent a good night's sleep; think about it, if your bedroom is littered with work items, you may have a difficult time shutting off your brain. The items that are directly in your sight on your bedside table are especially important to declutter.

What is sitting on your bedside table can affect not only your sleep but also how you wake up. Waking up to reminders of uncompleted tasks or clutter causes immediate stress and leaves you feeling anxious for the rest of the day.

FIGURE 7-1:
Minimalist
bedroom.

Bedside tables can be excellent places to store essential items you use every day before bed, or they can turn into bedside junk drawers. My advice is to keep only essentials in them, or better yet, get tables with no drawers to prevent the latter from ever happening. Chances are, what you use every day, such as an alarm clock, lamp, book, glasses, and a bottle of water, will be on top of the table, so why do you need drawers, anyway?

If you want to keep using the drawers of your bedside table, stick to these tips to keep them decluttered:

>> **Reading material:** A great way to end or start the day without the glare of screens! Have only the current book you're reading on this table and declutter the rest.

>> **Tech gadgets and electronics:** These actually shouldn't be stored close to your bed because the light they emit can affect the quality of your sleep.

>> **Other accessories and stuff:** I can't imagine what else you have in your bedside table, but go through it. Do you use it at least once a week while you're in the bedroom? If not, put the items where they belong.

>> **Preventive measure:** Clean the drawer and put in a few books or another large item to stop anything else from going into the drawers. This will help keep your drawers clutter-free.

Figure 7-2 shows an example of essentials on a bedside table. Without drawers, clutter has less of a chance to accumulate out of sight.

FIGURE 7-2:
Decluttered
beside table.

Considering hidden storage areas

I love unique space-saving storage solutions, especially for those who live in smaller quarters. I also suggest investing in quality storage systems or built-in systems if you can, so that you don't have to have boxes or bins in your home permanently. The bedroom can offer lots of unique storage solutions, but I also caution that these can be clutter traps if they are not treated properly and evaluated consistently. Firstly, ensure that everything is placed away neatly. When you know what you have, you'll be less inclined to add unnecessary items or keep collections that have little or no use. Then, watch out for these common bedroom storage areas:

>> **Under the bed:** Always check under your bed for monsters and clutter; that is my motto. Today's modern platform beds don't have an "under the bed," which helps to prevent dust and clutter buildup! I highly recommend this type of bed. However, some clever companies have invented storage by lifting up the mattress for hidden items. Check this place quarterly if you use if it for storage. Some beds also offer built-in drawers, which is genius for storage, but the same decluttering rules apply!

- » **Headboard storage:** Some headboards offer built-in or add-in storage solutions. Be wary of the clutter that can accumulate here and only keep what you actually need to reach for while in bed.

- » **Storage benches:** I love a good bench for sitting down and being able to tie my shoes. Today, they offer sneaky storage solutions, and they come in a variety of colors and designs, many of which can match your bedroom furniture and be placed at the foot of your bed.

- » **Behind doors:** There are lots of over-the-door organizers for shoes, jewelry, or any other accessory you feel would fit in its place. This is a great storage idea, but make sure that when you close your bedroom door, nothing you're looking at is clutter. Evaluate this extensively.

- » **Baskets, boxes, and bins:** These are great items that can provide extra storage if needed — and *only* if needed! Go through the items in these boxes and determine whether you actually need and use their contents.

Cutting clutter from corners

You may think this is an odd heading as every room or space in your house has a corner! For some reason, the bedroom corners seem to accumulate clutter like no other. It would be unusual to toss your laundry in the corner of your kitchen, but in your bedroom, it could be normal practice. I want you to examine the corners of your bedroom and remove the clutter. Please, stop using your bedroom corners for clutter from this day forward!

Once the clutter is removed from your bedroom, corners can actually be reevaluated as they can offer additional storage or seating areas in your bedroom. Again, for selected items, not clutter! Corners in your bedroom can be great for hanging corner clothing racks if you don't have a closet or enough closet space. They can also be a great place to hang your outfits for the next day so that you are prepared and organized.

Detoxing the digital zone

I know you have heard that your bedroom should be free of tech gadgets, especially your phone. And if you're like me, you have ignored this advice many times over and still do. I admit, I always think I have to have my phone beside me just in case. However, because of our constant need to be connected, this has now turned our bedroom into a stressful place. What's worse is that the bright screens affect our quality of sleep.

One study done by Harvard Researchers breaks down the detrimental effects from having your phone in your room. Here's how it impacts your sleep:

>> It takes you longer to fall asleep. End of story.

>> It messes with your natural sleeping rhythm, which can affect everything from appetite to stress levels, to the likelihood of getting a disease!

>> You feel more tired and your alertness is reduced.

I hope these reasons provide at least a bit more motivation to at least think about moving your phone out of the bedroom.

Furnishing for the Win

Now that we have identified a few reasons to clear the clutter, including technology, it's time to talk about a few other items and habits that are also important to keep the restful bedroom setting going. The more functional your furniture is, and the better organized it is for your lifestyle, the less likely clutter is to build up. I am not suggesting you go and buy all new furniture, but ensure that your next purchases are well thought out and fit your space, needs, and functionality.

Your bed

Another tip I would like you take from this book is that you should make your bed every morning! Although an obvious life lesson, which you may have learned during your upbringing, making your bed every morning sets the tone for your entire day. I reread this tip from Tim Ferriss's blog, which has become one of his main productivity tips. He claims that you automatically accomplish one thing once you have made your bed. Plus, it makes your bedroom look less cluttered. Make this a habit as you do with daily decluttering.

Also, your bed makes the best, largest surface for helping you fold and organize other things.

Your bed should take up the most space in your bedroom. It should be the piece of furniture that you have paid the most attention to when selecting, and it should have lots of space and not be cluttered with items beneath, on top of, or generally around the bed. Make your bed the most important piece of furniture in your bedroom and spend time finding the right bed and mattress for your bedroom's size and design, your preference, and your storage needs. Investing in a quality bed will likely last decades. As always, the simpler the better!

What goes on your bed is just as important. The following chapter goes into detail about decluttering linens, so skip ahead if you're curious about this now. As you can imagine, I try to keep it simple. A bed with 20 pillows you have to remove before you even crawl in is a bit too cluttered for my taste.

Essentials

Determine what the essentials are in your bedroom. By now, I'm sure you're aware that I encourage keeping the bare minimum of items in most spaces, especially the bedroom. It is more important in the bedroom to really ask yourself what you need, and whether or not it's conducive to ensuring you get a restful night's sleep.

Here are the bedroom essentials:

>> Bed

>> Sheets

>> A few surfaces to put some lamps on

You probably have many more items of furniture than this in your bedroom, and I encourage you to review each item of furniture that is taking valuable real estate in your sleeping haven. This is one of the first times in this book I ask you to really review furniture items, but furniture can also be clutter. We usually hang onto bedroom furniture because it came as part of a set, or because we are conditioned to think we need to have those bedside tables and dresser. However, if you don't use them, they are clutter.

AUTHOR SAYS

Simple is key for the bedroom. Figure 7-3 showcases my simple bedroom furnishings. I am influenced by European design and furnishings, which tend to be much simpler when it comes to bedroom linens and furniture. Lower beds create an illusion of a larger space, and so do duvets with classic sheet sets. Fewer pillows and more functional versus decorative ones are best. If you want to learn more about decluttering sheets, skip ahead to Chapter 8.

Encouraging your sleeping partner

After reading this, you may have some ideas that you want to put into action right away regarding how to make your bedroom a clutter-free, sleeping sanctuary. You may be sharing your bedroom and your home with other people, or even pets. I believe it is important to involve them in your decluttering process and share your new ideas so that you can collaborate and enjoy the sleeping benefits as a household.

FIGURE 7-3: My simple bedroom.

Here are a few things to remember as you share your new ideas and decluttering goals with your household:

>> **Be respectful.** With shared spaces, it's important to discuss and share ideas, as one person's clutter may be someone else's important paperwork or creative project.

>> **Explain the discomfort clutter is causing.** Be specific about the detrimental effects of having a cluttered bedroom, and the potential benefits of having a clutter-free environment.

>> **Negotiate.** It can take time for mindsets to change, and you may have to change your own first. Be patient and stick to what you believe will help make your bedroom a more restful sleep area. It will take time, especially to adopt the technology-free ideals into the bedroom. I'll be frank — I sometimes still keep my phone and laptop in my bed. It takes time to change habits, and you and I both need to be patient!

>> **Keep clutter styles in mind.** In Chapter 1, I discuss clutter personalities, and it's important to keep in mind your own style as well as that of the person you share your bedroom with. Clutter may be difficult to part with for your partner, so be gentle and kind when discussing these items.

THE BENEFITS OF SLEEP

This book focuses on decluttering, but I want to highlight the importance of sleep in this section. By now, you understand that having a clutter-free room promotes better sleep. I am passionate about health and wellness, and for me, sleep is one of the biggest and most important factors involved. Where we sleep has a significant impact on this.

I have read many journals, blog posts, and articles on the benefits of sleep. I have also read many health books that included the importance of sleep. But it was not until I read an entire book that was completely devoted to sleep that I really woke up about how important it is! The book, *The Sleep Revolution, Transforming Your Life, One Night at a Time*, by Arianna Huffington, offers medical evidence on sleep, showing how important it is for our overall well-being.

Today's society is busier than ever, and it has become a badge of honor to somehow get less sleep. Arianna Huffington calls this a sleep deprivation crisis! Coming to the office with the least amount of sleep is what people talk about instead of sharing how productive they will be with a full night's rest. Some companies are catching on that sleep can help to improve employees' performance. Here are a few extra tips on how to create a bedroom that's conducive to a good night's sleep:

- Create a bedroom environment that is dark, quiet, and cool.
- Turn off electronic devices at least 30 minutes before bedtime.
- Don't charge your phone next to your bed. Arianna Huffington recommends keeping all devices out of your bedroom.
- Stop drinking caffeine after 2 p.m.
- Use your bed for sleep and sex only, not for work.
- Keep pets out of beds.
- Choose a real book over an e-reader, and read something not work-related before bed.
- Make a list of what you are grateful for before bed. In my opinion, this is a sure way to happier dreams.

>> **Designate a clutter-free zone.** The best-case scenario would be to make your entire home, office, and mind clutter-free zones! However, that may not happen overnight (or ever). The bedroom can be one of those places you designate as a clutter-free zone and stick to for all the reasons mentioned in this chapter.

» **Make it easy.** I mention keeping "declutter boxes" in your home. If you get aesthetically pleasing baskets or boxes that can remain permanently in your home to ensure decluttering is top of mind, that will ease the process. Figure 7-4 is an example of these boxes that can be ordered from www. organzedjane.com.

FIGURE 7-4: Bedroom boxes for decluttering.

Image courtesy of author photocredit @lohmmedia

Chapter **8**

Decluttering Linens and Laundry Areas

N
ext to the closet chapter, this is probably one of my favorite decluttering topics, as I find linen decluttering extra fun. Stacked linens can look wonderful, and we spend so much of our time sleeping that we should take care of what we are actually sleeping on. If you read Chapter 7 on bedroom decluttering, you know that I am serious about getting a good night's sleep, and I believe linens play a big part in this. I don't give you advice on what type of linens you should buy because that is a completely individual preference, but I hope to inspire you to simplify your linens and find what really works for your style and sleep!

Having a linen closet is ideal, but don't worry if you don't have one. I give some practical ideas on storage solutions. Full disclosure, I didn't have a linen closet for years. When I finally got one, I was so excited that I would reorganize it almost weekly just for the fun of it! Whatever your linen storage situation, decluttering is a must, and a few quick tips should keep your linens fresh and ready for you or your next guest to use.

AUTHOR SAYS

I had trouble figuring out what to call a laundry room these days. You may not even store your linens remotely close to your laundry facilities; however, I still ended up bundling linens and laundry in this chapter and tried to organize it efficiently to make the most sense. If you live in a condo or apartment, perhaps your laundry machines are not in a physical room but in a closet or in your bathroom.

Or maybe you have a huge entryway room you call a "mudroom" where you also have your laundry facilities as well as an entire host of other items. When I refer to various laundry areas, keep in mind your specific situation. I try to give general tips. Some may not apply to you if you don't have a larger laundry area, but they may help you in decluttering your entryway even if they are not necessarily in the same spot.

Decluttering Your Linens

First off when I am referring to linens, I mean anything that goes on your bed. This obviously includes sheets and pillow cases, but I also talk about pillows, comforters, and duvet covers and briefly mention bed skirts even though I don't like these myself (it is a total personal preference). You might keep your towels in your linen closet as well, and that is great, especially if you have a larger closet or smaller bathroom storage space. If you want more information on towel decluttering, refer to Chapter 5 (bathroom) and Chapter 6 (kitchen).

The importance of linens should not be underestimated. A good night's sleep can cure most things, and sheets can help with that. I don't go into details about what thread counts look for, what fabrics you should buy, and so on — I am a decluttering expert, not a linen expert. In this chapter, I help you declutter and fold linens no matter what thread count they are.

I encourage you to gather up all your linens if they're not already in one place and go through them all while reading this chapter. The great news is linen decluttering should be one of the faster decluttering projects. And usually you are not as attached to linens as clothes or other items, so getting rid of them is a much smoother process.

Determining your needs

As with most of my advice, always start with what you actually need. One of the biggest reasons we don't get rid of linens is usually because they are still usable. Those old comforters you have from your college days are still in good shape even though you don't use them anymore. Or, those fitted sheets are slightly worn, but you keep them "just in case" you need them someday. The biggest culprit is when you discard the fitted sheet but keep the other parts of the set, and never end up using them again because it's not a complete set! There are many reasons that linen clutter builds up, but whatever the reason, there are few ways to determine what you actually need.

To determine your needs, first consider how many family members you have in your house. This should help you get more clear on your current needs. Each bed should have two or three sets if you don't do laundry that frequently. How many guest beds you have and how frequently you do laundry will help you determine whether you need one or two sets of linens for those beds. This is usually plenty, unless you have a serious revolving door of guests, in which case you likely need more sets.

Some people have summer and winter sheets that get changed seasonally. That is totally okay, even though you may be doubling the number of sheets you own. Again, limit the quantity to what you use and make it realistic for your lifestyle.

What do you need for each of the sets? That's a matter of individual preference, as some people like multiple flat sheets, comforters, or pillows.

For myself, I keep it as minimal as possible and stick to a fitted sheet, duvet cover, and two matching pillowcases. Not having a flat sheet may be the European way, but using a duvet rather than a comforter means you can wash the covers weekly.

WARNING

Emergencies and accidents do happen when it comes to sheets. If you have kids, maybe you need a few more spares. Mattress pads can also do wonders for protecting your mattresses, as you probably don't have many spare mattresses lying around, nor do you want to. Having a few extra linens is a great idea to mitigate accidents and emergencies.

Whatever your sheet set preference, ask yourself these questions as you go through your linens:

>> **Are they worn out, frayed, or stained, or do they have any holes?**

>> **Do they fit the beds you currently have?** Don't keep things because you might get a bigger bed or downsize in the future. Only keep what you currently need.

>> **Are any parts of the set missing?** What was once your favorite sheet set may now be missing a pillowcase and a fitted sheet. So why keep the remaining items if you don't use them?

>> **Do you like the way they feel?** Maybe the linens are itchy, not warm enough, too warm, or too wrinkly.

>> **Do you like the way they look?** If they don't match your bedroom theme or décor, donate them or give them away as they probably match someone else's.

>> **Do you have too many?** See the preceding advice to better determine how many you need.

Theming your linens

Linens often become cluttered because you don't have a specific décor or a set theme. I try to be as minimalist as possible with linens. Mine are all white, usually the same brand, and like I said, I stick to a fitted sheet, a duvet cover, and matching pillowcases. I don't use a flat sheet, but it's okay if you do.

Clutter starts to creep up when you add décor colors, bed skirts, varying comforters, accent pillows, random top sheets, and so on. I challenge you to try to keep it as simple as possible. I'm not saying you have to be as boring as me with my white linens, but stick to a theme for each room. This way the clutter won't build up in the first place.

TIP

I love labeling everything, linens included. This also helps me to stay decluttered. If I have to make new linen labels every month, chances are I am buying too many. I label my sheets by brand and size. For example, if the sheet set is a queen from Frétte I would label it like this. You also might want to label them by room or theme. For me, it is important to have the size on them because the last thing you want to do is have to open a perfectly folded fitted sheet to see if it fits a queen or a king bed. More on how to fold those pesky fitted sheets coming up. My labeled, themed linens in Figure 8-1 show what I have done for years.

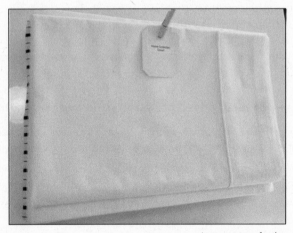

FIGURE 8-1:
Linens labeled by theme.

Image courtesy of author

Timing your linens

In this case, timing doesn't refer to how long it takes you to fold a fitted sheet or make your bed, but rather how long you keep your linens, pillows, and comforters.

Much of this depends on wear and how much they are used, but here are some general guidelines:

>> **Sheets:** There is no set guideline, as it truly depends on usage and how often they are washed. Stick to the tips in the preceding section to check for wear, frays, and stains indicating it's time to replace them.

>> **Pillows:** Generally, with daily use you should replace feather, down, and synthetic-filled pillows every 18 months; memory foam can last up to three years. Remember to also wash your pillows and follow the manufacturer's recommendations on this.

>> **Comforters:** Martha Stewart actually suggests that they can last for up to 25 years if you keep them covered when not in use and regularly air them. Obviously, replace comforters if they begin to look limp, flat, or start falling apart. Again, follow the manufacturer's recommendations for cleaning.

>> **Duvets:** Duvets should last longer than your pillows before they need to be replaced. The sleep council suggests most duvets can last five years and really good quality ones double that. There is no exact science to when you should replace yours, but similar to my other advice, if it is falling apart or getting lumpy, chances are you may need to think about getting a new one.

Folding your linens

Now that you have determined your needs, decluttered and maybe even themed your linens, now comes the exciting part of folding them. I try in this book to mostly focus on decluttering, but I really think it is important to add this section because linen folding really helps keep your decluttering sustainable, as you can see exactly what you have. Everyone who knows me knows that my fitted sheets are always folded perfectly.

TIP

My mom is still amazed by the technique I taught her for folding fitted sheets — and you can see the video on my YouTube channel. Look for "Folding a Fitted Sheet in Under 1 Minute (WITH MY MOM AS A GUEST)." You can go directly to my YouTube channel or under Jane Stoller or access it through my website organizedjane.com.

My short lesson:

1. **Place your hands in each of the corners, and place one corner inside the other.**

2. **Lay the sheet flat and perform the same action on the other side.**

3. **Now you'll have a rectangle shape that you can neatly fold into thirds, and then double over once or twice for the perfect fold.**

If you have a laundry room with a huge folding table, this would be an ideal place to fold fitted sheets. Few of us, however, likely have a laundry room that large. I usually fold my fitted sheets on top of my bed, as it's the perfect size. Alternatively, folding fitted sheets with two people is even easier. You each can grab two corners in your hands and meet in the middle. This can make fitted sheet folding fun, especially if you have kids in your home. Figure 8-2 shows what properly folded fitted sheet corners should look like.

The rest of your sheets should be a breeze after folding your fitted sheets. Flat and duvets can be folded in thirds or doubles and if you can fold them with someone just like fitted sheets, it makes the process easier.

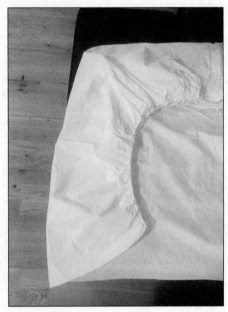

FIGURE 8-2:
A folded fitted sheet corner.

Image courtesy of author

Removing unneeded pieces

Now that you have a pile that no longer belongs in your linen closet, you may be wondering what to do with them. As with most of my advice, get the decluttered items out of your space as quickly as possible. The longer your clutter lingers, the greater the chances it won't leave. If your linens are in good shape, consider donating them to one of the following options:

- » **Car enthusiasts:** If your linens are in good shape, car enthusiasts love to use old linens as rags.

- » **Painters:** Old linens are useful for painters who need to cover furniture and floors.

- » **Animal shelters:** Donating your linens is a great way to help out rescue animals.

- » **College kids:** Anyone setting up a new apartment during college years usually welcomes linens.

- » **Homeless shelters:** These are often a much-needed, welcome addition to their donation supplies.

I have never donated sheets to or bought them from a thrift store, but donating them may be an option as well if the preceding options don't seem like a good fit.

Decluttering Your Laundry Room

As I note earlier, maybe you don't have an entire room for laundry, but chances are whatever area you store your laundry in has clutter. Where you keep your washer/dryer is less of a concern than what surrounds it. It's truly amazing how quickly stuff can accumulate on top of, below, behind, and in all the nooks and crannies around the washer and dryer. Instead of storing laundry items on top of your washer and dryer, store them on a shelf, in a caddy, or in a basket. If they are stacked too high, are difficult to reach, or even keep you from opening the washer, you need to reevaluate your current system.

With laundry rooms, the key is to dive in and get started because it usually involves less strategizing, inventory taking, or thinking compared to other areas of your home. The first step is to take a look around your washer/dryer and remove immediate clutter, lint, and dirt that has accumulated. Remove clothes that are clean, put them away properly, and wash ones that need to be washed. I bet you know you have already decluttered ten things without even thinking about it! Now the real fun can start.

Categorizing items

You may still have clutter around your laundry area even after your quick ten-item decluttering, so it's time to organize everything properly. This starts by following the usual decluttering principle: If you don't need it, get rid of it. Going a bit further, I encourage you to put items into categories similar to those that follow:

>> **Laundry items:** Generally, anything related to doing laundry is considered a laundry item. This includes detergents, lint removers, fabric softeners, clothespins, and so on. If you find a stain stick from 2008 that has yet to be opened, it's safe to say it should go. Or if that spray has never been used in ten years why do you suddenly think you need it now? Again, get rid of anything you don't use or need.

>> **Cleaning supplies:** If these are stored in your laundry room, take note of what you have and go through them.

>> **Outdoor stuff:** If your laundry is located closest to your entranceway, it is amazing what can accumulate. Be mindful of this clutter trap.

>> **Other miscellaneous items:** Anything else that has seeped into your laundry space should be evaluated. Determine how and why it is here, and what can you do to declutter it.

Don't forget to find proper homes for everything other than your laundry staples, which we work on next. Figure 8-3 provides an inspiring glimpse of truly decluttered and organized laundry supplies.

FIGURE 8-3:
Organized laundry supplies.

Image courtesy of Instagram author photocredit @dwell.organized

MOPS AND BROOMS

If you don't have a dedicated spot for mops and brooms, get one! And if you don't have a special way to hang up your mops, either with clips or hooks, install these and do it right away. Without these tricks, your mops and brooms will forever not only look disorganized but will linger longer than they should and end up being clutter. The following photo is an example of a simple hanging solution for mops and brooms.

© *John Wiley & Sons, Inc.*

Organizing by cleaner type

If you have one detergent for all your clothes, skip this section — you're already decluttered!

If you have a detergent for cold water, whites, delicates, colors, and so forth, then start planning how to best organize these. If you're lacking space, you may want to consider multi-purpose detergents or finding smaller bottles/sizes. If those are not options, then you will have to make do with your space and add shelves, hanging baskets, cubbies, or racks. The key is that nothing should be directly on top of a washer/dryer, nor should anything be laying haphazardly on the floor.

I suggest also decluttering by frequency of use. If you continually reach for your all-purpose laundry detergent and only use your delicate wash monthly, place these items accordingly due to usage.

Creating a sustainable system

You likely have some sort of laundry schedule or routine. Maybe you do laundry every Sunday or Wednesday evening, or every day because you have five kids. You have likely formed a habit of some sort because laundry is a task that never goes away and is a constant in our lives, whether we like it or not. Create a similar system for the items you keep around the laundry room.

The biggest and most obvious tip that is posted on every laundry room Pinterest board is to have labeled baskets for colors, whites, and whatever else is a big washing topic in your house. This saves you time and forces others in the same house to follow suit when sorting laundry.

Other things that are helpful when creating systems are to have your space prepared in the most efficient way possible. I am *not* telling you to get more clutter; however, some items that are helpful for creating a laundry system can include:

>> Labeled laundry bags or bins

>> Drying racks

>> Hanging racks

>> Laundry baskets

>> Large see-through containers for clothespins and laundry detergent

>> Hooks

>> Ironing boards

>> Irons

>> Baskets

>> Folding tables

AUTHOR SAYS

One of the keys to enjoying the never-ending task of laundry is to try to make the space and process as fun and as efficient as possible. With the right tools, you can add in hooks, labels, and jars for your items that make your space more visually appealing. Most people, maybe you included, don't like ironing. I love it and love ironed clothes, sheets, tea towels, you name it! However, I don't like wasting time fiddling with the ironing board. Having it handy makes all the difference for your time and your appearance. I say wrinkles have never been in style and never will be! Figure 8-4 provides a small space-saving way to store your ironing board.

FIGURE 8-4: Space-saving ironing board.

© John Wiley & Sons, Inc.

REMEMBER

Make your laundry system so efficient that it becomes routine and maybe even fun somehow.

Determining efficient storage

Having a dedicated laundry room is a luxury that many North Americans are used to since growing up in larger dwellings. In Europe, people live in smaller condos, and some places have a washer/dryer that are two-in-one and also placed wherever they have space (usually in the kitchen). Figure 8-5 is an example of a washer/dryer combo in the kitchen.

FIGURE 8-5:
Space-saving
washer/dryer
combo.

Dinh Ng / Unsplash

The reason I bring up Europe's space-saving washer/dryer combination is that today our laundry rooms have become too full. All you actually need is a washer/dryer and some detergent. It's even possible to use household supplies to make your own detergent if you're really against chemicals.

If you do have a large laundry room, make it as efficient as possible with folding tables, a stable ironing board, and the best cleaning supplies with labeled caddies.

For smaller spaces, see what you can do to use the space most efficiently by installing shelves or hanging baskets. You can use corner shelves, hooks, and over-the-door hanging storage to store items such as detergent, lint removers, fabric softener, clothespins, and so on.

REMEMBER

Whatever your solution, remember the basics of decluttering and don't get carried away with so much storage and then declutter and realize you have nothing to store (even though this rarely happens).

Washing using the "less is more" mentality

Make sure that what you are washing is actually dirty. Do your bath towels need to be washed every time you use them? Likely not. Jeans and sweaters only need to be washed after multiple wears. Your sheets and other towels will depend on their frequency of use and the activities they're used for.

Be mindful of what you're washing to preserve the environment, your clothes, and the decluttered atmosphere in your laundry room.

Mudrooms and Entryways

The entry from the outside world into your home is where a lot of clutter can build up. Large and small houses always seem to have clutter problems upon directly entering the home because, let's face it, coming home tired after a long day of work or activities makes it easy to drop your stuff, and it can easily be forgotten or placed in the wrong spot.

Here are my top tips for decluttering mudrooms and entryways:

» **Clear the clutter regularly.** This point may seem redundant here, but when I say regularly, I mean daily. From mail, to broken items, to trash, to books, to trinkets, it all enters here, so stop it from staying by being consistent in your decluttering efforts.

» **Be mindful of floor safety.** Get the right mats and flooring to protect your floors from dirt and moisture before they enter your house.

» **Designate zones for individuals.** Give everyone a dedicated spot and don't let them exceed this precious real estate with their items.

» **Get creative.** Use baskets or bins and decorate and label them. Use stickers, signs, and keep a declutter box on standby so items can be tossed in this box immediately upon arrival into your home.

The items in this spot in your house should be the easiest to put away quickly, and this area should be the most tailored to the individual so hanging up that backpack or putting the paperwork in a dedicated spot is a no-brainer.

Figures 8-6 through 8-8 offer some entranceway inspiration.

FIGURE 8-6:
FIGURE 8-6:
Spacious built-
in entranceway
organizing
system.

Douglas Sheppard / Unsplash

FIGURE 8-7:
Space-saving
entranceway
hooks and
storage chest.

© John Wiley & Sons, Inc.

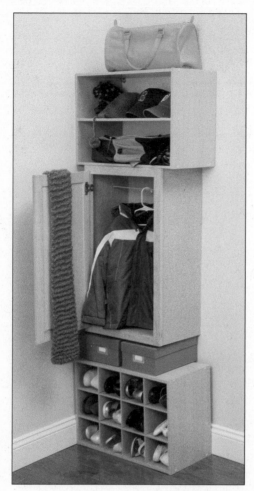

FIGURE 8-8:
Functional
entranceway
shelving and
cupboards.

© John Wiley & Sons, Inc.

Chapter 9

Decluttering Your Kids' Areas

S ome people have an easy time decluttering their kids' stuff. Their kids outgrow their clothes, books, toys, gadgets, and they toss or donate them depending on their condition. For others, the mere thought of giving away the sock that your child once wore is craziness! Plus, many parents often think about the what-ifs, such as what if they have more kids or their grandkids can wear and use the items someday. Both of these examples relate back to Chapter 1 where I ask you to determine your clutterbug style. However, there is even more justification for keeping your kids' items than there is for your own, which makes this a very challenging and sometimes emotional topic.

I am not going to tell you what you need to declutter in terms of "stuff," but this chapter can help you hone in on your decluttering mindset, as well as that of your kids'. This process helps you both become more comfortable with decluttering and help to shape our children's minds and influence them positively when it comes to clutter.

I also dive into the reasons why kids have so much stuff in the first place. If you're reading this and thinking that when you were five, you didn't have nearly the amount of stuff as your child does, you're probably right. Clever marketing tactics and technology have made our kids more aware of what is actually available to them. Last time I checked, five-year-olds don't shop online or have the means to pay for items yet, so their guardians and other loved ones are responsible for all the "stuff" that works its way into their rooms in the first place. This stuff actually comes from all angles for kids. From family members at every occasion offering presents, to McDonald's Happy Meal toys, dentists' offices, and Halloween goody bags, which seem to be getting filled with more than only candy, kids are consuming more than ever. Our consumerist society emphasizes the normalcy of presents and such for most holidays, which gives retailers the opportunity to sell more and more.

Of course, not buying things in the first place can be an easy solution, but I know this is easier said than done with all the external influences affecting kids today. Therefore, I am truly trying to change kids' mindsets first instead of tackling this huge societal issue.

AUTHOR SAYS

Because I don't have kids at the time of writing this book, I decided to do the next best thing to help me write this section. Many of my clients have families, and I have learned from them about kids decluttering. Plus, I have many friends with kids whom I asked for advice when writing this chapter. I was overwhelmed with the response, and surprisingly, everyone had the same tips, which were to declutter consistently and get everyone on board! Everyone was supportive and agreed that something had to be done to change not only the ways clutter gets into the home but also the entire mindset around decluttering. Therefore, you don't have to take my advice but the advice of the countless mothers and fathers whom I asked to contribute in this chapter, all of whom wish their kids would have and get less stuff.

Changing Your Kids' Decluttering Mindset

I truly want to establish that it may not actually be only you or your child's fault that they have too much stuff. Together, you and I can stop this from recurring and causing future clutter challenges for kids, who are our potential leaders of the future. Don't send your kids to clutter camp just yet, because there may be a few tricks we can work on together to get you started on helping to change not only your mindset but also societal norms, which are the largest influence on what comes into your home.

Why so much stuff?

I don't want to keep nagging on this point that back in the day kids didn't have that much stuff. But it is true — for them, and for us as well! However, now that we're aware of our consumerism habits, we have the opportunity to do something about them.

You may always be trying to keep up with your friends', family's, and even neighbors' purchasing habits. Plus, your kids are likely confronted with mass amounts of marketing and see the stuff their friends have, which makes them more inclined to accumulate more clutter.

You still need to instill the values of decluttering even if poor Sally and Tommy don't even realize they are on the verge of becoming clutterbugs or are well on their way to being featured on the show *Hoarders* in ten years.

WARNING

The problem is that not only does trying to keep up with consumerism lead to overconsumption, but it's also extremely damaging to the environment. Even if we toss items eventually, they still had to be produced and shipped, only to end up in a landfill. And don't even get me started on gift giving. Do you give gifts because you are generous or because you are conditioned to give in to the material demands and wants of society?

The following sections offer a few ways you can change your kids' decluttering mindset.

Leading by example

The *Washington Post* ran an article about why kids have so much stuff and how to deal with it. One of its suggestions was to lead by example, giving the example of not handing out plastic goodie bags at birthday parties. At first when I read this I thought, "OMG no, kids love the goodie bags." But then I kept reading and asked myself if they really do love them, or if they only love them for five minutes until they are on to the next thing. Plus, it went on to say that parents don't even like them because then they have to take them home, or worse, if it's their kids' birthday party, they have to find the sub-par junk to put in them.

REMEMBER

Leading by example starts with the people kids are surrounded by most — not only parents but also other relatives and friends who play an important part in shaping the amount of stuff that enters kids' brains and physical spaces.

It may take some tough conversations with your family and friends, as let's face it, most of us like giving more than receiving, and there is nothing like seeing a kid's face light up when opening a present.

TIP

Offer experiences or quality time instead of physical items, or pool funds to give one present instead of five. Events, activities, creative dates, and whatever other ideas you and your team around your kids can come up with will probably end up being more memorable to your kids in the long run, anyway. I remember playing cards with my grandmother for hours, but I can't remember what she got me for Christmas in 1995.

Sustainability also comes into play here. If your kids see you bring your own reusable grocery bag to the store, they will think this is normal. I grew up recycling, and I couldn't physically throw out a can or glass jar without thinking it was bad or that on some level I would get in trouble. Those values were instilled in me from an early age and have become part of my normal way of life, like brushing my teeth; I just do it.

If you can show your kids how you donate or repurpose items, they will think that is the norm. Try scheduling monthly donation drop-offs and bring your kids along. Getting other moms you're surrounded by to jump on board can help you stay consistent and make it more fun. Trust me, there are lots of other parents who wish someone with less stuff would make their way into their homes.

You also need to keep in mind who else is leading your kids, such as teachers, nannies, friends, and grandparents. If someone spends a significant amount of time with your children, these are all teachable opportunities related to decluttering. Let your tribe who spends time with your kids understand the way you and your family feel toward clutter and encourage this mindset. You will be surprised by how many people want to help with this quest and will be excited to help in any way they can.

Making decluttering fun

Kids and adults like to do things that are fun. For kids, the fun factor is even more important as they have a shorter attention span and less discipline to stay on track when given tasks.

Making decluttering fun is the single best way to get your kids involved. You want to help them equate donating and decluttering with having fun, instead of considering it an annoying or stressful task. This single change in mindset can be the way to create more ease and sustainability around getting rid of excess stuff.

I got my niece and nephew into decluttering at a young age, as I loved sharing my organizing and decluttering advice. Surprisingly, they seemed to always listen. When my niece was eight, we got together and made her own donation boxes, which she decorated and kept in her room. It was a fun activity and made the decluttering process fun, plus she always remembered the activity and why we did it. Figure 9-1 is an example of her decluttering process. My nephew has monthly decluttering challenges with his family going around on his hoverboard with my labeled bins collecting items. Figure 9-2 shows smiles all around.

FIGURE 9-1:
Using a donation box helps make decluttering easy and meaningful.

FIGURE 9-2:
Making decluttering fun!

Teaching that decluttering is a priority

A few years ago, I read a blog about a challenge to only have 20 toys. As soon as your child reaches the 20 mark, then he is to evaluate them and donate what is no longer needed. Therefore, he will only ever have 20 toys, which means he is likely to play with one for more than five minutes before moving on to the next. This may seem daunting, and to be honest and upfront, I have never known anyone to implement this rule successfully, but what I have known is parents who have dedicated bins for toys that, once full, signal that no more toys are allowed. Both of these examples offer kids a valuable lesson in not only decluttering but also valuing and using what they do have and donating the rest.

Again, remember that parents are not the only ones teaching kids these days. Be mindful to ensure everyone around your kids is aware of your decluttering goals to help create a sustainable system.

Here are a few more tips to help you:

>> **Immediately put anything broken in the trash if it can't be repurposed.** Get rid of what is now useless and clear precious real estate in your kids' spaces.

>> **Find a new home for anything that hasn't been played with in the last month.** This will help your kids value what they have and be more mindful with what they use.

>> **Give experiences.** I mention this earlier — activities and experiences are a big hit!

>> **Store some toys for later.** With the number of toys that kids have these days, they can be overwhelmed with what to play with. Storing some and taking them out every few months allows your kids to focus on what they have for the moment and really use it. Then when they are done, they can donate it and play with the other toys that were stored.

>> **Make homemade gifts and costumes.** Encourage your kids to make their gifts for others. And when plays and Halloween roll around, making costumes can ignite creativity in your kids and also help keep the clutter down!

Creating donation challenges

I could have easily made this a bullet point rather than a heading, but I feel very strongly that the earlier we are taught the joy of giving and helping others, the better our communities and the entire world will be. As an only child, my parents tried very early to teach me the values of sharing and giving, and they have stayed

with me. I also received so many great tips from parents about this section —
following are my favorite ideas:

>> **Being charitable with allowance money:** When kids get their allowance,
consider setting up not only a money jar for saving and spending on the stuff
they want, but also another one for giving. Help your kids identify which
charity or cause they can give this money to in order to instill a giving mindset.

>> **Giving away an item before holidays:** Before holidays, encourage your kids
to give away something they own before they receive a new gift. This can even
become a family tradition.

>> **Instituting a no-gift rule at birthday parties:** This tip was given to me by my
nephew who had this idea. He told all of his friends instead of a gift this year
he would like everyone to bring ten dollars. He then donated that money to
the local school for updated sports equipment. This is a super idea, and the
donation can be anything that your child or her group of friends is passionate
about.

>> **Creating challenges/games:** Give your kids a point when they donate a
certain amount of stuff, or perhaps set a monthly challenge to donate five
items to their selected donation spot.

>> **Taking advantage of libraries:** Get your kids to use libraries and other
resources that still exist today! Libraries are a great way to get kids to read
books and then return them when they are done. And many libraries offer
more than just books. Your kids can borrow from the library's DVD and
CD collections, which also can minimize the media clutter.

>> **Conducting thrift store challenges:** Instead of always buying new, some
parents are encouraging kids to find items at local thrift stores to understand
that "new" isn't always necessary.

These are just a few ideas, and I am sure you have lots more. Focus on making
donating and its benefits top of mind.

Repurposing toys and clothes

Repurposing can be more than fun for kids; it can be a serious life lesson. We are
so used to going on Amazon when we need or want something, and we usually get
it brand spanking new.

However, wouldn't it be great if our first thought was, "Can we make this instead?
Or do we have something similar to use?" When I was a kid, I thought like this
and was uber creative. It was in large part because I grew up in a very rural area of
Canada where going to a shopping mall required a 60-minute drive. And that was

before online shopping — the Sears catalog was all we had, and it took forever to get your items sent to you.

In came creativity. I would paint, bedazzle, glue, and fix anything I needed and had some genius creations. One of them I still use in my bathroom entailed painting flower pots for my makeup brushes. I even made some of my own clothes — jeans to jean shorts, dresses to scarves — and I fixed holes in my socks. I was resourceful then, and I still am today. My first book is filled with tips and tricks that I label budget organizing; however, today if I were to rewrite the book, I would call it sustainable organizing. Budgeting aside, we should first try to repurpose before we buy new, not just for our wallets but for the environment, society, and, to quote from the first section of this chapter, to be a good role model.

Here are some tangible examples of what you can repurpose for kids. And if you search this topic online, you will get hundreds more. You can even ask your kids to come up with the ideas! Here are three to get your creative juices flowing:

- » **Sock puppets:** Yes, it is still fun to repurpose socks into puppets.
- » **Planters as toys:** Help your kids discover how to grow things, from flowers to food.
- » **Dinosaur toothbrush holders:** Any toy can be used for this — it is genius and can also be used for pencils, paint brushes, and so on.

For more inspiration, check out www.architectureartdesigns.com/30-fun-diy-repurposed-toys-ideas/.

The key is to get your kids excited to reuse their existing items. This skill will not only enhance their creativity but will also make them more resourceful in all aspects of their life.

Hand-me-downs that never leave

Some kids only get hand-me-downs, while others have never experienced what gently used clothing is. This largely depends on family size, proximity to thrift shops, or the willingness of friends to give away their kids' old clothes.

One important thing to remember is that hand-me-downs also need to be decluttered as efficiently as possible. Often, they don't fit or we take them just to be nice. Many parents I talked to said they were given bins of hand-me-downs they don't need that are now taking up space! It's okay to say "no" to hand-me-downs if you won't use them.

Also, get rid of the ones that are too worn or used. They may be okay to further donate or hand down again if they are too well-used, or they may be fit for use as rags or other repurposing before they are eventually tossed.

REMEMBER

You don't have to keep everything that you were given or that was donated to you. Just because someone gives you her clutter doesn't mean it has to turn into your clutter. This goes for anything — not just kids' stuff.

Storing Toys Efficiently

A big part of decluttering is organizing what is left. This is an important step for kids' stuff so that kids can begin developing this habit early. Often kids have more different kinds of things than adults do. They usually have tons of crafts, which should be kept together so that your children can see what they actually have, and also so that they're able to easily get creative and repurpose items. Kids also usually have lots of different types of books, from coloring, to picture, to reference books depending on their age. These should also be sorted — magazine racks can do wonders!

Most kids usually have too many "stuffies," or stuffed animals. And when I asked parents what their biggest kids decluttering challenge is, they usually say stuffies and clothes! Find a way for your kids to organize their stuffies so they can actually see what they have. If they have hampers or baskets overfilled with stuffies, they're likely to forget what is on the bottom.

Many kids also have excess costumes — but how many do they really need? Can you borrow and rent costumes instead of always buying new ones? A tickle trunk for dress-up is always fun, and of course, I don't want to limit any creativity or future actors/actresses in the making. But if they don't use the items in the trunk, there is likely another kid who would be excited to use them.

Organizing by optimal height

I always hung up my jacket when I came home from school as a kid, and I still do today! In my house there was no way around this. My coat had the same spot in our entranceway, and I was the one who took part in this decision of where my coat went and what it would hang on. I painted the hooks, and my parents hung the hooks right at my eye level. My mom loves hooks, and for kids they are life-savers. I remember these hooks fondly and I remember painting them, making them, and using them every day for my backpacks and many jackets — living in Canada, you needed lots of different jackets.

Hanging stuff on hooks that your kids can reach and also enjoy using makes a huge difference. The stuff that is hung on hooks should be used constantly. Once it stays on the hook for longer than weeks or months — it should never get to a year — it's probably best to declutter and make room for items that need those hooks.

Organizing by labels and favorite colors

Certain colors make people happy. I spent a significant amount of time learning about different colors when I was designing my brand. Colors can affect our behaviors in many ways, and they affect our kids' behaviors too. Colors have the ability to soothe, inspire, excite, and even heal in some cases, so working them into kids' spaces is important. You can research various colors' properties and work these into your children's playrooms and bedrooms. To get your kids more involved and excited about decluttering, ensure that your their "declutter" boxes are labeled and in their favorite colors, or decorated with their favorite superheroes or pictures that they associate with donating. If your kids like these boxes, it will increase their chances of using them. Plus, if your kids have dedicated spots and boxes for their items with a limit such as a lid this will encourage decluttering. These spaces can also decorated by your kids or with their chosen theme to encourage organizing. Figure 9-3 shows an example of these decorated boxes.

FIGURE 9-3:
Kids' labeled box and easy-to-reach stuffies.

© John Wiley & Sons, Inc.

LABELING FOR LIFE

On the topic of labeling, I suggest getting your kids started early. I love labeling, and label and relabel like it's my job. In grade school you had to label your notebooks and such, and this is a good practice to instill. Today there are tons of label makers, and you can get labels in different colors, use emojis, or do whatever makes your kids excited about labeling.

Just imagine if everything in your kids' room was labeled and went back to where it belongs at the end of each day. This may be a pipe dream, but why not try to make it a reality one small label at a time?

Today, you don't even have to make your own labels; there are many sites where you can buy labels that are ready to peel and stick, including washable and waterproof ones for all your kids' stuff. Here are two digital labeling sites I use:

- **Mabel's Labels:** http://mabelslabels.ca
- **Kids Labels:** http://kidslabels.com

Sentimental items

It can be hard to say goodbye to your kids' items, and rightly so, as they grow up so fast. If there is something that you truly want to keep, treat it like your other sentimental items and put it in a labeled box. Also, be mindful of things that you think your kids will want. They probably won't reuse their old clothes and the like. I can't tell you what is sentimental because that's different for everyone. My mom kept one of the dresses I wore all the time that she made, and I still have it today and keep it with my sentimental items. Everyone's definition of sentimental is different!

Involving your kids

Most of this chapter reflects the reasoning behind getting your kids involved — not only involved in the process but setting up the systems, as this will ensure that habits form and can transform into adulthood.

Involving your kids early around the idea of "giving" can go a lot farther toward helping them than giving them more toys and games than they can physically ever play with.

Young children can donate their gently used items and already see reactions and understand the benefits to others. As parents, we can explain the benefits of how their donations will be used to help other people.

As children get older, the focus can shift from donating stuff to also volunteering their time. From food shelters, tutoring, elderly home visits, or whatever is available within their community, decide as a family where to volunteer. This can become a meaningful experience that sticks with your kids for life. Your children may have new ideas of where time and donations should be spent, and it's important to allow them to contribute, as it is also their community and the future of their planet.

Sustainability

As your children get older and grow, their organizing and decluttering habits also should evolve. The more you stay on top of this, the more likely they are to continue to declutter throughout their entire lives. Some final last words to help keep decluttering top of mind now and as your children grow into adults:

>> **Teach them to clean.** They need to know how, so don't always do it for them.

>> **Declutter regularly.** Monthly is best for kids with the amount of stuff they get. Put reminders in your calendar.

>> **Remember that less is more.** Teach this from an early age. They don't need more stuff, but quality items they love.

>> **Purge after holidays and parties.** On occasions where mass amounts of stuff come into the house, declutter right away and encourage giving or donating.

>> **Designate a home for everything.** The same concept applies for adults. Make your kids understand this concept.

>> **Allow messes.** Yes, I said it. Kids are creative and sometimes messes happen. When they are done, they can clean up!

>> **Use bins, cubbies, and baskets.** Get them in the habit of using storage containers (and, of course, labeling them).

>> **Buy less.** Kids watch what you do. If you're constantly shopping and have lots of stuff, your kids will think this is normal.

>> **Clean up before bed.** Make this a habit for life.

>> **Use time cubes.** Your kids will be thankful to discover young that time is a valuable asset that needs to be treated properly. Focusing on the task at hand is another valuable lesson. Head to organizedjane.com to get yours.

>> **Have 20-minute challenges.** When clutter builds up, make fun challenges and give everyone chores.

>> **Accept kids.** You will likely not be able to live the same minimal life you had before kids. Kids do need stuff, and you have to accept that, but you can work in your values around decluttering.

Chapter **10**

Decluttering Your Garage

I understand that garage decluttering is tough, since most of us use the garage as a dumping ground for clutter. Similar to the attic or other storage areas, the garage is one of the first places we put things we don't need or want to toss. Meanwhile, these items generally never leave the garage, which causes clutter to build up. The garage also has no boundaries; it can basically be a home for any-thing and everything, from cars to clothes to Christmas decorations. There's no limit to what can go in a garage!

Garages can be dirty and cold, or they can be works of art with tiled floors and framed photos of hot rods. Garages are often thought to be a man's favorite place, but women also have grown fond of their uses, from storing sporting equipment to setting up crafts and hobbies.

For those of you who don't have a garage (maybe you park on the street and are dreaming of a garage, or you live in the city and don't have a car or even a storage locker), bear with me. This chapter outlines tips for general storage that you can apply to your future garage if you eventually move into a home with more storage.

One thing is for sure: Garages are made for vehicles, and if your vehicle doesn't fit, it's a sure sign of too much clutter.

REMEMBER

Getting Real on What You Actually "Do"

Giving advice on garages is especially challenging because everyone has a different idea about what does and doesn't belong in the garage. To start, I want to go back to Part 1 where I talk about fitting your stuff to your lifestyle.

I want you to be really honest with yourself through this entire chapter — more honest than you have been throughout the entire book. Without a doubt, the garage is going to bring up some emotional discussions that will make you realize you can't ski anymore due to your knee injury. Or you are not allowed to go on motorbike trips anymore because you're now responsible for four kids. Whatever the reason for not using use the stuff in your garage anymore, it's likely a sore spot for you to deal with. No one likes admitting their age or that they're getting older. The belongings you hang onto must reflect the stage of life you're in, as well as any changes to your lifestyle. Perhaps it's time to get rid of your camping equipment if you haven't slept on the ground for fifteen years, or the toys you hang onto because you might use them "someday." Trust me: It's better to get rid of these items. If it turns out you need something you got rid of, you can always purchase it new or used, or even rent it or borrow it from a friend.

TIP

Before we begin, instead of the usual pretty boxes I've recommended to help you in the decluttering process, I suggest making sure you have some heavy-duty trash bags, a heavy-duty broom or vacuum, and a general big basket or box for items that have made their way into your garage but don't belong there.

It's time to get real about what you no longer need or use, and the following tips should help:

>> **Do an overview clean.** Do a basic cleaning to get started, moving similar items together (and tossing as you go, obviously). Remove items from the floor and clean any stains, cobwebs, and dirt to make it easier when you do a thorough declutter.

>> **Get your trash bags ready.** As I mention earlier, you can forgo the pretty decluttering boxes and get bags ready instead. Label the bags "Toss," "Keep," "Donate," and "Repurpose."

>> **Think about creative storage.** As you're doing your garage sweep, think about how to make your storage more functional. The garage can be the best place for creative storage, from using pegboards to PVC piping for garden tool storage. From ceiling to walls, the possibilities are endless.

A GARAGE DECLUTTERING SUCCESS STORY

I grew up with a real garage in the country, like the ones you see on TV. It was not attached to our house, it had a dirt floor, and there was no fancy door — it always remained open. However, that did not stop stuff from making its way into the garage. Our garage became a place for things that were forgotten, and since it was constantly exposed to the harsh Canadian elements, that stuff became unusable. At 16, when I learned to drive, I decided to make it my mission to declutter the garage so I could park the car I sometimes used inside to keep it cleaner and out of the snow. It took me days, but after I was done with my garage decluttering session, the car fit and you could almost eat off the dirt floor. This was short-lived, as my parents sold that house and built a house shortly thereafter that included a two-car, heated garage attached to the house. I thought we had won the lottery and was excited for the perks of heated parking.

My dad, being a car enthusiast, had dreams of restoring old English sports cars in that garage — MGAs to be exact, if you know English sports cars. With this hobby came more stuff that filled our garage, in addition to the many sporting goods and typical gadgets that already accumulated in this space.

When I returned home from Europe in 2017, I was on a decluttering mission to help my parents. At this point, I had the ability to work from home. I was starting my organizing business, and I truly knew that with less clutter their house would be a happier place and easier to maintain as they got older. The garage was one of the first places I discussed with my dad. I did not go in and do what I sometimes do and help people declutter. I simply started a discussion. We sat together and discussed his challenges with the space, where he wanted to improve, the projects he was working on, and what other ideas he had to make the garage more efficient going forward. It was easy for my dad to admit during this exercise that he had too much stuff, and he became excited to declutter so that he could restore more cars!

My dad is a shining example of where, if applied correctly, persuasion through involvement with decluttering proves to be most efficient. My dad's tools are now labeled, and he has room for a lift, and my mom can also use parts of the garage. It also houses an organized recycling system. The garage has photos of cars in frames, old license plates on the wall, and is home to a well-used and organized space that brings joy to everyone who steps inside it. The cherry on top is that my dad tells everyone about his organized garage and how he decluttered it to be more efficient.

The reason I am sharing this story is to give you insight into my garage decluttering experiences. We often forget about the garage as a space to declutter, when in reality it's home to some of the fondest memories of cars, sports, and toys. You are likely more attached to your garage than you thought.

Decluttering Seasonally

I encourage you to declutter in one of two ways: either seasonally or by categories. If you live in a place like California where you have one season, skip this section and go to decluttering by category instead of season.

Spring/summer

You probably move and store items twice a year: once for spring/summer and again for fall/winter.

I'm not sure about you, but I love it when seasons come and go. I love it when the warm spring weather comes and bright colors begin to become a staple instead of blacks and browns. I also love being able to get out my summer rollerblades, bikes, hiking shoes, and paddleboards. All of these things are typically stored in a garage or some type of storage locker if you live in a climate with winter.

When you uncover all your fun spring and summer items, you may get excited to use them, but be realistic about whether you actually will. This is the best time to sell these items to make money if you are not going to use them; typically, people start looking for specific sporting items at the beginning of the current season and will typically pay more for an item then than at the end of the season. Once you have assessed what you will actually use, store it efficiently.

When you're getting out your spring/summer items, it is also a great time to declutter your winter items. Often, I get so excited to use my new stuff for the current season that I forget to do this. I am assuming a few of you are also in this habit. However, this is the most important step.

REMEMBER

Before you unpack, fix, and clean your stuff for the current season, declutter and properly store your items from the previous season! Read this a few times so it really sinks in. I think this may be one of the best pieces of advice in this entire chapter!

REMEMBER

Here are tips for storing your fall/winter gear:

>> **Evaluate before you store.** Did you use those skis this season? Did you wear that parka? If you didn't wear, use, or need it this fall or winter, why are you storing it? Donate or discard it fast before you change your mind.

>> **Protect your equipment.** For skis and snowboards, put a thick coat of wax on them before you store them so that next season you can scrape it off and

be ready to go. Plus, wax helps protect your gear from drying out. Sharpen skates, clean hockey equipment, polish helmets, and make sure nothing is damaged before you store it. Whatever items you used in the winter and are keeping, you should clean, protect and store.

>> **Deep-clean.** On the same page as protecting your items, this is a great time to deep-clean your outerwear. You can use special wash for gore-tex or water-proof outerwear, and consider taking your cashmere and special jackets to the dry cleaners. For your base layers, this is a great time to give them one last hot wash before they are stored.

>> **Determine appropriate storage.** Storage should always be clean and dry, and your sporting items are not excluded from this. You don't want your items to smell musty or be ruined when you need them again. Make sure you find a good spot for storage that's not too difficult to reach, so next year it won't be a pain to grab your items. I suggest labeling your boxes and even taking a photo of what is inside if the boxes are not see-through.

>> **Replace what isn't fit to store.** If some of your items are really worn or could be replaced or fixed, do this now. If you replace your items at the end of the season, they'll likely be on sale versus having to purchase them at a high price at the start of next season. Plus, you'll be ready to go instead of scrambling to get your gear prepared.

TIP

Winter items can be bulky to store, especially big jackets. Getting some compression or vacuum pack bags can really help reduce the bulk, and these can be found at most hardware and department stores now. Even Ziploc makes them, and Figure 10-1 shows the amount of reduction achieved when compressed.

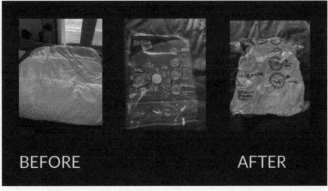

FIGURE 10-1:
Example of compression capabilities.

Image courtesy of author

Fall/winter

The reverse happens in fall/winter as you get excited to wear deeper, darker colors and enjoy the crisp, cool air. If you are a winter sports enthusiast, you probably get excited for the first snowfall or count down the days until the lake makes a giant skating rink. Being from Canada, I am a winter sports enthusiast (you basically have to be, since most of the country is under frigid conditions for the better part of the year). Growing up, I had tons of winter gear, making me an expert at storing it.

Assuming you stored your winter gear properly at the end of the previous season (see the preceding section), it should be a breeze to get it out and use it right away.

When taking out your winter equipment, make sure you have the proper storage for it. Winter items usually should not be left outside due to the temperature, but they're also likely to drip and be wet so it's a double whammy. You need to keep your items warm and the house dry. Install drip trays and hooks, and find unique places to hang/store larger items.

Again, the most important part of fall/winter storage is taking the time to properly store your spring/summer items, no matter how busy or excited you are to hit the slopes.

REMEMBER

The keys to storing your spring/summer items are as follows:

>> **Evaluate before you store.** This is the exact same advice as for the other seasons. Just do it.

>> **Protect and clean.** Certain floatable devices, summer clothing, and even wetsuits should be cleaned and may even need repairs before they are stored.

>> **Determine appropriate storage.** Label containers and make sure you also take photos of what's inside, especially if you might take a trip to a warmer climate midway through winter and need to access these items.

>> **Replace what isn't fit to store.** Same as the previous advice. Check floatation devices and floaties, as these often don't have long life spans. Replace what you'll really need next year; otherwise, consider tossing. Sporting equipment should be tested to make sure it still holds up and is safe to use.

Decluttering Categorically

You may have skipped directly to this section, especially if you don't have seasons, or maybe because it's easier for you to declutter this way. Whatever the reason, the categories I list are the basics, but you may have lots of others, so feel free to keep decluttering by whatever categories you have. The main thing is to stay consistent, and start small by either decluttering for a few minutes every day or tackling one category at a time. And remember, be honest and realistic about what you actually use now, not what you previously used or think you will use someday. Also remember your age; the sports and activities you did in your twenties may not be something you regularly participate in at this age, so there's no need to hang onto unnecessary items. Keep in mind that technology moves fast with sporting equipment, and make sure to always store similar items together.

Decluttering sporting goods

I love sports and fitness and think that everyone should make this a part of their lives. However, I don't think we need the thousands of new gadgets and the newest version of everything each year. If you are a professional or training to be a professional, then yes, you may have different sporting items for certain conditions or purchase new things more frequently. For the general population, though, get real on how much you actually do the sport and how much stuff you actually need.

Go through what you have and declutter what you don't need. The wonderful thing about sporting goods is that these items are great to donate because lots of kids are in need of these items.

Really think hard about what you keep. If you haven't used your figure skates in four years but know you will skate someday, then why not rent the skates next time? They will surely be newer and likely have sharper edges than the ones you are holding onto. Plus, you could be passing on those skates to be used right away by someone who needs them!

REMEMBER

A few tips regarding sporting goods:

>> **Store bicycles up and away.** Bikes should be stored inside to prevent corrosion from the elements and so they are not stolen. There are lots of nifty ways to store bikes on walls and from the ceiling today. This is the best option because you will actually see your suspended bike more, which may make you go biking more often. Plus, bike lifts can free up space in your garage. Figure 10-2 shows a bike lift that attaches to your ceiling and uses an easy pulley system to raise and lower the bike down.

FIGURE 10-2:
Suspended
bike storage.

>> **Consider hallway lockers.** If you have a family with lots of sporting equipment they frequently use, hallway lockers may be a great way to give them their own space and also the accountability to keep their stuff organized and decluttered. They can only fit so much stuff in a locker before it won't be able to close!

>> **Place a bench in the garage.** A bench will not only make your family happy to put on their sports gear, but some benches even come with storage underneath, which will entice your family to keep these items in the garage rather than trekking them into the rest of the house.

Decluttering camping supplies

Camping supplies have always challenged me. I used to camp when I was a kid; I loved it and have wonderful memories from camping. My parents, on the other hand, did not enjoy it because it's lots of work — first, to get all the camping equipment, then to set it up, take it down, clean it, and store it for the next time you go camping. I am by no means saying don't camp. If you love it and it brings you joy, then keep camping and keep your camping gear. But camping stuff has a funny way of working itself into your life even if you don't camp. You may have the best intentions to camp all summer but only go once due to your kids' baseball, soccer, gymnastics, hockey, and whatever other sport seems to take up every weekend for kids these days.

WARNING

I am always in shock about the amount of camping equipment and new technology available today. Venture into any outdoor store and you will be amazed at what new camping invention has arrived to make the experience more enjoyable. Even people who don't camp will want to buy this stuff, so be careful when going into outdoor stores (unnecessary gear can quickly turn into clutter). Even the most well-heeled city dweller can be enticed by the newest gadgets.

Here are a few tips on decluttering your current camping supplies or new gear (if you didn't take my advice and went inside an outdoor store):

>> **Avoid immediately replacing items due to the potential "empty garage syndrome."** Decluttering your items can make you feel lighter and more organized, but it won't immediately change your purchasing habits. Make sure you stay mindful to avoid impulsive purchases post-camping decluttering.

>> **Envision the rewards of not only how much time you will save in your garage, but how much better you will feel with the carefully selected pieces that remain.** Make sure your camping gear is specific to how often you go camping and your camping style, as well as the time of year and conditions you camp in.

Decluttering car accessories

How many car accessories you own depends on how much you care for your car inside and out. If you wash your car weekly, I assume you have a healthy selection of shampoos, brushes, and cloths. If you try to do some maintenance on your car, you may also have specific tools for this. The same principles apply here to car accessories and supplies: If you don't use them and/or suddenly don't need them anymore, get rid of them.

Along the same lines as the stuff *for* your car is the stuff *in* your car. Firestone tires has concluded that the average American spends 600 hours each year in his car. And this can lead to a cluttered car if you aren't careful.

In addition, clutter around the driver's area can be very dangerous. Today there are many great solutions for car storage, including specialty cargo organizers, back-seat organizers, and if your beloved pet travels with you, a variety of items including pet hammocks.

I include this quick section for the importance that it has related to safety. In the first few chapters, I go into detail about the distraction that clutter can cause for your mind. And I know that distracted driving is a very dangerous thing, so keeping your car clutter-free will improve your driving and your ability to focus! Safety and clutter-free go hand in hand in my books.

Decluttering miscellaneous items

I could make a 30-page list of what else you could have in your garage, but the main thing is to be practical with what you're keeping. Here are some ideas on how to store your items:

>> **Work wonders with shoe organizers.** For spray paint cans, spare tools, mittens, and winter items, shoe organizers are an easy and cheap option for storage — the possibilities are endless with these genius inventions! And the beauty of them is that you can hang them wherever and store them when the season is done.

>> **Use magnetic strips.** I talk about these in the tool section, but think beyond tools. You can get empty metal cans to store paintbrushes in and hang them. Plus, they're easy to replace.

>> **Invest in gadgets you use daily.** Invest in making your garage as user-friendly as possible. As I state in the introduction, this is the place where clutter can often build up, such as recycling, boxes, and items that should be fixed. Consider which items you are always needing, and make a commitment to yourself to always have these on hand. For example, are you always using packing tape? Make a section for this. Also, get recycling boxes and label them to help your family get in this habit.

>> **Make your entranceway in your garage.** More often than not, our garages are just a place for stuff and our cars. They are not pretty or warm or fun places to hang out (that is, unless you are a car enthusiast or have a man cave). Creating an entranceway in your garage can help keep the clutter and dirt out of your home in the first place. Use benches, hooks, rugs, and whatever will entice the people in your household to use this as a first stop before entering your home.

>> **Install wall racks.** These can be great for storing everything from cleaning supplies to extra produce and drinks to gardening supplies. Using baskets is also a great way to ensure you see what is in the racks and prevent clutter from building up.

>> **Employ bungee cords.** Another staple in garages is bungee cords, which are a great way to secure sporting balls, hang up random items, and fix things. The possibilities are endless, and they are a great item to have on hand.

>> **Lock up dangerous items.** Your garage may be home to chemicals or sharp tools, and it is best to keep these in a locked cabinet.

>> **Create zones or areas.** It's easy to make zones for your sports equipment, car supplies, and other specific categories I address earlier. Consider other categories of items you have as well, such as crafts, painting, recycling, gardening tools, recycling, exercise equipment, and so on. Dedicate a specific area to each category of stuff you have.

For all your miscellaneous items, I recommend not buying storage units or items until you declutter. Take a really conservative approach and use what you have, install a few shelves, and go from there. It's easy to get carried away in garages with all these extra items, but remember to evaluate them first.

Decluttering Tools

Wondering what tools you should keep? The ones you use, obviously! Still, it can be difficult to decide which items to hang onto. Following are the basic tools to consider keeping:

>> Hammer

>> Wire cutters

>> Pliers

>> Screwdrivers (multihead are the best)

>> Wrench (adjustable)

>> Knife (retractable for safety)

>> Cordless drill (super handy)

>> Staple gun

- » Nails, screws, nuts, and bolts

- » Plastic anchors (especially for hanging things)

- » Hooks

- » String (or fishing line)

- » Tape measure

- » Level

- » Stud finder

- » Pencil

- » Sandpaper

- » Duct tape

- » Strong glue (like Gorilla or Krazy glue)

- » Flashlight

- » Safety equipment (glasses, gloves, and so on)

I'm sure I have missed many items on this list and included some you may not need. If you're a contractor or work with tools on a regular basis, your list will be much longer than this. And if you do no home repairs and outsource everything, you may have nothing on this list. This is just a very general guide.

If you have a lot of tools, keep the ones you regularly use. If you get a new tool, don't keep the old one. Get rid of duplicates right away as well as tools you don't know how to use (let's face it, if you haven't tried to learn by now, you likely never will).

Tools that are broken should be discarded and replaced if needed, so truly determine the frequency of use of your tools. Determine whether you can borrow or rent tools instead, as this is a sure way to minimize clutter (and save money).

Make sure the tools you decide to keep are well organized, as nothing is worse than starting a project and not being able to find the tools that you know you have to complete it. Figure 10-3 shows a well-used and well-designed tool storage board.

Lastly, label everything — tools are no exception!

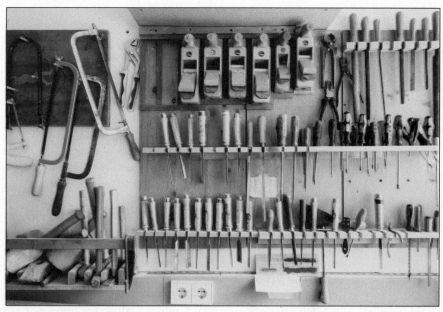

FIGURE 10-3: Tool storage.

Labeling your items

Labeling your items is good advice for literally any area of your home, but it's especially important for your tools because you generally need to grab them quickly. Having dedicated spots and labels for your tools will help you to keep them ready when you need them and also help you stay clutter-free. As with anything, if you find yourself creating 20 new labels a week, you're accumulating too much stuff that can lead to clutter.

Figure 10-4 shows my dad's labeled tool box. With so many different types of screwdrivers and wrenches, labels are needed!

FIGURE 10-4: A labeled tool-box makes it easier to find and use your many garage tools.

Renting versus buying

Today there are lots of options to rent tools — more so for larger equipment than your basic toolbox and screwdrivers. Your local hardware store is usually happy to show you what they have for rent, and you can then do the cost analysis of whether it is worth it to buy or to rent these items. When you're doing your analysis, you have to remember to factor in the cost of potential breakdowns and also assign weight to the precious real estate you give up in your home to place that tool. I am a big fan of renting items when you don't need them on a regular basis, because when you rent you are usually using more up-to-date equipment and don't have to worry about maintenance.

The biggest thing with tools is truly to maintain the system you create. Once you're organized, you will feel accomplished the next time you reach for that Phillips screwdriver. But you need to keep your organizing scheme going, and you may need to do a seasonal, monthly, or even weekly organizing of your tools depending on how often you use them. Make sure that the people who may borrow your tools know the system and where items belong. Nothing is worse than having your tools perfectly organized only to realize that someone has not put something back in the right spot!

Decluttering Big Kid Toys

The items I am referring to may not be toys, and may very well be useful motorized equipment. As with all my advice, if you use it, keep it! If you don't, declutter it. The value and the size of your items don't matter — it's the value they bring to your life in terms of usage and benefits that do.

Decluttering boats, trailers, snowmobiles, and four-wheelers

I am not saying you should immediately get rid of all your small motorized devices. What I am suggesting is that you evaluate them and determine how often you use them. In addition, I advise you to review the motivation before purchasing these items. In my experience, for example, Sea-Doos or small, personal watercraft are fun until you realize you only used them twice the entire summer. Did you buy them because your neighbor had them? Because you thought you would use them every weekend? Get practical as you evaluate which items you want to hang onto and which items you're willing to declutter.

Small motorized equipment that is for pleasure and does not serve a purpose should be well-thought out purchases. Don't give into the latest fad, and make sure you purchase within your budget. Be ready to sell if you end up not using them.

Answer these questions honestly to help you better determine your needs for your items:

>> Do you use them?

>> How often?

>> Is this for pure fun or does it also serve a functional purpose?

>> What is the cost analysis of renting instead?

>> Could you share with your neighbor?

Again, I am not suggesting you should not have these types of items; I just want to make sure they are well-used if you do have them!

MOTORCYCLES

I could have looped in motorcycles to the preceding section, but I want to call them out in this sidebar. Motorcycles are usually a hobby, but if they are your main mode of transportation, then that is a different story. I used to ride motorcycles and love the feeling of an open road. With motorcycles comes lots of decluttering, and the motorcycle itself is one of the items to declutter. With many of us living in cities with no garages, storage becomes an issue. Many places offer motorcycle storage over the winter, for a fee, of course. If you have a Harley-Davidson, for example, your local Harley dealer may offer this service. This is a great storage option if you don't have the space, and most dealers usually service the motorcycle for you. Factor the cost of storage into your budget before you purchase a motorcycle to determine if it will fit your lifestyle.

(continued)

(continued)

If you only use your bike a few times a year, is it worth it to have one? Today there are many options to rent bikes, so keep this in mind before you rush to purchase one. In addition, make sure you declutter the "stuff" that comes with your motorcycle, such as the following:

- **Tools:** Make sure you have what you need and discard the rest. Same goes for your bike cleaning supplies.

- **Clothing:** You should definitely have specialty clothing for both comfort and safety, but go through your clothing every season and toss/replace items if they are worn. I also recommend donating or selling what you don't wear.

- **Other stuff:** With being a bike enthusiast, chances are you get lots of gifts or even buy yourself trinkets related to motorcycling. Be wary of what you receive and buy, as these likely have no bearing on your actual biking activity but rather are dust collectors. I mean, are you actually going to use those Harley clocks your friends keep buying for you? Again, be practical. The following photo shows an example of the amount of space a motorcycle and its tools could take up in your garage.

SplitShire / Pexels

Decluttering lawn and snow equipment

If you have lawn and snow equipment, you're likely living on a property with a lawn or driveway requiring snow removal. Be grateful you have the space and are able to do this. City dwellers may dream of having space and yearn to do yardwork on weekends, while those from the country wish all they had to do was drive out of their temperature-controlled garage and have a cocktail instead of mowing the lawn on Saturdays.

AUTHOR SAYS

If you have a lawn and/or driveway, you need stuff to take care of it, unless you want to completely outsource this, which may make more sense after you do a cost/benefit analysis. Many companies offer these services, and the added benefit is that you don't need to store the items, maintain them, or take your precious time to do the work. I truly believe that outsourcing can be the best approach, but this is a personal choice.

TIP

Review your lawn equipment after the season and either declutter or replace items. Do the same for your snow equipment after the winter.

Of course, all the usual rules apply — you need to have a dedicated spot for these items, and they should be as close to the exit as possible for ease of use.

Little kid toys

If you have kids, refer to Chapter 9 on decluttering kids' areas. The garage can be a place that kids' stuff can accumulate, especially outdoor toys and seasonal items.

>> **Sand toys:** Kids often have toys from their sandbox or outdoor play areas such as buckets, toy trucks, and small gadgets. Decide what they still use and then donate the rest.

>> **Water toys:** If your kids play in the water or if you have a pool, then you likely have accumulated many water toys. From floaties to pool noodles, decide what is still in good shape and discard the rest. Be careful about donating these items because normally they only last for one or two seasons.

>> **Sporting equipment:** Yes, your kids' tiny basketball net is cute, but do you really need to keep it now that they are in college?

Apply the same principles as in Chapter 9 to whatever else your kids may have in the garage. Don't forget to involve your kids and make their garage storage space easy to reach and clean. *Remember:* The more involved they are, the more likely they are to keep up the organization.

Decluttering Boat Garages

Not everyone has a boat house, boat, or partakes in any of the activities surrounding this, but I wanted to add this section for the few who do. I talk about decluttering your boat itself, but I start with general themes of boat houses and fishing supplies.

Creating boat house rules

If you don't have a boat house, you will likely skip this section. However, if you're thinking of getting a boat (even if you don't have a boat house or a spot on the lake yet) and are planning on mooring it or keeping it in the driveway, continue reading.

A few rules I have for boat houses:

>> **Keep items off the floor.** This is not only for organizational purposes — if weather causes water to seep above the docks, keeping your stuff off the floor will protect it.

>> **Check wet suits and life jackets annually.** Ensure they still fit and meet safety standards.

>> **Keep floaties in check.** I am all for the newest Instagram-worthy blow-up swan to place in the pool or bring on your boat for a dip in the lake, but take the photo and pass it on, because blow-up floaties are rarely used more than once. Better yet, borrow one for the day, and definitely don't keep floaties for more than one season.

>> **Discard pool noodles annually.** They lose their buoyancy.

For the boat itself, here are some tips to keep clutter at bay and ensure your items are up-to-date for safety reasons:

>> **Take inventory.** Make sure you regularly check what you have in your boat at least annually and make a list. This is a great time to remove what you don't need and/or replace/update what you do need. Your must-have safety equipment depends on the number of people and the country you are in, so make sure you have a checklist on hand and review it every time you go on the water. Trust me, it is easy to forget a life jacket if you have an extra guest, and that can result in a hefty fine or danger if there is an emergency.

>> **Invest in stowaway bags and lockboxes.** Keeping the items in your boat tucked away protects them from wear and tear and also keeps them safe.

>> **Utilize unused space.** There is lots of hidden, unused space in a boat, and you can attach things like winches and wallets so they don't fly overboard and can be easily removed when you need them once on shore.

>> **No junk drawers allowed.** Similar to my kitchen advice, your console should not resemble a junk drawer. Keep your boat tidy and don't let bits and bobs accumulate. Take anything you don't need or use off the boat.

Fishing stuff

I had to add this as my parents owned a fishing resort for 20 years, so I am well aware of what fishing stuff entails, and it is much more than a rod and a few lures. One thing about fishing is that it is often laden with memories, like old times fishing with your father or colleagues. If you like or love fishing, it likely has something to do with your memories, making the decluttering process more emotional.

Go through your fishing tackle, rods, and gear after each season and determine what you are still using and what needs to be replaced.

REMEMBER

You may have sentimental fishing items in your cabin or lures from your grand-father that have special meaning. That's okay, but don't keep these stored with your fishing items. Rather, keep them in your sentimental box. Plus, you likely don't need to keep all 100 of his lures; keep only one and trust that your memories will last forever.

Another thing to remember is to hang up your rods. I once saw a great invention of using a pool noodle with slits in it to keep them in place — a simple and cheap way to store items rather than building a big, complicated system.

TIP

I love tackle boxes for lots of things other than fishing tackle. Tackle boxes can be used to organize so many items, and the bonus is many are usually see-through so items can be easily found. Figure 10-5 is an example of a tackle box that happens to be filled with tackle.

Here are a few examples of unique things to store in tackle boxes:

>> Batteries

>> Jewelry

>> Snacks

>> Makeup

>> Small tools (screws, nails)

>> Electronic cords (think earbuds)

>> First-aid supplies

>> Office supplies

FIGURE 10-5:
A fishing
tackle box.

Sarah Labuda / Unsplash

Chapter **11**

Decluttering Your Storage Spaces

This is a tough chapter, and I am not going to lie. Decluttering storage spaces isn't easy or quick. Storage spaces are likely the spot where you put everything — not just items that you know you will use annually, like Christmas decorations, but items that you've postponed decluttering because the thought is too stressful to deal with.

Also, decluttering your storage items usually means making a bigger mess, so you need to carve out the necessary time to tackle this project. Decluttering storage spaces requires removing items that may be dusty, dirty, and have been stored for years, so be prepared for a big job. (This is not the quick ten-minute decluttering session that can instantly improve your living room.) You are going to need to dedicate some serious time and effort to this, but trust me, the results are worth it. Having all your stuff crammed into storage spaces is useless because you can never find what you need, and you've probably forgotten about it altogether, which renders your items useless.

I am a fan of storage spaces, and I think having a designated spot for handy and/or occasional use items is necessary. What I'm not a fan of are these spaces becoming dumping grounds for anything and everything, making it impossible to get the occasional use out of items that you need.

In this chapter, I give general tips for tackling these spaces, whether you have an attic, basement, rented storage locker, or a space under your stairs for storage. This chapter applies to wherever you store "attic-like" items. I also drill down a bit deeper into the most common items that tend to be stored in attics or similar places, and why I don't even recommend storing them in attics at all!

Tackling Storage Spaces

My advice usually centers around starting small a few minutes a day, making slow and steady progress, celebrating your successes, and then sustaining your systems. However, your storage spaces are a different story. If you declutter for ten minutes a day, it may take you years to finish these spaces because just the process of getting into your storage area and moving items around can take you ten minutes. I warned you already that this is going to be one of your more dedicated decluttering missions, and I wasn't kidding.

TIP

I would attack this space full-on. Clear your schedule, enlist support, and start decluttering. Even though you don't see this space, knowing it is free and clear of clutter can also help clear your mental space. Hiding clutter doesn't mean it doesn't exist and doesn't enter your mind. Even thinking about the clutter in your attic for one minute a day means you're thinking about it 365 minutes a year — time you could have taken to just declutter it and make room for other thoughts. With this final warning, it's time to dive in.

I want your storage space to be a place you love going to because you know exactly what is in it, you can easily access items when needed, and you have peace of mind knowing where everything is located. More often than not, our storage spaces are a pain in the butt for us and we dread even the thought of going in them. The practical tips I share can help to change this entire mindset.

First of all, I want you to feel grateful that you have a storage space. And if you literally have no storage space — not even a storage locker in your building — feel grateful that you don't have to spends hours on end decluttering it!

If you don't have any storage space, you still need to find a way to store items that you occasionally use. I not only highlight some common items that are found in storage spaces, but I even recommend other spots for them in the future. Storage spaces are really for storage of items you sometimes use, and that's it.

Getting started with a handful of steps

Before I dive into the categories of what may be in your attic, I want to focus on a few steps that are really important to help you get started:

1. Safety first!

If your storage is in an attic or basement, you want to be extra cautious when starting your decluttering mission. Make sure floorboards are safe, put on a mask if there could be something dangerous in the air, and wear gloves to protect your hands. I am also a big fan of lighting in my storage spaces, and chances are you can improve the lighting in yours. Wear a clamp-on headlight if you don't have lots of light and/or bring additional lighting with you until you find a more permanent solution. Make sure to watch your head if there are low ceilings or beams!

2. Take everything out.

There is no way around this and it may be a terrible task, but you have to do it. Take out boxes, baskets, furniture, and whatever else you may have stored. You may need help with larger items, and if something doesn't fit through the door, you may have to take it apart to get it out of there!

3. Clean.

Your storage space will inevitably be dusty. Remove dust and clean the empty space because there's no better chance to do this than when everything has been removed. Vacuum and sweep all the nooks and crannies.

4. Inspect and fix.

You want to make sure there is nothing dangerous, from mold to loose floorboards. Do a thorough inspection of the space and fix what is required. Also take note of the temperature — is it frigid or so hot you can melt an ice cube in 30 seconds? Sometimes your storage spaces are not insulated property, and this is important for what you will be storing in these spaces.

5. Practice prevention.

After your efforts in cleaning and updating your space, make sure you prevent dust and mold from accumulating in the first place. Seal cracks to prevent moisture and dust from coming in. You may even want to seek professional support if needed to help with this.

What I did not mention in these steps is to build special racks or shelves or invest in expensive storage units. Your storage spaces should really be for items you use only occasionally, and therefore you don't need fancy devices or shelving for these to be stored on. You need to store less stuff and really make sure you keep only those items you use at least once per calendar year.

What shouldn't be stored but likely is

I hope now all your stuff is outside your storage space and ready to be decluttered! This is my favorite part, and I hope it can become yours too. There is nothing like being able to give your gently used items to someone else who will appreciate them more than you do.

I am going to talk about items that you may have in your attic but really shouldn't, but I am not going to list what you should be storing. Christmas decorations, seasonal items, and selected sentimental items are my basic suggestions, but you're on your own to make this list for whatever occasional items you have.

REMEMBER

Storage takes up precious real estate and should be an extension of your home. If you're paying for a storage space outside your home, you have an even bigger reason to declutter and save your money.

To start, look through the following list to see whether you removed any of these items from your storage space and declutter them. Don't put them back into storage, as I don't think these belong there in the first place.

>> **Clothing:** You can keep clothing in your storage area if you wear it and are only storing it for seasonal purposes or to avoid anything getting ruined. You should not store clothes you're never going to wear again. Donate these immediately so someone else can wear them today! Clothes you think you might wear one day also don't belong in storage. These should be in your closet and decluttered with the rest of your clothing. Also, the more fabrics you have in your storage, the greater the risk of moths and mice.

>> **Paperwork:** Don't put paperwork in your storage space. Skip to the next section to get more details on what to do with paperwork.

>> **Furniture:** Furniture should be used, not stored. If you don't use it, why are you keeping it?

>> **Too many sentimental items:** If you have stacks and stacks of memory boxes, you can't possibly enjoy all the stuff in them, and you probably don't even remember what is in them in the first place. I discuss strategies for dealing with this later in this chapter.

>> **Packing material and empty boxes:** Get rid of these ASAP.

>> **Electronics:** By the time you find them, they are either too old, are no longer relevant, or have been ruined by dust or the elements. Technology moves fast, so don't store electronics. And if you love records, then keep reading because later I give advice on what to do with electronics you want to keep.

» **Old travel bags:** Not a week goes by that I don't see an ad for the latest new travel bag or suitcase that is lighter, more functional, has wireless charging, you name it! Holding onto old suitcases and travel bags is unnecessary. Keep your travel items up-to-date if you travel frequently, and if you don't travel, then why do you have these in the first place? Plus, airlines are getting stricter with weight and sizes, so traveling with your old huge and heavy suitcases probably isn't the best idea.

» **Photos:** It always bothers me when photos are stored in attics because no one can ever see them! Photos are meant to be viewed, especially if you took the time to print them. They should be taken care of, not stuffed in a box where they are likely getting ruined. More details on physical photo storage follow, and in Chapter 15, I give strategies for both physical and digital photo storage.

Getting realistic

As you're going through your items, I want you to get realistic with the things you have stored and ask yourself these questions:

» Why did you store it in the first place?

» How long ago did you store it?

» If you use an item occasionally, how often? Monthly? Annually? Every five years?

» Do you need this?

» Would you miss this if you didn't have it?

» Can you rent or borrow this?

» Does it cost you to keep this maintenance-wise?

» Is there a new version that is more efficient?

Make sure those items that make the cut after going through this list are properly packed before you re-store them. For example, you use your Christmas decorations every year, so make sure they are all together in a large labeled tote and that you only keep the stuff you actually use every year.

TIP

If you do have a large attic, this does not mean you have to fill it with stuff. A larger storage space isn't a free ride to more clutter.

Recycling packing material

How often do you keep boxes from your old or current TVs, microwaves, and teeth whitening systems? If you never do, then great! If you have all three of these sitting in storage, it's time to finally get rid of them. Retailers are great at taking returns, but usually they only need to be in the original box if returned within the first 15 days. So, keep the box in your home front and center until you decide to keep the product, and then promptly recycle the box. I have never needed the original box to send back an item to be fixed. If you have, then maybe keep the box, but I would really question why the original box is necessary. Look into store policies to ensure that you can make an educated decision as to whether you keep or toss an item's box.

It's not uncommon to move often; no longer do we spend 30 years in the same house, let alone the same city or country! You can decide how many boxes you plan to keep depending on how often you move. If you move every year and are a serious do-it-yourself mover, then maybe you should keep a few moving boxes. However, in my experience, boxes tend to become weathered even after only one move. Plus, you can buy used moving boxes quite easily as people usually list these for sale right after they move, which is a great idea — and you can do the same.

I have moved many times and I have even lived out of my wardrobe boxes for months when I was in transition between apartments. I do love wardrobe boxes — they are the boxes that have a hanging space for your clothes. These are usually a bit better quality and expensive. I keep these and use them for storing my seasonal items when not in use. Figure 11-1 shows a couple examples.

FIGURE 11-1:
Repurposed wardrobe and moving boxes.

Image courtesy of author

Keep your boxes and packing material if they can serve an alternate purpose and don't clutter up your space.

Determining a Strategy for Sentimental Items

I'm not going to lie: This is the section I have been dreading since I started writing this book. Not because I don't love organizing my sentimental items or sharing my advice on this topic, but because it is and always will be an emotional topic for everyone — myself included.

Everyone's definition of what is sentimental to them is different. I will never tell you what you should or should not keep, which is why I take a different approach. I try to focus on a strategy for helping you declutter your sentimental items rather than saying what those items should or shouldn't be.

AUTHOR SAYS

Memories and items, especially from past loved ones, are precious, and I completely respect that and want you to keep whatever brings you the most happiness.

Time to talk strategy!

How much is too much?

Sentimental items can bring you lots of joy until you end up with so many that you have boxes and boxes filled with ticket stubs from every concert you ever attended and every drawing your kid ever made you. I recently had to declutter my grandmother's belongings and determined she was a serious sentimental clutter-bug; I found every single postcard that she had ever received. There were literally 20 shoeboxes of them, and the sad part was she never once looked at them. There were simply too many!

The key is to be selective in what you keep. Had my grandmother selected five special postcards out of the 20 boxes of them, she would have been able to look at them regularly and enjoy the memories from each one.

Going through your sentimental items should be a joy, and the more selective you are about how much you keep, the better the process will be.

Still, people continue to ask me questions about the number of sentimental items they should keep.

Here are a few guidelines I follow for my own life. By no means do you have to follow these exactly, but they can provide a framework to help you in your decluttering process.

>> **Your childhood memories:** One or two boxes should suffice.

>> **Your kid's mementos:** Some parents keep their kid's room as-is with all their stuff in it. Others keep a few boxes of their favorite items. There is no way to determine an amount here, but asking your kids for insight can help determine what to keep.

>> **Relationship mementos:** If you're still together, creating a sentimental box may be a great project to discuss with your partner and do together. If you're separated, don't keep these items and move on.

>> **Parents' or grandparents' items:** I have one large box labeled, "Grosi (Grandmother in German) Sentimental Items." My mom and I together made this box of our most treasured items from my late grandmother. We often look at it together.

>> **Career memorabilia:** You really should not keep paperwork from courses or your previous work. Consider maybe digital storage if you actually do reference them. Awards, diplomas, cards, and trinkets are best kept at your office in sight versus storing them. After your career ends or when you're starting a new one, think about what is really important to you as you don't want to be starting a new job and hanging onto ten boxes of stuff.

>> **Miscellaneous:** Be selective and understand that the less you have, the more you will really appreciate those items.

Saving only the best

On the same theme of determining how much you should keep, I encourage you to change your mindset and keep only one of something where you have many and make it count. Hanging onto multiples or bulk saving will not make your items more special.

Go through your items and pick the ones that bring you the most memories or happiness and keep those. Discard the rest.

Giving it time

I know it is hard to part with sentimental items, and it may take time to do this. If something is obviously trash or broken, it's likely easier to get rid of even if it is slightly sentimental.

If you are having trouble determining what to keep and what to discard, put those items in a box labeled with a big question mark. Store this for a maximum of six months and consider this a grieving period for your sentimental items. I know letting go can be emotional, and I want you to really be ready. Put a note on your calendar to revisit your question boxes once you've had time to reflect on the items before you decide if you will keep them or declutter them.

As an alternative, take photos of items and create a photo album titled "Sentimental." Often this is better than keeping the items because you can access the photos from anywhere and share them with others. Figure 11-2 is a screenshot of my sentimental album on my phone photo albums.

FIGURE 11-2:
My "Sentimental" photo album on my iPhone.

Image courtesy of author

Where to store them?

If your items are precious enough to keep, then why are you storing them in some musty attic or damp basement?

I recommend getting serious about these items before you decide to keep them. Here are a few tips on how to store the items you've decided to hang onto:

>> **Get a nice box.** Ensure that the items you're keeping have a nice home. This box, basket, or whatever other item you use to store your sentimental items should be pretty enough to be on display. I keep my items in white round hatboxes with labels on them. Figure 11-3 shows an example.

>> **Label the items.** Even better, take a photo of the box or basket so you know what's inside.

>> **Make them easily accessible.** There is no point in keeping items if you can't access them.

>> **Schedule time to use/look at them.** Why not make a date with Mom to go through your childhood memory box? This will make a fun evening and encourage you both to look at these items.

>> **Show them off.** Give your items a new home and bring them into your everyday life so you can actually see them.

FIGURE 11-3:
Sentimental box.

Image courtesy of author

Sorting Your Books

I hope you don't keep your books in storage; if you do, that's not a great way for anyone to read them. Books should be read and enjoyed by as many people as possible, and this is why I think it's important to address them during this chapter. I mean, you are physically reading this book and I don't expect you to keep it forever. I actually encourage you to pass it along to others or recycle it once you have taken all the tips you need for your lifestyle. Since it is a reference book, you may want to hang onto it for longer than most until you have mastered all the techniques, but then it is ready for a new home!

Reading and decorating OR reading and decluttering

Books today can be read, reread, donated, recycled, and used for decorations. In this section, I am primarily talking only about *physical* books, not the ones on your tablets or e-readers, but I talk about those in Chapter 14.

Start by gathering all your books from all locations and sorting them. This may be a big job, and if your books are literally too far away, then you may have to go room by room to where they reside.

The way you sort will depend on what genre of books you have. If you have fiction and nonfiction, begin by sorting into these two categories. Typically, you read fiction once and then you can pass it along. You can further sort nonfiction by types of books, from self-help, to reference, to biographies. Nonfiction books that you keep going back to for reference should generally be kept accessible. Nonfiction that you only read once can be passed along!

A few other tips about book storage:

>> **You can save your favorites.** You don't have to get rid of all your books because you've read them already. The books that you truly love and keep reaching for can have a permanent spot, but you have to set some boundaries as to which ones actually are your favorites.

>> **Go digital.** They take up less space, which is especially helpful when you're traveling.

>> **Use books as decorations.** As you can probably tell, I don't like too much stuff around that can collect dust, with the exception of books. I love the way books look on a bookshelf, coffee table, and as accent decorations. However, be mindful

that they do get dusty, and unless you are committed to dusting them regularly, you should not have them as decorations. Be sure to switch it up — donate the ones you have had for some time to make room for new ones.

>> **Remove references or sections.** If you are interested in a page or a part of a book, why not remove that section or take a picture of it with your phone instead of keeping it in its entirety?

>> **The book is not the memory.** Remember the joy you got from reading the book. It's not always necessary to keep it.

>> **Forwarding books is the biggest act of kindness.** It feels good to be able to enhance someone else's life with books. Libraries and fundraisers are always happy to accept gently used books!

>> **Lend books.** If you're not ready to fully part with your books yet, try lending them first to see the joy they give other people.

>> **Declutter a book a day.** I once read advice somewhere that if you declutter something every day, you will have decluttered 365 items over the year. This is an especially great concept for books and can provide you and/or your family a good challenge.

REMEMBER

Your book collection does not define how smart you are or how much knowledge you have. Keeping books for only this purpose and not actually reading them is a total waste of space. Keep this in mind as you declutter!

Decluttering electronic and audio books

I am a huge fan of both books on my Audible app and on my Kindle. I love being able to instantly buy a book and read it right away. I also love being able to carry all the books I want to read with me on vacation, and I love listening to audio books, especially when doing mundane tasks or working out. However, my love for these types of books can also lead to a cluttered mess. If you buy many of these, consider forming a group so you can share them by giving each other account access or getting memberships to keep the costs down.

If you do have many saved and downloaded, be aware that this is also taking up valuable real estate on your hard drive, which will need to be decluttered.

With the ability to store literally 10,000+ books at your fingertips, getting clear about how you organize them is important from the start. I sort mine by genre. Thinking about lending your device to a friend may be a good motivator for you to properly declutter and organize your electronic and audio books. Figure 11-4 is a screenshot of my Kindle with my folders for book genres.

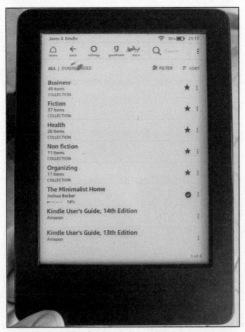

Image courtesy of author

Decluttering Furniture

If you have furniture stored, I advise you to get rid of it. You may be keeping it because "someday" you might need it for your bigger house, or your kids might need it for college, or because you've moved and literally kept all the furniture you've ever had.

Much of the furniture you have may be left over from moves or even given to you by relatives, but the problem is if it doesn't fit in your space now, then it's only taking up storage space for something else. And worse, if you actually are trying to use it and it doesn't fit, you are blocking the way to a better piece of furniture that could be providing added benefits to your space.

Lots of people are always looking for used furniture, so it's a good idea to put an ad out or donate it to a rustic resort or shelter. Furniture should be carefully selected for the space you're currently living in; otherwise, it only looks like clutter and is an eyesore.

IS IT REALLY ANTIQUE?

You may be holding onto furniture because you think it could be worth something someday, or because you love antiques. If you love them, you should be using them in your house rather than keeping them in storage. Old and new pieces can work well together, and there are no rules about this. The main thing is that your furniture — new or antique — has to fit your lifestyle and hopefully also be functional.

If vintage discoveries and antique collecting is your thing, then by all means, I am not stopping you. Just make sure you keep it for the same reason as your other stuff — because you actually use it.

To determine if your antiques are worth something, you may have to do some research, starting with the mark, label, and/or signature, if your item has one. On furniture this is usually inside drawers, on the back, or under the sides of the piece.

Identifying the style period of a piece of furniture is important and many look similar, so you may need professional help with this. There are also lots of reproductions so you need to test your antique for authenticity, and finding the right antique handler or guide can definitely help.

Electronic Items

If your computer, laptop, TV, and other electronics were made before 2000, chances are they can't be refurbished and it's time to let them go. Maybe some of the parts can be used for things or by scrap metal collectors, but make sure you dispose of them properly as they don't do well in landfills.

Chances are you are also keeping lots of cables and power cords. Part of the problem is that we do need different chargers for different devices, and these can quickly accumulate. Gather all your cords together and discard what you don't need and any that are frayed. If you don't know what the cord is for, get rid of it — you can always buy yourself a new one if you need it. Use the same approach for other tech gadgets and accessories. Just remember to recycle them.

Finding a designated space for your tech accessories is the next step, as they should not be in storage. You really must do this to help keep them organized; otherwise, you will waste time when you need them. Maybe each member of your family has a designated spot for electrical items. Rubber bands work wonders for keeping cords together.

Apart from the items that we keep just in case our phone breaks or just in case we need that extra landline phone cable, electronics — from mixed tapes to family home videos on VHS — can be full of memories. The thing is, technology moves fast and you need to keep up; otherwise, you won't even be able to view your memories anymore.

As I was writing this, I was thinking about my old family movies on VHS. I did some research and I was able to successfully get them onto a memory stick. I found out through my research that there are actually a few ways to modernize your old videotapes and even places that do it for you, including Walmart, Walgreens, and Costco. There are also a few do-it-yourself ways, but then you need some equipment such as a DVD recorder and VCR combo. It may be worth it depending on how many you have to transfer.

Try to modernize everything you want to keep. You don't need duplicates on a CD and in your iCloud library. And music can be downloaded, so why keep physical records, tapes, and CDs? If you do have a record player and enjoy it, then keep your record player and records in a spot in your home, not in storage.

Once you have your music stored digitally, remember that this can also quickly become a cluttered mess. If you are a serious music fan, then you should have an idea on how to best organize your music by genre, playlists, or artist. Whatever you decide, make a system and stick to it. Declutter weekly if you're accumulating many new songs on a regular basis.

Decluttering Paper and Printed Photos

I need to address paper and photos, both of which I don't think should be shoved at the back of an attic. I also want to encourage you to modernize your paper and photos going forward as much as possible, keeping them digitally decluttered, of course.

Dealing with paperwork

If you have a business, you likely have boxes of your accounting documents because legally you need to keep these for a certain number of years (the number is dependent on where you operate your business). Yes, keep these documents until they are ready to go to the shredder, and if possible, don't store your business records in an attic — you will forget about them, and they will stay well past their due date. Skip ahead to Chapter 13 to find out how I digitally store all my accounting records. Other paper you may have in your attic should also not be stored here. If you keep every single document from a training or client contract, you should be able to have this in your office space, not your attic, so you don't forget about it. Any important documents regarding finances, wills, and insurance should also not be stored in the attic or hard-to-reach storage areas because when you need them, they should be easily accessible. If you really want to get technical, they should also be in a fireproof safe!

Managing magazines

I love magazines of all genres. I now have an app and read them digitally for a lower monthly fee than when I used to buy the physical copies, and this has also significantly reduced my clutter. The one caution I have is that with digital magazines you can often be lured into online purchases, making other potential clutter come into your home easier.

If you do have physical magazines, storing them is useless unless you really have a good storage system that allows you to reach and read them frequently.

I gave this challenge to my parents as they have kept every single *National Geographic* magazine since 1979. And they were all over the place, mostly in the attic and not sorted or stored properly. I asked them why they keep them, and the response was because they learn so much from them and they have beautiful, timeless pictures. If this truly is the case, then you need to invest in a system to keep them and actually look at them to make it worthwhile.

My parents now have slipcovers for each year and look at their magazines often. They don't keep any of their other magazines, and my dad now reads the paper online to reduce clutter. Figure 11-5 is an example of these properly stored *National Geographic* magazines.

AUTHOR SAYS

I still don't advocate keeping magazines, especially not fashion, gossip, or hobby magazines, as the content and trends change so quickly that they will soon be out-of-date. If you really love an article or photo in a magazine you're reading, keep that page or take a photo with your phone and store it in the appropriate album. Pass along magazines to friends or doctors' offices and/or recycle them.

Image courtesy of author

Sorting albums

Photos are memories that should be sorted and properly cared for, and they should not be in an attic for no one to see. Jump to Chapter 15, where I discuss photo decluttering in detail, both physical and digital.

3
Decluttering Your Workspace and Digital Life

Store files, reduce office supplies, and utilize software to better communicate with teams and increase your efficiency.

Shift your mindset from paper to digital forever and make virtual storage clutter-free.

Declutter your online life to keep up with emails, social profiles, and digital items.

Tackle photo decluttering (both digital and print).

Chapter **12**

Decluttering Your Office

I am very passionate about having a clear workspace, almost as passionate as I am about having a decluttered closet. This is because any lingering clutter in your workspace makes you less productive, less creative, and more stressed.

If you want to be *more* productive, creative, and less stressed, then follow my simple tips to declutter your office.

Throughout this chapter, I also want you to think about shifting from a paper-based mindset to a digital one. I discuss focusing on eliminating paper altogether in the next chapter, but I give a few tricks for your actual office to start.

Following are some helpful tips on the basics of office decluttering:

» **Determine what you use.** Don't save things for "just in case" like cables, files, or other work items, whether physical or digital.

» **Declutter daily.** At the end of your workday, spend a few minutes clearing your workspace and planning for the next day. Also, most of your office is actually about storing files and that requires you to keep on top of your system and declutter weekly or even daily depending on the amount of information that comes in.

» **Sort and donate.** As you do with any of your spaces, it's a great idea to donate what you no longer use. Often someone else could use that chalkboard that you haven't used in a decade.

>> **Rearrange what doesn't work.** Pay close attention to your space and make it as efficient as possible. *Remember:* Don't immediately buy new supplies because after you declutter, you'll want to shift more of your systems to digital, requiring fewer physical items that take up space. In Figure 12-1, you see a desk, computer, and clear workspace that can be your reality if you commit to decluttering.

FIGURE 12-1: A decluttered workspace.

Storing Files

Think about your current files on your desktop, in your filing cabinets, in your binders, or wherever else you keep files. Are you already getting a bit stressed thinking about all the places your files could be? Are you anxiously wondering about the amount of time it will take to go through your files? Yes, it may be stressful, but you need to do this. Working with cluttered files surrounding you is likely the main reason you waste time looking for things, and your workflow and creativity are guaranteed to also be affected by this.

The good news is that amazing things will happen once you declutter your files. You will spend less time looking for what you need, and your train of thought will not be distracted by clutter. As an added bonus, your team and bosses will be impressed and think that you're naturally tidy and clutter-free — which you will be after reading and implementing this chapter!

First, I address those folders that have been sitting idly, maybe for years.

Decluttering your files

With office files and emails, I want you to be brutal and do a total purge of what you don't need or is outdated (more on inbox decluttering in Chapter 14). First tackle your physical files (if you still store things physically) and then your digital ones. The same principles apply to both.

Wherever your files are located, bring them to one spot in your office. If they are all on a computer, you can skip this, but you will want to make sure they are accessible, so bring your hard drive back-ups.

Decide what to keep and which files to discard. This can be a quick and hassle-free process. Have two piles: one for recycling and one for keeping. You may want to hold onto old projects or information, but trust me, you won't need them later. The quicker you are, the more brutal you can be.

The following sections give you more advice on determining which files to declutter and which to keep.

Future learning

If you're saving files for your employees to learn from, give them to them now! In my experience, when my boss gave me a stack of boring files to review from courses or projects, I didn't really give it much thought other than a perusal. If you're a manager and feel that something is worth teaching to your employees, customers, or other staff, then set up a 30-minute training and go over the documents. This way, they can then review the files and decide what to hold onto.

Projects you're proud of

I get it: You may have worked hard on that slide deck you presented to the executive committee back in 2012, as it literally took months of sweat and tears. Don't keep all the versions of the project, but do consider keeping the latest version and make it digital. I also recommend saving it under "Sentimental Projects" or something like that.

Info for taxes and audits

You usually need to keep accounting documents for around seven years, depending on your filing location. I suggest storing these digitally, and I share more on this in the next chapter. You may also need to keep other records, such as safety, quality control, maintenance, and process documents. These should be stored together, labeled, and easily accessible.

Figure 12-2 is an example of a folder of all tax-related information. You will notice no receipts, as I suggest storing receipts digitally for a variety of reasons (see more on receipt storage in the following chapter).

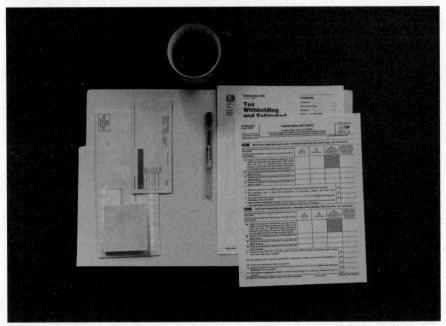

FIGURE 12-2:
Keep folders for related information.

Kelly Sikkema / Unsplash

Keeping records

Keeping records is only worthwhile if you know where to find them. Seriously, if you have an audit for whatever reason and you can't find your necessary documents, you could be in serious trouble.

Examples of records you may need to keep include taxes, safety, health, quality control, environment, and more based on your industry. Not being able to locate these or having them damaged could result in serious fines and even jail time in some very serious cases (especially regarding safety).

Be very conscious of important files and how you store them. I highly recommend keeping them digitally as well to prevent damage in the event of a flood, fire, or other loss.

I don't joke about office fires, as one of my good friend's printing businesses went up in flames and they lost everything. However, now they keep all files in a digital format, which is a good recommendation for anyone.

KEEPING DILIGENT RECORDS

I am not a lawyer or accountant, but if you start your own business, I would suggest meeting with both regarding the type of records you should be keeping and how to store them in order to protect yourself, your business, and your employees. Lawyers usually recommend keeping all things documented — even phone conversations — and following up with an email so that everything is tracked appropriately.

I don't begin to list the possibilities of what different businesses should document, but keeping good records based on your industry and business is a good practice. Even a daily journal containing notes on certain things such as the weather, sales, interactions, and other topics can be useful if an issue arises.

Storing effectively

Now, what about all the other files you should be storing? For your digtal and physical files, you want to store them so you can easily find them and they take up the least amount of space.

How you create your folder system depends on your business and your needs.

Here are some general guidelines to help you get started:

>> **Folders for meetings:** If you go to or plan lots of meetings, then it is best to have a folder dedicated to all the items around those meetings, like notes, presentations, and tasks.

>> **Folders for people or projects:** If you have staff and/or customers, you likely have info on these people and it should be filed together. Same with projects.

>> **Training/reference folders:** It's a great idea to have all your training documents together so that you can easily refer back to them.

>> **Accounting/business records:** As mentioned in the preceding section, these need to be filed, and you have to be able to find and access them quickly if they are requested.

>> **Personal documents:** You may have some form of personal stuff that has made its way to your office, especially if you have a home office. Also make folders (and even sub-folders if needed) for these documents.

As you go through your files, you'll probably realize that you have worked hard over the years. Take time to be proud of everything you have accomplished. Your files are likely a reflection of your accomplishments and various roles/jobs/

customers, and they can bring up lots of emotions — both good and bad. Decluttering is always a great time to embrace what you have accumulated, keep the memories, and then declutter the stuff that no longer serves you.

REMEMBER

Be brutal when deciding what files to keep both digitally and physically. Make sure the files you really need have a dedicated spot so you can actually find them later. When you're designing your new systems, set yourself up for success by keeping the files you use 80 percent of the time within easy reach and label everything. I also realize you may not be able to declutter your files all at once, and that's okay, but try to tackle as much as possible before getting distracted. I recommend using a time cube to help you stay on task. You can purchase one at www.organizedjane.com.

Simplifying Your Office Supplies

I am always shocked at the number of office supplies that people have and never use. Even kids often have way too many school supplies. The funny part about having so much stuff is that when we need a pen or a paper clip, we never seem to have one on hand. This is a mystery I will likely never solve, but I can try as much as possible with the tips that follow.

Firstly, gather all your supplies for your office and your home, even if you have items in several spots. Make sure you get them from all the possible hiding corners, especially if you have some in junk drawers, which, if you follow my advice in Chapter 6, you no longer have — only essentials!

Once you have them all in one spot, start getting rid of what you know you don't or won't ever use.

Determining your daily needs

Now figure out what you actually need. What do you use on a daily basis? Your answer to this question can show you what should really be on your desk. If you only use paper clips once a month, they don't deserve that real estate.

From the remaining pile you've already decluttered, take out your daily needs. They may be only a pen, a calculator, or a time cube (which is my number one productivity tool).

Store everything else in a drawer and if you haven't used that drawer in a month, consider decluttering it more.

Getting rid of your office junk drawer

Don't keep an office junk drawer! I don't believe in junk drawers because they are one of the main clutter traps that waste space. If you have many items in bulk, you can keep these stashed in a drawer, but the drawer should only have the essentials, not a bunch of items you never use.

I am always amazed when I walk into corporate stationery storage. It's like seeing dollar bills everywhere. It's funny how when it is not our own money we tend to buy more items "just in case" or supplies that we don't actually need or use. Whether you have your own business and are very conscious of every penny or work for a corporation where you are given carte blanche on office supply spending, only get what you really need; otherwise, it will cause a mental clutter block and cause you more work to organize it.

And don't think just because your office has procured the best deal with Staples or wherever you get office supplies that you need to order the 5,000 paper clips. Be intentional with your purchases not only to save money and mental space, but also to help reduce your environmental impact. Figure 12-3 is an example of the main daily office supplies consisting only of a pencil and a journal.

REMEMBER

Focus on the items you use every day and keep those.

FIGURE 12-3:
Simple daily
office supplies.

Plush Design Studio / Unsplash

Managing Your Calendar

Calendar management is very close to my heart. I have loved planning since I was a kid and would always pride myself on my agendas and the intricate details I would put into planning, from color-coding my tasks to planning in advance. I loved my agenda, and I loved the new year when I could get a brand new one and start the process again.

Fast forward 20 years and I love my digital calendar just as much, if not more, because it offers more options that increase my productivity, such as sharing it with others, which has been a serious game changer.

You may not think that calendar management belongs in this book, but I know that if your calendar is cluttered or inefficiently used, you are probably not planning your time wisely. And it's not only about calendars but about your schedule as well. Even with the best of intentions, you can end up with an overwhelmingly cluttered schedule.

Optimizing your time management skills

Your time certainly shouldn't be cluttered, because then you're unable to properly focus on tasks and it's likely to take you twice as long to get them done.

Following are my top tips for time management:

>> **Clarify the 80 percent rule.** Your time should be spent on revenue-generating activities for your business or the company you work for. Review where you spend your time and make sure that at least 80 percent is devoted to this; otherwise, declutter a few things by delegating, outsourcing, automating, or finding another way to eliminate tasks that don't generate revenue.

>> **Shorten your meetings.** This one has literally changed my life. I never schedule hour-long meetings; rather, I ensure that they are 45 minutes or less. This strategy immediately frees up time in your calendar and your life. Plus, it makes you and all the people you have meetings with more efficient. Shorter meetings force people to come better prepared and stick to the agenda.

>> **Eliminate unnecessary commitments.** This one really has to do with dedicating your valuable time to the most important revenue-generating activities in your business and to the activities that bring you the most personal joy in your nonwork hours.

>> **Use a time cube.** This is a simple timer (shown in Figure 12-4) that can help you stay focused, especially on digital tasks. For example, when you want to work on emails, set the timer for 30 minutes and only work on emails. Don't check Facebook or answer the phone or even get up! It's a funny thing, but this blinking time cube staring at you for some reason helps to keep you on task and focused until the timer goes off.

I also recommend using a time cube instead of the timer on your phone so that you aren't distracted by your phone when you're trying to focus on decluttering.

FIGURE 12-4: Time cube — the key to time management.

Image courtesy of author

Discovering the art of clutter-free calendar planning

The biggest reason calendars become cluttered in my experience is because to-do's are mixed in with meetings and appointments. Sort to-do tasks away from meetings, appointments, and recurring tasks.

Actually, stop filling your calendar with tasks altogether. You should have a to-do list somewhere — maybe you use digital notes or a journal — but don't put in your calendar each task you have to do. For example, if you have to conduct several follow-ups, you can label a 30-minute time block for this and put details in the notes. Better yet, use customer relationship management (CRM) software where the follow-up is automatically prompted once you send a task.

Some things are habits that you don't need to actually put in your calendar, such as brushing your teeth or walking the dog. However, if you're trying to commit to a morning routine that includes meditation, movement, and drinking lemon water, you may want to schedule 30 minutes and label it "morning routine" until it becomes a habit!

Try assigning specific tasks to certain days of the week. This is super easy on digital calendar. For example, every Tuesday you might create your social media content. Put this in for every Tuesday at the same time. This not only helps your calendar stay efficient, but it also makes these recurring tasks habits.

Organizing Your Shared Workspace

Today lots of us don't have our own office, as the open-concept office or shared workspace has become the norm. This is a blessing for former clutterbugs, who literally have no more space to store stuff. This also forces you to modernize your working documents and also your mindset as you can no longer make a mess. Instead, you have to be tidy and efficient, and you can learn from those around you.

Going digital

I cover going digital in depth in the next chapter, but when you have a shared workspace, you need to do this ASAP. This is especially important if you are not using the same working spot every day, which often occurs in a co-work environment.

You need to have everything on your laptop in order to access it from anywhere. There is no way around this.

Creating a system

You need to have an impeccable digitally organized filing system in addition to a quick daily system to set up your office.

Having a routine can help you stay organized and efficient. For example, perhaps as soon as you arrive at whatever version of office or workspace you use, you set up your computer with a charger, and get out your pen, notebook, and phone charger. You likely have a reusable coffee mug and a routine to get coffee. This is simply one part of creating a systemized routine; the other part is creating a sustainable system for your digital files and organization. Having a routine helps you stay consistent and productive in all that you do.

Understanding how to adapt

If you're now using a coworking space and have been used to a traditional office for your entire life, it will take some adapting. The reasoning behind a coworking space is to encourage collaboration and reduce the barriers that can often form between different teams. And if we get down to profitability, it's likely a less expensive option as you can have smaller spaces and not have to put in expensive walls. Many companies don't even have physical offices anymore and rent office spaces for their employees at coworking spots instead.

It may be a good idea to try to embrace this culture as I don't see the shift changing back anytime soon. I am even seeing high-level executives and CEOs moving to shared office spaces and utilizing meeting rooms for confidential calls and meetings.

When learning to adapt, try to see the benefits of teamwork and also renewed inspirations from hearing other ideas and conversations from your co-workers or other employees and business owners from different industries! What may seem daunting or annoying at first may become a great way to network, generate inspiration, and gather ideas for your own projects.

Chapter **13**

Shifting from Paper to Digital

I n this chapter, I discuss shifting your entire mindset around your office and the paper that is likely cluttering it. I focus on eliminating paper altogether and storing your files digitally.

REMEMBER

Before we dive into eliminating paper clutter, remember the basics of office decluttering that can apply:

» **Determine what you use.** Don't save things for "just in case," like cables, files, or other work items, whether physical or digital.

» **Declutter daily.** At the end of your workday, spend a few minutes clearing your workspace and planning for the next day. Most of your office is actually about storing files, and that requires you to keep on top of your system and declutter weekly or even daily depending on the amount of information that comes in.

» **Sort and donate.** As you do with any of your spaces, it's a great idea to donate what you no longer use. Often someone else could use that chalkboard that you have not used in a decade.

> » **Rearrange what doesn't work.** Pay close attention to your space and make it
> as efficient as possible. *Remember:* Don't immediately buy new supplies
> because after you declutter, you'll want to shift more of your systems to digital
> media, requiring fewer physical items that take up space.

Ready for the fun stuff? It's time to get rid of paper once and for all, one tree at a time. This shift may not be easy, and it probably won't happen overnight, but it will make you more efficient and is the way of the future. Going digital not only helps save paper, but it also saves space and can be more reliable since it's harder to lose digital files than physical files.

Eliminating What You Can

Before I dive into switching things to paper, you first need to go through what you have, which you may already have done if you've read the preceding chapter. Please do this as a first step, as making a switch to digital can be cumbersome and time consuming. For example, it takes work to scan and then digitally sort documents, so you only want to do this with items that are worth keeping in the first place.

The next few sections go over some ideas to help you eliminate unnecessary items.

Deleting unneeded photos

In Chapter 15, I give tips on how to declutter physical photos. Before you embark on a digital photo mission, declutter digital and printed photos first. This is extremely important as you only want to organize and digitize priority photos; otherwise, you will never get anywhere.

Deleting unneeded files

The goal of this chapter is to get you to change your mindset completely — to eliminate the paper you have and store it in alternate ways. I realize that you may have lots of paper already, and you are going to have to sort through your paper piles. It may not be pretty or fun, but you have to do this to avoid misplacing important documents or keeping things you don't need.

I suggest getting three bins and labeling them recycling, important (for your personal documents you need to keep), and filing (this box contains the paper you will turn to digital with upcoming steps). You may have already done the sorting part when you decluttered your office, but if you didn't, now is definitely the time.

You'll come across certain documents and paper that have personal information on them that you may need to keep, such as documents with signatures or original copies. It's a good idea to shred these items, or you may choose to keep them in an organized manner. Shredding does require an additional step. if you have a shredder in your home or office, it's no big deal, but if you don't, then you have to physically take the documents somewhere so really assess whether the documents need to be shredded in the first place.

For the other paper that requires filing, here is the fun part: You can file them the old-school way (which I don't recommend), creating folders and keeping them in a filing cabinet or binder, or you can modernize them and make them digital.

Now I have some quick tips to help you decide what to keep and what do get rid of when it comes to paper. These tips are not set in stone but hopefully can get you started on thinking about what to keep:

>> **Tax returns and supporting tax documents:** Typically, you should keep your tax documents for about seven years, but there are exceptions, so check the guidelines for your local area. There are ways today to totally digitize your tax documents, and I share more on that in the next section.

>> **Owner's manuals:** If the manuals are available online, you really don't need to keep them. And I would be shocked if they were not online.

>> **Warranties:** Gone are the days when you need to actually keep those warranty cards. Receipts are usually required, but those can also be stored digitally.

>> **Receipts:** These can be super tricky as they can fall into so many different categories. I suggest organizing your receipts digitally so that you have a defined system for taxes and future returns. (See the later section "Working with Receipts" for more info.)

>> **Personal documents:** From birth certificates to land deeds to contracts, there are things we should keep, and they should be filed in a special place. I suggest backing these up digitally if you need to keep the physical copies.

Deleting all junk

Do a serious sweep of all your stuff and be even more brutal. Get rid of anything and everything that is a junk document — end of story! Go through your inbox and files twice to really declutter — we tend to keep many files or emails "just in case" because they don't physically take up space in our home, but they do take up space in our precious online world.

Once you've deleted all of your junk, you should be left with the files that you can modernize into paperless files! Technology really is a wonderful thing when you put in the time upfront to create the digital system. I guarantee it will save you hours of hassle in the long run. Plus, your document quality will be preserved, and moving will be much easier.

Eliminating Paper and Storing Everything Virtually

With your files ready to go, it's time to get the digital process started. You may wonder why I'm so keen on keeping things digital. I am a major fan because it not only takes up less space but your documents are also easier to access and share, and they won't fade over time or get damaged. If you have super-important documents that are not stored digitally, then they should be stored in a fireproof safe to avoid damage. Now, do you currently do this? I am thinking not. So, store them digitally and back them up, maybe twice if they are that important.

Scanning your paper files

If you have paper files you want to make digital, there are really only two ways to do this that I know of: scanning or taking a photo of them. Taking a photo may not give you the best readable quality, so scanning may be your best option.

You can get a scanner app on your phone, but if you have more than a few files, this can be cumbersome and you'll need to use a real scanner.

WARNING

If you have never scanned anything before or have many piles of documents that need to be digitized, I suggest getting help from a friend, co-worker, or professional at a copy store. This will save you not only hours but lots of headaches. You can even bring entire boxes to the copy store, and they can scan them faster than you can scan a few pages. Enlist support with this step if you have lots of paper files and are serious about going digital.

If you are ready to tackle scanning on your own, here are my top tips:

>> **Scan to PDF.** Get in the habit of creating PDFs versus printing whenever possible. But also remember to consider whether you really need to keep the document because your digital files also need to be decluttered.

>> **Going forward, scan right away.** This way paper won't pile up, and you won't have to do a massive scan like you are doing right now!

>> **Utilize backup and clouds.** I keep everything in iCloud, but I also back up my entire computer and files quarterly onto an external hard drive for an added measure of security.

>> **Organize.** Keep all files organized, make a consistent naming system for your files, and make sure you have the most used ones the most accessible. I start by sorting by year and then making subcategories for my work and personal items.

I don't have a lot of advice on which scanners to use or get. I have one combined with my printer (which I use mostly only for making labels).

Whether you need to buy a scanner or use your smartphone is up to you. Keep in mind that many offices and even co-working spots usually have a scanner.

Rethinking printing

After you've spent hours scanning or paid someone to do it for you, I think you might be done even looking at another paper document! This attitude can help with this next step, as this section is about a mindset shift.

Likely you have seen on so many emails for years now the words, "Think before you print this email," which makes sense for the environment and for your clutter.

In my first job after university in 2005, I remember my boss would print every single email and file it under "customers" or "employees." It was so much that she had to hire an assistant to keep up! Can you imagine if we did that today?

Before you hit that print button, think about whether you really need to have it on paper or whether you can simply save it to PDF.

TIP

If you get the majority of paper from your mail, contact the vendors and switch to paperless communication.

Using clouds, drives, and memory sticks

Now that you have gone through your paper, I want you to decide on a way to digitally store your files. I prefer the cloud as it is the best way to share info, and it doesn't take up space on your hard drive and/or in your office. Plus, you can access the cloud from all your devices.

MY RECOMMENDED SCANNING APPS

I have tried several scanning apps because I like to be able to scan wherever I am, even though with my newest iPhone, I find the camera takes photos that are just as good for scanning purposes. Regardless, here are my favorites:

- **iScanner:** www.iscannerapp.net

- **Adobe Scan:** https://apps.apple.com/us/app/adobe-scan-mobile-pdf-scanner/id1199564834

- **Abbyy FineScanner:** https://www.abbyy.com/en-ca/mobile/

One of the great benefits of these apps and most others is that you can export anywhere. Share them so quickly through email, clouds (including Dropbox), and social platforms. The following figure shows my iScanner app with the export function after I scanned a document.

Image courtesy of author

I am not sure when you will be reading this — maybe memory sticks won't even exist anymore, or maybe there will be some new invention to replace the cloud. As I am writing this in 2019, clouds, drives, and memory sticks are the normal ways to store digital documents.

Clouds and internal drives

If you're wondering what cloud storage is, I am not talking about the fluffy white ones in the sky but the ones that are used to store documents in a remote server-based storage. For example, we used to have to download media, but now we can stream from servers. I use the words "cloud" and "drive" interchangeably because Google Drive is technically a cloud server system. And to get really basic, the cloud means that you are storing your files on someone else's hard drive rather than your own. The data is usually encrypted for security, and you can access the file through some type of app or software installed.

The biggest advantage of cloud storage is that you can access your files anywhere on most devices. Plus, you reduce storage on your hard drive. In my experience, I can store everything I need in the cloud, from word documents to PDFs to photos. Plus, today my computer doesn't even have a USB drive, nor does my cellphone, so sharing documents via the cloud is much more efficient.

The key to making the cloud super efficient is to sync all the data you store. If you don't do this already, I suggest doing some research because your cloud storage needs depends on the devices you use and how much stuff you want to store. Also, the level of security and how tech savvy you are can help you determine which type of cloud storage is best for you.

There are free storage services, but usually when you reach a certain size, a monthly fee kicks in. Still, these fees are worth it because you have to pay for space one way or another for your digital stuff, or buy memory sticks you can easily lose. The best part about cloud storage is that you can easily share large files.

I still get asked what the best cloud-based storage system is, and again I say it depends on your needs, comfort, and maybe what you may be dictated to use at your company. I use iCloud for all my files to be synced and stored. For my business, I share documents and house them on Google Drive, and many of my customers and employees use Dropbox, so I am familiar with all of these. There are tons of options; the key is to find the one that works best for you.

I remember when Google Drive first came out. My corporate office had just switched to Gmail, and it was a big transition from the old Lotus Notes. If you don't remember Lotus Notes or are too young to have been exposed to it, consider yourself lucky. It was one of the worst user interfaces, in my opinion. But when this change came to the office, everyone was freaking out! After some training and testing, Gmail did come out for the win, and I think everyone has long since forgotten about Lotus Notes. Along with Gmail came "the cloud." I put this in quotes because it was really something that people did in the office. They used air quotes to describe it because it was a bit unknown. And everyone was super scared of the cloud. They were scared that all their files would disappear or that they would not be safe. However, the cloud was used. And in all fairness, clouds can become a cluttered mess unless you set up a system and follow it. But one thing is for sure — they are wonderful for keeping and sharing documents.

Don't be scared by tech words such as "drive" or "servers." Once you do a bit of learning about cloud-based storage, it won't be scary and can be very user-friendly. You may be worried, but you've likely spent time already using cloud systems, as I am sure you have used Dropbox and Google Drive or at least heard of them. I would encourage you to do a bit of research and get familiar with these systems because they are becoming the way most businesses are sharing and storing documents. I promise — if I can do it, you can too.

Memory sticks and external hard drives

If I have not convinced you yet about clouds, maybe you want to stick to saving your files to a memory stick. The size depends on how much you have to file and how many large files you have, such as high-resolution photos and videos. You may need to get a large external hard drive for all your storage needs. I recommend one anyway for a second back-up of your files as well.

I would recommend getting a 500 gigabyte (GB) memory stick or hard drive to start with because it doesn't cost too much and fits most of your needs. You also need to make sure your computer has the right connection port for the type you get.

My final warning in this section is that you need to store your files somewhere, not only on your computer, because then you will lose them eventually. Please don't store files only on your laptop, which you could lose or which could break. Today there are lots of options to keep your digital data safe, so I encourage you to do this.

Creating a password system

Security Magazine stated in 2017 that the average business user has 191 passwords! How is anyone supposed to remember that many passwords?

There are alternatives that are coming, such as fingerprints, biometrics, and facial recognition, but many of those still require passwords for back-up and they are not yet 100 percent secure.

It's a good idea to ask yourself if your passwords are secure. I bet some of you still use 123456 and your mother's maiden name or your kids' birthdays as your password. The level of security that your passwords should have is not my business, but I do think you should protect yourself and your data by creating a more complex password to ensure your data's security.

It's important to declutter your passwords, and you have to pick a system to do this. I was totally against password keepers and password managers for a long time. I'm not sure why, but last year I had enough with passwords and now I use a manager, which automatically helped me declutter my passwords. Now, they are all stored, and even better, they are more secure than before.

MY RECOMMENDED PASSWORD MANAGER PROGRAMS

The real importance of a password manager is that the passwords are much more secure than your own, which protects your data. This is extremely important in today's society with the amount of confidential information we store both personally and professionally. Plus, next time you fail a login because you forget your password, you'll be thankful for using a password manager. Consider getting a password manager; it is a lifesaver. I recommend the following:

- **Dashlane:** www.dashlane.com
- **Keeper:** https://keepersecurity.com
- **LastPass:** www.lastpass.com

Working with Receipts

I felt receipts deserved a bit of discussing as they are annoying, can be tricky to store both physically and digitally, and you likely never know what to keep or don't remember where they are if you did keep them. It's not uncommon to be unable to find the one receipt you actually need. I've been there, and I think it is safe to say that we all have.

Which receipts to keep

I don't keep the receipts for everyday personal purchases. If you're budget tracking, then maybe you want to keep them to help stay on track. Or you may want to keep a receipt if you feel like you want to return something (although most stores now also have records of purchases). Give yourself a deadline if you think you might return something. I like giving myself a week to decide whether or not I want to keep a purchase. Sometimes we forget to return things, which adds to our clutter. Even if the store has a policy of 90-day returns, make it a point to give yourself that one-week timeline.

I generally keep the receipt for anything valuable or expensive, such as large electronics or jewelry, for insurance purposes.

It's a good idea to keep some receipts for your personal tax return, whether you have a business or not. Different tax laws will dictate what you can add to your personal tax return; for example, healthcare, travel, and anything you had to buy for your job could be deducted. Check with your accountant, as they will be able to tell you what you should keep for your personal tax return. If you have a business, you are likely aware that you need to keep all receipts for your business from restaurant bills to supplies to advertising. You need to keep them to be able to write off purchases, which is important for businesses.

From today onwards, start a system. I have a system that categorizes work, personal, and short-term purchases (for anything I might return, which I only keep for one week in my wallet). Under work, I keep all my receipts for business expenses, and under personal, I keep anything of value for insurance purposes.

Once you have your system, stick to it. If you want to tackle the receipts before you start this system, carve out 15 minutes a day with the help of a time cube purchased on www.organizedjane.com until you're caught up. If I'm being honest, this will be a painful task and will motivate you to never let receipts pile up again.

Don't be nervous to get rid of receipts. Usually, you don't need them and many retailers store them electronically. The most important thing is to set up a system and stick to it going forward. Also, if you find a receipt that doesn't fit into any of your categories, you likely don't need to keep it.

How to store receipts

You can go old-school and create bins and envelopes and continue to have to deal with your receipt clutter for years, or you can simply go digital.

You guessed it: I recommend digital receipt storage. Actually, I say it is a must because these days, if you decide on the old-school method and you actually need to use/find one of the receipts, I guarantee one of two things: You either won't find it, or when you do, it will be so faded that you won't be able to read it.

Get an app and go digital. Avoid scanning receipts, as this can take hours. Instead, use your phone to take a picture from the app for it to automatically upload to software and be stored in the cloud. I use the NEAT app, which then further connects to my accounting software. If you use the Google receipt app, you get tons of choices. Once you find an app, the key is to create a system and declutter receipts regularly.

Figure 13-1 depicts how I scan my receipt and then what it transfers to onto the app. The information is automatically populated. You can even have humans verify the information for a small fee. The nearby sidebar lists my favorite receipt apps.

FIGURE 13-1:
Scanning receipts into an app is super easy.

Image courtesy of author

Get in the habit of taking the photo with the app and then moving the photos on a weekly basis to the folders you created for your system. Be committed to this system and schedule weekly time in your calendar for this step. Then, when you do your annual taxes, you can quickly delete by month, year, and so on, and they will never build up.

Most of the apps keep the receipts in the cloud, so there is no need to keep the physical copy. If you feel safer keeping a copy on your hard drive, that is also an option, but I trust the cloud.

MY RECOMMENDED RECEIPT TRACKING APPS

There are tons of options for tracking receipts. Here I share my top three from my usage and trials with them:

- **Neat:** This was actually the company that used to sell a portable scanner. I saw them all the time in airports. I use NEAT because it is simple to scan with my phone, and it connects to my accounting software, which is QuickBooks. `http://neat.com`

- **Expensify:** This is one of the most popular receipt tracking apps, and I found it very easy to use. `www.expensify.com`

- **Zoho Expense:** This app offers many business software solutions, including a CRM that can also be linked to receipt tracking. `http://zoho.com`

Chapter **14**

Decluttering Your Online Life

With the rise of technology and social media, the topic of online decluttering is only going to become larger and larger. If you're not being as productive as you'd like, it may be because you spend too much time online and don't have strong boundaries around the use of your phone or social media. Often, our phones and computers are necessary for our jobs, careers, and businesses, so it's no wonder we spend so much time using our devices. If you have been decluttering your home and physical spaces, your online world should be no different. Having hundreds of files on your desktop, multiple tabs on browsers, and — god forbid — hundreds of unread emails, is very stressful. Think about that red number that shows up on your phone with the number of unread emails. I can't stand that, and I choose to turn off notifications before I let a big number stare at me every time I pick up my phone — you're just asking for stress in this case.

This chapter helps you get real with a few big topics, including email management and your online presence. Both are likely causing wasted time and mental clutter. I encourage you to really take a good look at your entire online life and treat it with the same decluttering lens through which you see your closet or office.

TIP

If you're not ready to dive into the online world just yet, maybe start with these quick tips:

>> **Clean up your downloads weekly.** Yes, I said weekly. You likely download items multiple times a day; therefore, you need to keep them under control to remain decluttered.

>> **Clear your cache history.** Along the same lines as clearing your downloads, get in the habit of also clearing your history.

>> **Clean out your inbox.** I talk a lot more about email decluttering, and this one is a must.

>> **Close browsers while working.** Having too many browsers can also significantly slow down your computer and overwhelm you.

>> **Close tabs and hide toolbars.** This helps give the illusion of a bigger working space. Plus, it feels less cluttered.

>> **Delete videos, podcasts, and audio books that you've downloaded and finished watching/listening.** You can always go back and redownload these if you bought them, so there's no reason they should be taking up valuable space in your digital life.

>> **Get rid of music you no longer like.** Delete what you don't need on a monthly basis. These days, there are many playlists on Spotify that don't even require you to download them at all.

>> **Use cloud-based storage.** This can help remove all those unorganized files and folders on your desktop and keep everything contained and sorted in one place that you can access from many devices instead.

>> **Focus on business.** Remember your computer and digital space can be for fun, but they should primarily be used for work. Declutter and organize it accordingly.

>> **Don't forgot about social you.** Even if you don't want an online presence, it likely already exists. Keep things up-to-date and tidy.

Cleaning Up Your Computer

Your computer should be treated with serious respect, as I think it is one of the most powerful tools that you have in your home and office. If you have a Ferrari, you may disagree; however, I still think your computer is the ultimate tool because your Ferrari can't research the nearest late-night yoga studio or serve as the gateway to online shopping. It should not be a dumping ground for files or the cause of feeling stressed and overwhelmed when you open it. Rather it should be a clean and organized space that helps to inspire you and keep you on task with minimal distractions.

I first tackle what is taking up most of your computer space, which is digital files.

Organizing digital files

What comes first, decluttering your files or inbox? I choose to start with files so that you can create a system and then move on to your inbox. You may be more inclined to better delete and tackle your inbox once you know what files you have on your computer and how you will then further organize it. But ultimately you should do what is best for your system; just pick one to start.

If your files are already mostly digital, that's wonderful news, but be sure to treat them with the same decluttering methods as physical files and delete what you don't need or use. Here are a few tips to help get you started:

» **Sorting your files:** I always start with personal files because I have fewer of those than work files, and it is also more fun. I have two main folders on my computer, Work and Personal, and I divide everything into those two categories. For example, I sort my work by year, projects, and people.

» **Theming all sub-files:** I always make sure to have sub-files. If you get more than ten documents in a file without a sub-file, things can get cluttered. For example, under a file labeled "2019," you should likely have sub-files. These sub-files may be months or customer names or whatever helps you sort your files faster.

» **Backing up your files:** As I mention in Chapter 13, I recommend using a hard drive, or even better, a cloud system. Get an external hard drive for your back-ups and any files that you may only use occasionally. Even though I save everything to the cloud, I back up my entire computer quarterly. I have this task in my calendar to hold myself accountable.

Your digital filing system should be adapted and changed to your needs all the time, even daily if needed. Nothing is set in stone, and that is the beauty of digital files. You can easily change names and locations fast. Your system should make you feel calm, allow you to waste no time searching for documents, and be decluttered on a consistent basis.

TIP

Become friends with clouds. Like when you were a kid and you used to marvel at the different shapes of the clouds in the sky, today you can marvel at the wonders of technology and how you can literally store anything in the cloud without taking up space.

Looking at inboxes

The other day I saw a really good Instagram post saying that there are two types of people in this world with regard to our inboxes, and that our inboxes can say a lot about us! This post also probed me to research more about our inbox personalities.

I'm not sure where the image originally came from; it was tweeted back in March 2015 and then re-tweeted over 20,000 times. I couldn't find the originator, but Figure 14-1 is my own attempt to portray the same meaning.

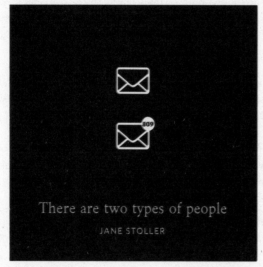

There are two types of people

JANE STOLLER

FIGURE 14-1:
There are two types of people in this world.

AUTHOR SAYS

This similar image caused serious drama in the social world. Apparently, people are very sensitive about their email habits. Hence, I include the following disclaimer: Email management is a sensitive topic, and I am in no way saying what you are doing today is wrong and that you should change. Do what works best for you. I do my best to give you decluttering strategies that work for me and my clients and according to my research. I don't want this section to cause depression or defensiveness about the current state of your inbox. I simply want to help where I can.

The reason the image got so much attention is that how you manage your inbox can be highly personal. However, no matter how disorganized or organized you are, it actually has no reflection on your inbox maintenance. I know extremely disorganized people who maintain their inbox at zero and are very proud of this. I also know many organized people who could not control their inbox if they spent hours working on it.

The reason I am so passionate about inbox decluttering is not so that you can just delete all your emails to get to zero, but for a deeper reason: Emails can become a total waste of time if not managed properly.

Most of us spend way too much time working through our inboxes and letting them manage us. I hope that is not you, but if it is, don't worry — you can change that. For the longest time, I struggled to manage my inbox; I would respond to emails as they came in and was constantly distracted throughout the day. I was always baffled that come 6 p.m. I had not completed any real work.

Can you outsource your emails to someone else or even automate them? Many entrepreneurs and CEOs of companies do this to improve their time management and productivity.

I am sure that some of you still feel you need to tap every stroke of the keyboard to reply to your emails, and I am the same. I have outsourced and given more control to my team, and they have access to my emails to help with response times. To tell you the truth, they do a way better job at responding than I do. If you have a good team and/or assistant, you won't have any problems.

If you still intend to do your own emails, check out the practical tips in the following sections.

Devote hours to clean it up

There is no way around this, and it sucks, but I promise it will pay off. To get your emails managed, you need to devote hours to clean it up once and for all. After this you will never let it get back to its original state. Have a glass of champagne; it may help to loosen you up for faster deleting (at least, that's my method!).

Delete

Delete and don't think twice. You may want to just delete all 15,000 emails and start fresh. I certainly think that's a viable strategy, and I'm not saying you shouldn't do it. If you want to go through them all, then you need to be fast and brutal. If you use Gmail, try highlighting the entire page and then quickly scanning and checking the ones to keep. Mass deleting can help you to get your email total to a more manageable level. Be heartless and ruthless when you delete. No one will notice — trust me.

Out-of-office statuses and vacations frequently contribute to email clutter. Often, people go away for a week and then never actually get back to their email management.

AUTHOR SAYS

I need vacations to recharge, and so do you. I actually think that is why Switzerland is more efficient than North America, and I learned this from spending a few years living there. Obviously, I know that this is a huge generalization, but there, five weeks is the minimum vacation time, and employers encourage employees to take the time off. You are never punished but instead celebrated for recharging. I believe that taking time to recharge only makes you more productive in managing everything in your life, even emails.

Be diligent about deleting emails when you're back from vacation, and when you're on vacation, maybe set a time limit to check emails if you must. Better yet, hire someone to look after them for you! Someone in your office may even do it for free, and then you can return the favor the next time that person goes away. If you're truly operating a work email, no personal stuff should be filtered through anyway. Give up email control for vacations and let yourself relax!

Don't worry about junk

Most people get a lot of junk and/or spam. Junk mail will probably only get worse. The great news is that today you have lots of ways to handle it. From intuitive email programs that only let emails from your trusted contacts come through to fancy unsubscribe buttons, it's easier now than ever to filter your junk mail.

If someone's email lands in your junk mail, who cares? If it is important enough, that person will ask you if you got the email and you will say no and check your junk mail. It's really as simple as that, so don't waste your time overcomplicating the process. I used to scroll through my junk mail searching for important ones that slipped through. In the years I did that, I moved only a few to my inbox and the world would not have ended had I not done that. Junk is junk — just forget about it.

Unsubscribing

Free up your inbox to get only what you really need. It may take some dedication to unsubscribe. Try Unroll.Me (`https://unroll.me`) to help speed it up. And think carefully before you give your email addresses. If you have to for something you buy, unsubscribe as soon you as you get the first newsletter if you're not interested in hearing from them.

Set up a system that can last forever

When you're doing a mass decluttering session of thousands of emails, delete and make categories so you can file what you need to keep. Don't respond to the emails you're going through during your mass declutter; pick another time to batch all of these together since it will be a more efficient use of your time.

Archive, star, and color code

Have you ever taken the time to become familiar with your email system? Discovering everything your email can do is usually eye-opening. From offering massive amounts of archive space, to starring emails for quick finds, to making your email look beautiful and automatically coloring emails from contacts and sorting them accordingly, it's a highly intuitive system. You can also integrate it with CRM software like HubSpot for free to better track email reads, make templates (a godsend if you're rewriting the same thing over and over again), and help you effectively file and sort everything.

Spending some time getting to know your email system's functionalities and creating a system may seem daunting. You may think that you don't have time for it, but in the long run it will save you time. Do it as soon as possible. And if you're thinking, "What a waste of time because I will probably switch email providers someday," be practical and think about how often that actually happens. Gmail will be around a bit longer, and if a new system comes along, I can only imagine it will be even more intuitive.

Set a limit

Once you finish your many hours of getting your inbox to zero, take some time to reflect on how good it feels before you are bombarded with the next few sets of emails. Then, set a target, such as a number that you will never exceed in your inbox. Many people I have talked to about this say their limit is 50. Mine is 20, and keeping this number of emails helps me stay stress free.

You can only maintain your decluttered inbox and keep it manageable if you deal with it daily or hire someone to deal with it when you're away.

I also make sure I don't check my emails all day long on my phone. I use my time cube and I check emails twice a day for a set amount of time. It helps me focus, and I get them done in half the time without interruptions.

Establish an email mindset

Decluttering your email may require a mindset change. You have to be motivated enough to do something about it and also concerned about your emails in the first place. It's also a good idea to help change the mindset of your customers, co-workers, friends, and whoever else is used to your habits. If you usually respond back within an hour to most emails and then suddenly stop, some people may be worried or frustrated. It's a good idea to let people know about your shift in email practices.

Write an out-of-office message to automatically respond letting everyone know about your email mindset shift. The first example that follows came from Tim Ferriss's blog at https://tim.blog/2014/07/14/autoresponse/.

> *Thank you for your email. To increase my productivity, I am only checking emails at 10 a.m. EST and at 2 p.m. EST. I hope you will understand my shift for increasing productivity so I can focus more on my tasks.*

Here's an example for when you're on vacation:

> *Thank you for your email. I am on vacation and recharging for the upcoming productive fall season. Your email will be read by [insert name], my assistant, and she will help you with your inquiry.*

Dodge the dreaded chains

Yes, I am talking about email chains, not other types that you use for towing cars or whatever else you use chains for.

They can seriously clog up your inbox. Delete email chains after you respond, and also let your teams or co-workers know about other tools for scheduling meetings. For example, you can share calendars through your email provider or with tools such as Calendly that allow for meetings to be booked efficiently and without hassle.

Beware "reply all"

Accidentally hitting the dreaded "reply all" button can happen, and the only thing you can do is to be conscious when you reply. I used to work for a huge company with over 100,000 people, and a few years back there was this email chain about some IT problem, and then suddenly people were replying all. First of all, it was a glitch that you could even do this, but all the emails were in the address bar. It was hilarious; people were literally saying "stop replying all." It took over a week of productivity as the company was dealing with these threads of people replying from India to Canada to Indonesia to New Zealand. After this I am really conscious of reply all because it can reach up to 100,000 people, not to mention it makes you look silly!

My final email advice

If you really hate email, don't have time for it, continually mess it up, reply all, or do weird formatting things, outsource. Your business and customers will be happier, and so will you. If a personal email comes through about your kids, I am sure your virtual assistant will text or call you. If you get an embarrassing email or, god forbid, a nudie, then she will likely also tell you and you will deal with it.

Again, these are tips. If you continue to have 1,978 unread messages and you feel uncluttered, that is okay too.

Addressing apps on all electronic devices

This is a no-brainer, but delete the apps you don't use. You can get them back instantly if you ever need them again. A former colleague of mine said he doesn't like to have more apps than what fits on the first page of his iPhone because it helps him feel clutter-free.

I have also used this philosophy, but I have folders on my phone for apps so that I can easily access apps. For example, I have folders for Travel, Social, Maps, Music, Shopping, Accounting, and so on. Figure 14-2 is a screenshot of my phone app folders.

Every week, I go through my phone and delete apps and things I don't need. I do this when I do my weekly photo organizing. Yes, I said weekly; if I don't do this weekly, it turns into a big mess!

FIGURE 14-2:
Phone app folder screenshot.

Image courtesy of author

Keep all your devices and apps updated so that you will always be able to use the newest features and hopefully have the fastest speeds. Plus, it's super annoying when you keep seeing that update button. Just update your apps when needed, or even better, turn on automatic updates so that when you're sleeping, it will still work.

Sorting Out Social Media

Social media is a great tool, and I am not going to stay you need to get rid of all your social media! I actually give the opposite advice. When used properly, social media can be highly inspirational and great for networking, bring you customers, and provide a nice distraction when needed. I love social media, and I work hard to declutter it weekly to ensure I am only getting the proper inspiration, business leads, and happy feelings that it can create.

Your time and mind are two of the most important tools you have, and what you let into your life is totally controlled by you. If you regularly feel stressed or overwhelmed about your online time, then it's time to make a change, and decluttering can be just the change you need. Maybe you need to redirect your attention to something more productive because you can only take so many more cat videos or friends' baby pictures.

The good news is it is relatively easy to become focused with your social media. It takes some discipline, systems, and boundaries, but you can really work hard to cut the noise and clear your mental space with regard to your social media usage. If you have been reading this book, then you've hopefully been regularly decluttering your bathroom, closet, and kitchen. Your virtual life should be no different.

For this section, I want you to think differently about social media. Of course, consuming content that's relevant to your hobbies and interests is great, but it's easy to get caught up in the addictive nature of social media. Take back control of your social channels and use them wisely for making connections, actually being social, and engaging with inspiring accounts rather than mindlessly scrolling. The less you have and the more targeted the accounts you follow are, the easier this is to do.

Try to relish positive accounts, wisdom, and advice and join in where you can! It makes the experience more productive and useful.

Here are my top tips for keeping on top of social decluttering:

>> **Unfollow/block/mute.** It may be tough or awkward, but if you don't enjoy someone's content, remove it from your feed (even if it means blocking someone who may get offended). You are in charge of what you consume, and you totally have the right to consume any content that you like! Plus, be honest and get real — just because you were friends 15 years ago doesn't mean you need to follow that person. Muting is a way to avoid hurting feelings if you are worried about it.

>> **Declutter daily.** At the end of your day, evaluate whether you've felt any negative feelings from people on social media. If so, get rid of their presence on your channels immediately. This will help you feel lighter and less stressed and/or reactive.

>> **Set time limits.** Don't endlessly scroll for hours. Set up 15-minute time limits and get the most out of social media. It's amazing how much you can engage, respond, and be inspired when you have a short and focused window.

>> **Take downtime.** A perfect time to do your social media is when you are feeling most sluggish during the day. Instead of struggling to work on a project, schedule your social break and you may find renewed inspiration and energy afterwards.

Maintaining social profiles

I think you should be conscious of keeping your profiles up-to-date and not having them cluttered. Take time to clean up your social profiles because your first online impression and a cluttered profile can detract potential customers, friends, relationships, and network growth.

Delete items that are no longer relevant, keep your photos up-to-date, delete old Pinterest boards, and unfollow groups that are no longer relevant to your current career and/or business. Refresh your profiles to keep the online version of you clutter-free and current!

YOUR FIRST IMPRESSION IS ONLINE

For some of you reading this, it is very logical that your first impression should be up-to-date. Whether it's a customer or potential employer who lands on your page, it's important to regularly monitor your social profile to ensure you're giving the best possible impression of yourself. Of course, an online first impression can never compete with an in-person first impression, but it's a smart and proactive step to take if you're trying to build up your online presence or attract potential jobs and opportunities. Here are a few tips to help you get started:

- **Take a course or hire a coach.** If you don't know where to start or don't know how to use social media, then it's time to learn. Social media is continuing to grow, and even if you're a senior, you will likely need some kind of social media presence for something. There are thousands of courses and videos online to help you get started building up your profiles. If you want to take it a step further and really understand your social profiles and their potential impact, I recommend taking a course or hiring a coach to help you. We hire resume writing coaches, athletic coaches, and speaking coaches, and online branding coaches are just as important today. I used http://thinknatalia.com to help me up my social profiles.

- **Professional photos are a must.** Whatever your career or business, you need some sort of professional photos to help build a reputable image. They don't need to be traditional headshots in a pin-striped suit; the photos should fit your brand or industry. If you're a lifestyle blogger, your photos will likely be different, but they should still be professionally taken.

- **Declutter irrelevant or outdated information.** Only have the most relevant information on your profiles and declutter what isn't good for your brand. For example, perhaps the social world doesn't need to know that you were valedictorian of your high school and babysat on weekends when you now own your own bookkeeping business.

- **Be authentic and ensure everything is correct and up-to-date.** Just like an old-school paper resume, you can't put something false on it. Be authentic and keep things current. When you finish a course, update your profile, or if you're currently taking the course, say so.

Automating and outsourcing

If you use social media for business, then it can quite quickly become overwhelming, time consuming, and extremely cluttered as you may not be able to physically keep up with it all. That is completely normal. As soon as you get too busy and your social media is distracting you from your core revenue-generating activities, look for help! Use apps to schedule and plan, and use people to help you write content and increase your engagement. Don't be ashamed or afraid to ask for help.

Dealing with Other Digital Devices

I want to do a quick mention of some other useful digital tools that can also use a little decluttering — or maybe a lot.

Decluttering your phone

I already went through apps earlier in this chapter. Here are a few more ways to make your phone decluttered:

>> **Apps:** Delete what you don't use and anything that doesn't provide value.

>> **Music/videos:** Delete what you don't listen to or watch anymore.

>> **Notifications:** I turn all of these off because I don't want to be constantly bombarded and only want to check emails twice daily. If you're scared to do this, let your customers know via an auto response or let your friends know the times you check your phone. For example, I let people know that they can only call me in case of emergency.

>> **Screen time:** Do you know how much time you spend on your phone? It's important to know for your time management. iPhones usually tell you about your weekly use, but you can also get an app for this.

Decluttering your e-reader

Decluttering your e-reader is a bit different than decluttering your physical books because you can't donate them or give them to libraries or friends when you're done with them unless you're going to give them your entire device. I recommend deleting what you have read or making an organized system either by genre, last name, or whatever system you prefer because if you don't organize your e-books, you can't find them. Most e-readers allow you to go back and redownload the book from where you originally bought it, so it is never really lost. Plus, the beauty of an e-reader is that you can highlight and take notes of what you want to keep, which is easier to find again.

Decluttering your tablet

I tend to forget about my tablet because it is not my preferred choice; I use my computer and phone the most. However, I know lots of people who do everything on their tablets. The same rules apply to tablet decluttering as those that apply to phone or computer decluttering. Delete what you don't need or use, and be realistic. From my experience, tablets are usually cluttered first and foremost with apps, so go through these with diligence and be brutal. Remember, you can literally download any app again in 5 seconds.

Chapter **15**

Photo Decluttering Once and for All

My friend who is very organized and business savvy said to me the other day that the one thing that really clutters her mind is her photo organizing. I know many people struggle with this same issue. I want your new decluttered lifestyle to allow you to never think about clutter again. Sounds good, right? Just imagine being free of lost focus and time thinking about where to start since decluttering will already be part of your daily routine.

You are not alone in feeling overwhelmed about photo decluttering. The state of your photo organization, or lack thereof, is nothing to be ashamed of, but not doing anything about it after reading this chapter is!

Anyone who has ever had that annoying note come up on their smartphone when trying to take a photo indicating that their storage is full knows the frustration of having too many unsorted photos. This used to happen to me, and I would get so frustrated and stressed that I'd literally want to throw my phone out the window. The struggles are real, and I understand; it was not long ago that I too had about 8,000 unsorted, cluttered photos, and it gave me anxiety even thinking about them! It took me a while to get them sorted, but now I've created a sustainable system that allows me to easily access my uncluttered and neatly organized photos. Plus, I have vowed to never to let that happen again.

You may think going through your photos is going be fun, and at times you will smile at the wonderful memories and rejoice in the special moments of your past. It's also possible that you may never want to take a picture again after you have done a mass digital photo decluttering. All the emotions you may feel before, during, and after your photo decluttering are normal and okay.

The truth is, photo decluttering may be tough, but it's worth it. Once your photos are decluttered, you'll have less clutter in the back of your mind regarding your digital photos. And think about it: If you stress one minute per day about the messy state of your photos, you basically will have wasted over 6 hours in a year just over stress! Plus, think about all the time you waste looking for photos! You may miss your best photos or forget you even had them and will never be able to see how great you looked that summer day in 2009. So, take those 6 hours, sort your photos, and never waste time thinking about decluttered photos again.

Decluttering and Modernizing Printed Media

Decluttering and modernizing printed media, including slides, photos, and videos, not only frees up physical space but also allows you to organize them in a more accessible way.

REMEMBER

Modernizing does take time, collaboration, and resources, so therefore it's really important that the digital media you are keeping is worth it in the first place.

Slides

If you don't know what a slide is, then skip this section or ask your parents, as they may have some boxes in the attic to declutter.

I found four huge bankers' boxes of slides in my parents' attic, and I found a local camera store (yes, they still exist) and asked them if they convert slides to digital. They did and said it was one of their biggest services, which means lots of people are already modernizing.

I brought my slides into the store and two weeks later had a memory stick full of photos, which have brought my parents so much joy to view. They have been looking at these photos constantly over the last two years on their iPad and computers and even committed to decluttering them and making albums so they could find them faster. They made a big print for their bedroom and are happier than ever to have these. If I had not modernized these photos, they would likely not have been able to view them because they don't have a slide projector and they'd completely forgotten about them.

AUTHOR SAYS

This story is proof that decluttering can bring up wonderful memories that you would have otherwise forgotten. Decluttering can bring more joy than buying new stuff.

If you still have slides, I suggest taking them to a professional. Decluttering them can be difficult if you don't have a slide projector, and you may have to get them all converted and then declutter them after, as my family did.

Printed photos

This section covers my tried and tested photo decluttering strategies for printed photos.

REMEMBER

I recommend you take your time and sort your photos with care. For this reason, photo sorting can be a huge time investment.

To start, gather all your physical photos in one location, getting them out of storage forever. You will like viewing these photos, and that is what makes this process so emotional and difficult. My advice is much the same for digital photos, but following are a few quick tips to get you started:

>> **Get rid of duplicates ASAP.**

>> **Cull the bad ones.** Blurry, out-of-focus, or bad quality images need to go.

>> **Create a system.** Organize by year, person, or event depending on what the majority of your photos are about.

>> **Treat fragile ones with care.** Some older photos may be in bad condition, and you can take them to a professional for restoration.

>> **Curate and/or display them.** You will probably come across some real beauties that you want to display and share.

>> **Don't store them.** The ones you are not displaying should be placed in an album. If you know you are never going to get around to this, take them to your local camera shop or send them in online to get them converted to a digital format and give them your selected piles/titles so they can sort them in albums.

Videos

When decluttering your stored videos, get them into a digital format. You can do this yourself by buying equipment or even taking them to your local Walmart or similar department store.

Managing Digital Photos

One of the questions that I get asked the most is how I store my photos and what organizing strategies I use. Like anyone with a personal brand and business these days, I have a lot of photos that I need access to on all my devices.

Creating a digital photo strategy takes time and lots of patience for decluttering. Like I said earlier, it won't happen overnight, but it's worth it because photos are one of the best reminders of past memories (that is, if you can find them or remember that you even have them in the first place).

Photos on computers, clouds, and mobile devices

My biggest piece of advice is to streamline your photo storage to all devices. That can only be done with some sort of cloud storage system. In all honesty, I did not digitize my photos until September 2016. I remember this date so clearly because organizing my digital photos was always on the back of my mind, and I was embarrassed to call myself a professional organizer when I didn't even have my own photos organized.

It was easy for me before the digital age to make pretty albums for each year or occasion, and I still have my perfectly organized albums that I cherish and often look at. When we all had printed photos and film cameras, it was much easier to stay digitally organized. The whole process involved having to physically walk into a camera store, buy Kodak film that usually had about 30–50 photos on it, then take those photos, remove the film, bring it back to the camera store, and return later to pick up your finished products. This was not the era of 100 selfies before heading to meet friends. Long story short, it was easier to be photo decluttered.

Even though we are in the digital era, be conscious of how many photos you take because it takes time to declutter them later. When I am snap-happy with my iPhone and take 100 photos of the same latte, I regret it when I'm decluttering later.

When I started the photo decluttering process in September 2016, I was decluttering 16 years of photos. I won't lie to you; it took me nine months. Of course, I decluttered these in stages, but it was a serious commitment. Now I am overjoyed with my photo organizing. Figure 15-1 is how I organized my photos before I converted to a cloud system, and Figure 15-2 shows my albums organized in the cloud. I also waste no time searching for photos and can easily bring up a trip or memory when I need to. It is a wonderful feeling.

The moral of my story and my biggest advice is to make a strategy today to deal with all your current photos and be able to follow through with this strategy forever. You'll need to adapt. I was diligent from 2000 to 2016 storing the photos on my computer and backing them up on a hard drive, making an album every month. When I was ready to embrace iCloud (which was later than most people), I adapted this strategy to save my photos on all devices and still declutter my photos monthly.

REMEMBER

To create a photo decluttering strategy, it's important that you never miss a month. Repeat after me: "I will declutter my photos every month." Staying consistent is the key to staying decluttered.

In 2016 when I decided to declutter my photos, I decided I would declutter two years' worth of photos every month. For example, I started with the years 2000/2001 and went through all the photos. Figure 15-3 is an example of my photo decluttering schedule I used to keep me on track.

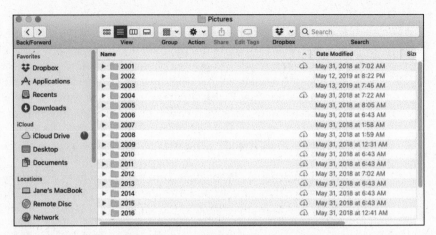

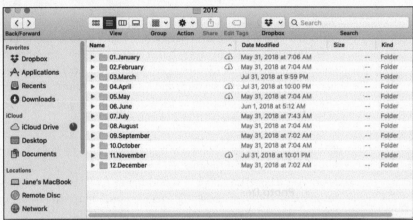

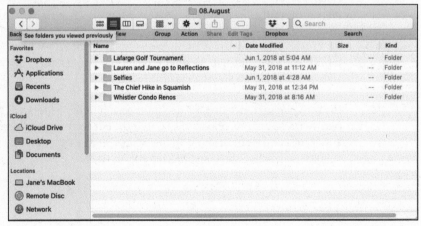

FIGURE 15-1:
My photo
album storage
pre-cloud.

Image courtesy of author

FIGURE 15-2:
My photo
album storage
post-cloud.

Image courtesy of author

Photo Decluttering Strategy.

Day	Years to Declutter	Complete	Notes/Missing
January	2001/2002		
February	2003/2004		
March	2005/2006		
April	2007/2008		
May	2009/2010		
June	2011/2012		
July	2013/2014		
August	2015/Current		
September	Videos		

ORGANIZEDJANE.COM

FIGURE 15-3:
My photo
decluttering
strategy
schedule.

Image courtesy of author

I made an album first for the year and then for each month and then drilled down even further to events.

I was faster for the earlier years because I didn't take as many photos in the early 2000s. The photo decluttering really became tedious when I got to years 2010 and beyond, as there was a shift to taking selfies, many more multiples, and in general more photos for social media. Instagram started in 2010, which helps explain why most people take so many more photos nowadays.

Multiples, photo bursts, and live photos

To add more complexity to photo decluttering, we often have so many of the exact same photos or almost the exact same photo due to photo bursts and taking live photos. Most people either never create time to declutter them or somehow think they may need that photo with a slightly different angle one day.

» **After you take multiples, pick your favorite immediately.** If you don't do this right away, you probably never will until you get the reminder that your storage is full.

» **Turn off live.** Turn off live forever to avoid taking up so much space on your devices. Live photos can be cool as you see a movement and can pick the best from a few seconds, but seriously, when have you ever done that? Once you've turned off the live setting, check it every few months because sometimes it will turn back on.

Dealing with Digital Videos

I used to keep videos because I thought I'd regret deleting them. But the reality is, I rarely looked at old videos on my laptop or iPhone. Rather, most of the time these videos took up precious space on my devices. I get how much emotion videos can evoke (often more than still images), and you don't have to delete everything to declutter your videos. However, I do recommend getting realistic with how often you actually look at your videos, creating a system similar to photo decluttering, and ensuring that you stay consistent throughout the process. The main tip to implement is to carve out time on a monthly basis to go through any and all videos you have on your devices and determine what needs to go.

TIP

Unless you're a professional video editor, properly editing videos is likely a time-consuming process — or you may not even know how to edit videos. Everything from trimming, to applying filters, to cutting out sections can take ages. Hire someone to help you with the videos you want to keep. If you keep only your best videos, then making them even better quality will aid in the decluttering process.

Another idea is to amalgamate videos from a special occasion and give them to a video editor to take the best parts and make one special video.

If you're wondering where to find freelance video help, I suggest you start with the following two sites, which I have used to find freelancers for so many digital tasks, including video editing:

» **Fiverr:** www.fiverr.com

» **Upwork:** www.upwork.com

ALRIGHT, IT'S TIME TO DELETE PHOTOS AND VIDEOS WITH YOUR EX

When you're going through your photos or videos, you're sure to find some of your ex (that is, if you have an ex; if you don't, you're really lucky).

Love should be celebrated, but if or when that love ends, get rid of the photo or video. If you really want to keep it because it was a great vacation or you happen to look phenomenal, keep it digitally. There is no need for your new someone to find physical photos of you and your ex.

Get rid of the photos with these helpful tips:

- **View and remember the good times.** Know that many more good times are coming in the future.

- **Appreciate the special occasion.** Maybe you took a once-in-a-lifetime vacation and want to keep those memories. Check back to see if you have photos or video with only you in them, and discard the ones with both of you.

- **Let go of the past.** Often, we have trouble letting go of things because we are holding onto the past. I am no psychiatrist or in no way a relationship expert, but holding onto those photos will remind you of the past, and it's best to move on.

4

The Part of Tens

Chapter **16**

Ten Reasons to Keep Decluttering

When writing this book, I was very concerned — you might even say stressed — that I was forgetting important points that are vital to the decluttering process. Every time I finished and submitted a chapter, I would think of other points I should have added, and I made notes to make sure to add them in somewhere.

In this final part of the book, I want to really get down to the important items that I think are integral to why you need to keep decluttering. It should become a continual practice that you incorporate into your daily life forever. Once it becomes a habit, it will seamlessly fit into your lifestyle. Soon, you won't even think you are decluttering; it will simply be part of your routine!

REMEMBER

The bottom line is I really tried to incorporate everything possible related to decluttering into this book. By now you know I believe that decluttering is not going to solve every problem, but the practice of changing your habits and mindset can help you achieve your goals and live better.

Smaller and More Expensive Dwellings

Even in Canada, where I am from — which is also one of the largest countries in the world — the houses are getting smaller. This is partly due to the fact that Canada is so cold that most of the population lives sprawled close to the U.S. border. Regardless, there is still lots and lots of space! However, the hottest markets are the big cities, which have less space and expensive real estate. Therefore, dwellings are getting smaller to be more affordable.

In a census conducted by PricewaterhouseCoopers in 2007, it was noted that Canada has the third largest dwellings in the world after Australia and the United States. This means many countries have smaller dwellings already!

In addition, increases in immigration in countries continue to put high demands on housing, and those arriving to countries such as Canada and the U.S. may not have such high demands for space because they're likely used to smaller dwellings. The shrinking sizes of houses and condos in most major cities in North America will likely continue to be the trend. It's imperative that you adopt your decluttering habits now, as smaller spaces leave even less room for error when it comes to deciding what to keep and what to discard.

Smaller dwellings mean you naturally have to declutter more, but I always say the size of your space should not determine how much stuff you have. Everything you own should be based on your lifestyle.

Freelance Work Lifestyle

The rising "gig economy," as it is often called, is representing a shift in traditional ways of working. Instead of going to an office every day and working for the same employer, people work remotely and can work for various employers on a variety of tasks suited to their skills. The gig economy is more flexible and allows more time for freedom and personal fulfillment while also giving businesses more options to hire people for a variety of tasks. The two largest websites currently promoting freelance workers are Upwork and Fiverr, and I have used both of them extensively with exceptional results.

So, what does this new way of working have to do with clutter? You no longer need a big office with massive filing cabinets; you likely only need a computer, Wi-Fi, and a comfortable place to work. You also have to be clear of mental clutter so you can freely focus on several tasks with perhaps several employers versus the traditional role of only working for the same employer doing the same tasks day after day.

Freedom of Life

Freedom is becoming a goal for most people. In my business, I ask people what they want more of in life. The answers are usually more money, more time, and more freedom, in no particular order. And all of those can be achieved by decluttering! Seriously — I am not joking on this one.

Freedom comes from a variety of things, some as small as removing physical clutter from your home daily. This helps give you more time versus wasting hours cleaning and trying to find your items.

Mental clutter can also keep you awake at night, causing you to always be tired, unprepared, and never really feeling like you can maximize your days.

Freedom in life can also be having more time to spend on the things you love doing versus always cleaning or working so many hours. Trust me: Removing unnecessary clutter both physically and mentally can grant you the freedom you desire.

Gaining More Hours in the Day

Decluttering helps you save time. And again, when I ask what people want more of, time is usually mentioned.

It makes sense that the more stuff you have, the more time you need to clean it, move it, and keep it organized.

The less physical and mental clutter you have, the less time you spend thinking about it. The less you think about it, the better you're able to focus on the important things in your life, increasing your productivity tenfold.

Pausing from Consumerism

Disclaimer: I love shopping. I probably always will, and I still do lots of shopping. The difference today is that I do my shopping on a conscious level, often scheduling trips and knowing what I need before I go out and shop aimlessly. Don't get me wrong: Sometimes I am still enticed by the latest marketers' schemes, need a little retail therapy, or simply end up with excess trendy items that I didn't need to buy. However, these useless shopping trips are always a reminder that unnecessary items quickly become clutter, and I try my best to be aware of these habits and not let them happen again.

I have also spent time living in other continents where shopping is much less of a national pastime than it is in North America. Some countries in Europe still close their shops on Sundays and have early closing hours, whereas in the United States you can literally shop 24 hours a day in most cities that have a Walmart.

The reasons that people are tempted to buy stuff are different for each person. Most people are aware that happiness is not directly related to things we have and that keeping up with the Joneses is not a goal we should be striving for. If anyone's last name is Jones, I feel very sorry for you as it has been used for years to describe keeping up with our neighbors' and friends' stuff.

In the early 2000s, there were more shopping malls than schools. The ratio was around 2:1 in 2000. Reading this statistic triggered me to do more research on the topic, specifically on the rise of consumerism. Without getting into a history lesson, shopping really began to increase in the United States after World War II. It was the first time that men and women could go into stores and buy exactly what they wanted. The rise of suburbs promoted people to buy homes and then fill those homes with stuff — often trying to find better and more items than their neighbors had. This trend has continued to this day.

Many articles referred to various countries' political systems and leaders to promote spending versus saving to help the economy. Whatever the reason for the rise of consumerism, there is no denying that shopping has become part of our culture. Think about how much we spend on mainstream holidays that have increased across various countries. The need to buy more gifts at Christmas, decorate scarier at Halloween, and purchase more Easter bunny stuffed animals continues to increase.

TIP

Here are some simple strategies that I used to help curtail my shopping habits:

>> **Have a spending plan and track it.** This may be more relevant to a book on budgeting, but it makes sense to have a simple budget to help curb poor spending habits and excess shopping.

>> **Get support.** Shopping is more fun with friends anyways, so why not grab a friend and tell her what you need so that you don't buy more?

>> **Leave it for a day.** If you are not sure about a purchase, leave it and see if you even remember it the next day. I use this method a lot, and it has saved me a ton of money (and clutter!).

>> **Don't shop when you're emotional.** Often, you'll buy more than what you need when you shop for emotional reasons. Save it for when you have a clear mind and stick to practical purchases.

>> **Remove temptations.** You likely know what clutter you have too much of and what you're in the habit of purchasing in excess. Don't go to the stores, read the magazines, or follow the social media accounts that lead to temptation. Minimize these distractions and focus only on what you need.

Inspiring Friends and Family

My goal for writing this book was to inspire everyone to read it and adopt some tips to start and continue decluttering in all facets of their lives. It truly is my hope that that you will also pass along your tips and encourage others to adopt similar strategies. I believe that a decluttered world will lead all of us to be less stressed, happier, and have more time to focus on our valuable contributions to society.

This last statement sounds like decluttering could help bring world peace, and on some level, I think that it could!

Understand your motivation for decluttering; likely, your friends and family have similar motivations, and this can offer a nice place to start the conversation. Once you feel more in control of your decluttering habits and what you are bringing into your space, you can extend this advice to others. When you can come together to work toward a common goal, you can achieve anything you set your mind to.

Finding a Better Home for Your Clutter

In most of my chapters, I try to give some practical tips on what to do with your clutter. The obvious ones are donating, selling, repurposing, and, if all else fails, recycling.

Chapter 18 provides my top ten destinations for your clutter. Five of those spots are related to donating. The remainder are ideas for selling, giving to friends, and repurposing. Again, my goal is to make decluttering a lifelong practice. Don't only declutter once, but rather make it a daily habit that helps keep you organized and grounded.

Skip ahead if you'd like to find the exact declutter locations, but following is my general advice for most physical items:

>> **Donate:** As Chapter 1 discusses in detail, donating should be at the heart of your decluttering mindset. Being able to donate your items to benefit others not only helps your closet but also helps you improve other people's lives. In our consumerist society, you need to be aware of not only the amounts you are buying, but how you can further your belongings' sustainability. Donating does not just mean giving away items to your local thrift shop; it can also mean giving items to neighbors, friends, or family.

>> **Repurpose:** An often-forgotten part of decluttering, a multitude of items can be repurposed.

>> **Sell:** This advice may sound contradictory to my first point about giving clothing to others who could benefit, but it's still very valid. There are many apps, online consignment stores, and retail stores that sell lightly used items. I normally sell items I've bought brand-new that have little wear and tear, and donate items that are more worn.

>> **Toss:** At some point, items become no longer usable. But as usual, see if you can repurpose these items first.

Paying It Forward

The more things you give away, the lighter you will feel. Plus, you may feel like your heart is getting bigger due to your newfound generosity in donating items that someone else can use and appreciate.

However, I want to go a bit deeper into this, helping others not to accumulate clutter in the first place. With regards to gift giving, birthday presents, and simply showing up with stuff for friends and family, a solution could be to check what they need or give them experiences versus stuff. It is up to all of us to solve even small clutter issues and not add to someone else's clutter collection.

Be cognizant of your own clutter rules and use the same principles when giving gifts or hosting parties. I mean, how many swag bags of stuff do you really want to be getting and/or giving? Pay it forward and don't clutter someone else's life.

Bettering the Planet

Today, you can't use a plastic straw without thinking of the impact that it has on the environment. From giving up plastic items to save our oceans to not printing paper to save trees, we know the impact that our stuff has on the environment.

Think of it this way: What ends up in a landfill is clutter, so don't accumulate it in the first place. Today, the lesser quality of items seems to call for constant replacing. From our furniture to our electronics, there are a ton of cheaply made items on the market that don't stand the test of time. Most of us look for the best deal instead of the best quality, but this mindset causes us to often accumulate poor-quality items that constantly need replacing, producing more waste.

Before you buy an item, think about how long you want it to last and whether the quality of this item reflects this desire. I always suggest quality over quantity for most items, from clothes to furniture to office supplies. Often technology moves so fast that some suggest this may not be the best option, but use this motto where you can.

I also believe that doing more of what makes you happy can better the planet. Focusing on experiences that bring you joy, such as getting outside, hanging out with good friends, or expressing your creativity, helps you to worry less about the possessions you do or don't have. Create intentions to consume less and enjoy the simple pleasures of life to mitigate your ecological footprint.

You Bought This Book, Didn't You?

If you bought this book for yourself, thank you — I really hope that at least one tip can help make your life easier and clutter-free for the long run.

I assume that if you bought this book, you want to make a change in your decluttering habits. You may be on the verge of applying for the *Hoarders* show, or you may actually not have any extra stuff lying around but you want to clear you mental or digital space, which can cause just as much stress.

If this book was a gift, please don't be offended. The person bought it as a nice gesture, and everyone on the planet can use some decluttering inspiration. Don't think that the person who gifted you this book thinks you are messy, disorganized, or super cluttered. They may have bought it simply for inspiration or because they needed it themselves and wanted to see you implement the tips first!

If you found this book in a donation bin, even better! This is a sure sign that its previous owner implemented a decluttering strategy.

Whichever way this book landed in your hands, I hope that it will truly make a difference and be one of the reasons that you start decluttering today and for the rest of time.

Lastly, remember your Clutter Danger Card, which was introduced in Chapter 3. Go back and take a photo and keep it on your phone when you need some extra decluttering motivation.

Chapter **17**

Ten Ways to Label Anything and Everything

While writing this book, I realized that in almost every chapter I talk about labeling. Labels are crucial in the decluttering process — even in digital decluttering! In this chapter, I give some practical tips and ideas about labeling.

If you've read previous chapters of this book, you likely know that I don't advise labeling things you don't use or that don't add value to your life. I constantly say that it is useless to have beautiful labeled boxes with items in them that you never use — this is just a clutter trap! However, labeling boxes of items that you actually use on a regular basis is a decluttering game-changer. Plus, making the boxes pretty never hurts!

Your lifestyle determines what labels you need, how long they will last, and whether they change regularly. Your lifestyle also determines the look of the labels and how fast you need them. You don't need perfectly color-coordinated labels with your personal branding or business logo on them for everything. Of course, they would look amazing! But when you're quickly labeling your fridge items or making a temporary label for a work project, speed and functionality take priority over aesthetics.

REMEMBER

Labels don't have to be forever. They usually only last for a certain period. I have not had many labels last more than a few years before an update is needed. I recommend updating them frequently and adding this to your regular decluttering routine.

The following sections cover different types of labels, ways to make labels, and recommendations for how you can use them.

Label Maker

I love my label maker. I really do. It sits beside me on my computer when I'm working, and I miss it when I'm traveling. I love making labels, and a label maker makes them all perfectly uniform to give my items a polished look.

Figure 17-1 is a picture of my label maker, the bigger version that the brand Brother offers. I also have a smaller handheld version that I keep in my Bahamas home, as of course I make labels there as well. Figure 17-2 shows how I always make sure I have at least two replacement label cassettes, as you don't want to be in the midst of a labeling project when your cassette runs out!

Label makers are great for quick labels and those that need to be changed frequently. My rule of thumb is that if you need to make ten or fewer labels at a time, then a label maker is perfect. Figure 17-3 shows an example of what a label-maker label looks like.

FIGURE 17-1:
My label maker.

Image courtesy of author

FIGURE 17-2:
Spare label
cassettes on
hand.

DECLUTTERING FOR DUMMIES

FIGURE 17-3:
Example
of standard
label-maker
labels.

Computer Labels

When my dad came to me and asked to borrow my label maker, I was ecstatic. I was not ecstatic when I saw him take five minutes to print one label and saw that he wanted to label his entire wall of small nails, screws, and washers. There were over 100 drawers, which would take him months! I instead suggested he sit down beside me for an hour while I made computer labels using a Microsoft Word document with the Avery labels template in size 1" x 2-5/8" rectangle labels.

I printed the labels, and an hour later my dad was happily placing them on all of his drawers. He is now forever able to find all types of screws, nails, or washers whenever he needs them.

**AUTHOR
SAYS**

The reason for this story is that there is a time and place for different labels. If you have to make more than ten labels, I suggest using a computer for faster results. Plus, you will then get to know the standard label sizes you are always reaching for and can keep those on hand.

In your Microsoft Word program, under "Tools," you can choose "Labels." Then, there is a drop-down menu of many different label sizes and the number it corresponds to from the supplier. Avery is the most standard one. This is the easiest way to create labels on the computer because the template gives you the correct label size.

I also use computer labels for mailing items. I rarely handwrite addresses; I use shipping and return labels, as they look more professional.

I always keep my most-used Avery labels on hand. See Figure 17-4.

The beauty of computer labels is they are fast and can be customized. The downside is that you can't throw a computer and printer in your purse to make labels on-the-go.

I suggest computer labels for anything you need to customize or want to look pretty. And of course, if you have to do ten or more labels, it's much quicker, providing you have a printer. You can also send them to your local print shop if you don't have a printer or if you don't want to make them yourself.

Figure 17-5 is an example of my customized computer labels.

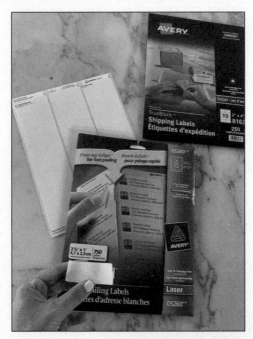

FIGURE 17-4:
Example of
my most-used
Avery com-
puter labels.

FIGURE 17-5:
An example
of a computer
label.

Handwritten Labels

I still love handwriting letters and labels, and I do this often. At the moment, I am planning a large lifestyle photo shoot for my business, and I wrote all the labels by hand. It's quick, and they are only being used for one event, so handwriting these is efficient.

REMEMBER

The term "label" doesn't necessarily have to refer to a sticky label. Figure 17-6 shows cardboard labels that can be attached with a string or slip over something, such as a hanger.

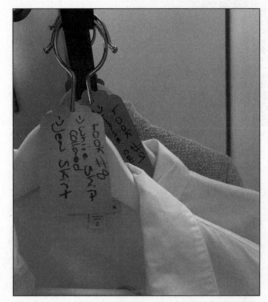

FIGURE 17-6:
A handwritten label.

Image courtesy of author

Permanent Labels

Sometimes you want to label something permanently. In this case, you want to engrave your items or use labels that are sewn or crazy-glued on, or done with permanent marker. When I think of permanent labels, I think of them on clothing or totes. For example, my luggage has a permanent label on it. However, make sure you only permanently label something when you are absolutely sure the name or letters will never change.

Also, many stores do personalization or permanent labeling for you. The store where I bought my suitcase, shown in Figure 17-7, offered this service.

FIGURE 17-7:
Suitcase label.

Image courtesy of author

Washable Labels

Perhaps you need to write something on a plastic storage container, but you need to change the label whenever a different food item goes in it. Getting a washable marker and keeping it within reach of where you label is a great idea. Then, once you don't need the label or want to change it, you can simply wash it off. This is also great for events on whiteboards where you need to label directions or entranceways.

Pre-Written Labels

You can order labels that already have words on them or make custom ones. My favorite site is Mabel's Labels (https://mabelslabels.ca), as she has already made a label for practically everything you can imagine needing a label for. Plus, she can give you great ideas and inspiration! This site is especially great for kids' labels, and if your kids start labeling now, they likely will continue this healthy habit into adulthood.

Picture Labels

Who said that a label has to be written? You can use photos to help identify what is in boxes instead of listing the item(s). Doing this was easier when we had Polaroid cameras; however, it doesn't take long to print the photos on your printer.

Check out Figure 17-8 to see how I quickly label my shoeboxes with a photo so I know what's inside.

FIGURE 17-8:
Photo labeling of my shoeboxes.

Image courtesy of author photocredit @lohmmedia

Digital App Labels

A label doesn't have to be physical. You can make digital labels on your phone using apps. I mention the app Snupps (www.snupps.com) in Chapter 4, which is basically an app to organize anything.

If you have a box and don't have any labels, why not start a shelf or list on your phone of what is inside? The great thing about this is that you can share the information or quickly edit it, and you even save paper. Plus, when you're away from home, you'll always know what you have.

Food Labels

Earlier I give an example of washable labels, which are great for food; your food containers' contents can change so quickly! Labeling freezer items is also very important. If you don't, you risk your items getting freezer burn. Use a marker or sticker label to simply label what you put in your freezer and the date you put it in. If the package isn't see-through, for example packaged meat from the butcher, make sure you label what it is and the date.

Danger Labels

If something is dangerous, it needs to be labeled to let people know. This can be for chemicals in spray bottles, medication, or larger hazards such as equipment or even where not to enter.

Ensure any hazards around your work and home are labeled to let people know of the dangers. Just because you know something is dangerous doesn't mean your kids' babysitter will. Be safe rather than sorry and label anything dangerous.

WHAT AND WHEN NOT TO LABEL

I love labeling, and I know it helps to increase efficiency! But there are some things I don't label because I don't want anyone to know what is in them. Here are some items I don't label or times when not labeling makes sense:

- **Jewelry:** Call me crazy, but I have this fear that if someone breaks in and sees a box or drawer labeled "jewelry," it will be the first thing they steal.

- **Money:** I believe in labeling folders for your personal documents, but if you keep a stash of money at home or the office, it's best not to label the envelope or box for the same reason noted in the preceding bullet.

- **Moving:** When you're moving, of course you need to label! However, if you are having professional movers move the boxes, or if your items might be exposed to the public on the street or during transit, it's best not to label valuables, such as jewelry (which you shouldn't have movers move anyway), valuable antiques, and whatever else might be enticing if someone sees the label.

(continued)

(continued)

- **Anything super personal:** If seeing a label may cause shock or curiosity in a potential guest, it's best not to label that item. Some things are meant to be kept personal, and if you label them, someone may find them alluring.

- **When you don't want someone to know your name or address:** When I was interviewing parents for this book, I found out that some parents don't like to put names on items that are seen in public, such as backpacks, towels, or clothes. A hidden label (for example, inside a backpack) is okay to help identify items; however, one mother advised not to label anything obvious because you don't want your young kids to think that strangers know them.

Chapter **18**

Top Destinations to Finally Rid the Clutter

talk a lot in this book about getting rid of stuff. Actually, most of this book is about this topic! That's why I thought I would go into a bit of depth about where you can actually get rid of stuff. I focus mostly on North American locations for donation sites and global locations for consignment options.

REMEMBER

Decluttering requires shifting your mindset and remembering that someone else can benefit from whatever you don't use, need, or wear. Donating helps someone in need, reduces negative environmental impact, and helps bring value into someone else's life. When you shift your decluttering mentality to helping others, it becomes much easier to let go of items. I encourage you to try thinking about the people you're potentially helping each time you are going through your items.

Donating Your Items

The act of giving not only helps others, but it also helps you feel good. Getting rid of items you no longer use frees them up for someone else who likely can use them. Giving brings others joy and is a great alternative to letting your items collect dust.

The act of giving can also be a chance for you to connect with your community and really become more aware of how you can contribute to making the world a better place.

Today I see donation bins and cans all over the place. From various Walmart parking lots to strip-mall entrances to schools, donation bins are becoming popular and convenient.

One problem that can occur after decluttering is that your stuff sits in your house waiting to be dropped off at the local charity or donation spot. Often, the worst thing possible happens: That stuff designated to give someone else joy stays in your garage for ages, or worse, makes it back into your house. This is terrible because someone else really may have needed your items, and now all the efforts you and your family went through to declutter are wasted.

A great option is to pre-arrange a pickup from a local charity. This forces you to have a deadline and ensures that your items actually get donated.

Following are five places in North America that have a pickup service, but I recommend checking with your local charity, as availability of this service differs by city.

>> **Salvation Army:** Most cities and small towns have a Salvation Army, so this is always your best bet to try first. This place has been around for over 150 years, so it is safe to say that they know what they're doing and are skilled at giving your items to others who likely need them more. They accept pretty much anything as long as it is in good condition, such as clothes, kitchen accessories, books, and appliances. If you live in the U.S., you can go to their website at https://satruck.org/donate/choose and enter your zip code to schedule a pickup. It's really that easy!

In Canada, depending on your location, residential pickup may be available. Locations and contact details can be found at www.thriftstore.ca/donation-pick-service.

>> **Goodwill:** Most cities also have a Goodwill. Contact them directly at www.goodwill.org to see if they do pickups in your area.

>> **AMVETS:** These are thrift stores that offer used clothing, household goods, and toys, and the revenue helps veterans' programs. Visit them at https://amvets.org/thrift-stores/.

- » **Habitat for Humanity:** This one is big in Canada, and you can even volunteer your time to help build houses for this organization, which I have done to help impact my community. What is great is that they offer furniture pickup, and they can even restore it for reuse. Often furniture is not decluttered because you can't physically move it out of the house easily, so this is a great option for furniture. Go to `www.habitat.org/stories/does-habitat-offer-furniture-donation-pickup`.

- » **Donation Town:** This service connects you with a local charity where they come and pick up your items. Find them at `www.donationtown.org`.

TIP

To keep donating top of mind, keep a box labeled "Donate" in your house. You can buy one from my website at `http://Organizedjane.com`. These boxes are prettier and easier to carry than cardboard boxes. See Figure 18-1.

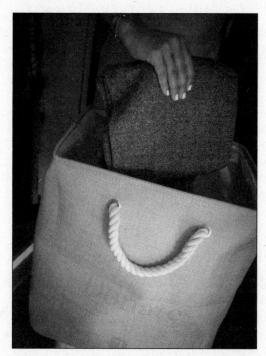

FIGURE 18-1: A "Donate" basket.

Image courtesy of author photocredit @lohmmedia

Selling Your Items

I resell lots of stuff and am almost always selling something. I have done this since eBay was invented in 1995. I was fascinated that there was a platform to sell and buy items in an auction environment. Now, I use a variety of online platforms to sell my items, from free apps to apps that charge a percentage per sale.

I always recommend selling items that are like new and donating items that have more wear. I still bring my items to a store to resell, and on occasion I have still placed something on a street curb, although this is a method I discourage as many streets don't allow it.

Selling direct to consumers

Some platforms allow you to sell an item to someone directly. You can use a third-party platform such as eBay to do this and pay a small user fee. Today there are so many sites to sell items that I can't possibility list them all. There are free sites, such as Craigslist and Kijji, as well as sites that take a small fee for each item that is sold, such as Depop (www.depop.com).

There is no excuse for not being able to sell your items if they are in good condition, and it's surprising what people will buy. I once even sold used soap dispensers because they were a reputable brand.

It takes only a couple of minutes to make an ad with your smartphone, and you can also ship items. As long as you have Wi-Fi, you can sell your items, no matter where you live.

Consigning

I consign my designer items and more expensive clothing. Some people ask why I do this instead of selling directly to the consumer. There are many reasons. For me, selling designer items can be tricky for both the buyer and the seller because there are many fakes or look-alikes that are causing problems in the luxury market. I buy lots of preloved clothing and accessories, but to be safe, I only buy them from reputable places that offer a designer inspection to make sure they are not fake. That is why you pay more to buy from one of these stores. If you are selling an item at a consignment store, there is a split between what the store takes and what you make. This split can be as high as 50 percent.

My favorite preloved stores for buying and selling are located in the U.S., the U.K., Canada, and Switzerland. All of them now offer online shopping and consigning:

>> **Fashionphile:** Their motto is shop, sell, repeat. And if you buy an item you usually get the option to sell it back for a certain price within a few months. It's like renting something, and it's a genius idea. www.fashionphile.com/

>> **Vestiaire Collective:** I am a major fan of this site because anything you buy comes with a stamp of quality and an authenticity check by someone on their team. This shop is based in the U.K. but ships and accepts items globally. https://us.vestiairecollective.com/

>> **LXR and Co:** I have bought and sold several items from LXR and CO, and now they even sell directly in stores such as the Bay in Canada and Lord & Taylor in the U.S. www.lxrco.com

>> **Turnabout:** My favorite physical consignment store in Vancouver, British Columbia, and now they also have online shopping options. https://turnabout.com/

>> **LUX Luxury Shops:** There is something very special about consignment stores in Europe. If you are ever in Zürich, Switzerland, this stop is a must. Also, in Paris there are many hidden gems. They really bring a new meaning to vintage and offer a European classic touch. www.luxury-shops.com

And lastly, don't walk into your local consignment shop with a grungy old brown box. Get one of my decluttering boxes and walk into the store with some serious consignment know-how! Figure 18-2 gives you an example. Having one of these pre-labeled baskets will encourage you to sell more and you can keep it alongside your "donate" bin. When it is full simply bring it to your consignment or store of sell them direct. The key is to have the bins as constant reminders.

Most people forget that many of their friends or acquaintances within their networks would love their stuff. They may not love all of it, but there are surely a few items that friends may need or can use. Plus, friends are more likely to cherish your items and appreciate them than strangers you sell to.

Garage and yard sales are also a great option to sell your items to your community. If your local flea market is a hit, this may also be a great option.

FIGURE 18-2:
A sell basket.

Image courtesy of author photocredit @lohmmedia

Hosting Exchange Parties

Why not host a party where everyone can bring things to give to someone? If the guest list is shared ahead of time, you will have an idea of who is attending and what their style is.

I call this a party because the more you can make donating and decluttering fun, the more likely you and your friends are to make it a habit.

One friend I know does not like these parties because she says she gets upset after she decides to part with clothes. She gets even more upset when she sees one of our friends wearing her items, and she usually wants them back. I always remind her that if she didn't wear an item or didn't feel comfortable in it, then it is wise to pass it along and be happy to be getting rid of clutter.

WARNING

Bottom line, if you haven't worn an item of clothing, or if it doesn't make you feel great, donate it. I guarantee it will look great on someone else, but that doesn't mean you should take it back. You gave it away for a reason, so stick to that. Plus, if it looks great on someone else and gives them confidence, that should be a great feeling for you, too.

Instead of a party, you could also do secret drops of items you know your friends will love at their houses. Facebook also has many selling groups that are becoming increasingly popular, especially among mothers.

Repurposing and/or Recycling Items

I am a big fan of repurposing items, and I was encouraged to get creative with repurposing as a child. I grew up in a very rural community in a small town in Canada, and we didn't have shopping malls that were close and there was no Amazon delivery back then. The only delivery option was the monthly Sears Catalog delivery, and even then, we had to drive to the hardware store 45 minutes away to pick it up. The struggles were real, but I had a lot less clutter!

In hindsight, this helped to make me more creative and resourceful, and for that I am thankful.

If you google "repurpose items," you will literally be bombarded with hundreds of ideas of things you can make and creative uses for your old stuff.

WARNING

I am not suggesting here that you keep stuff "just in case" you need to repurpose it, but if you can use it for something else, then do. I suggest repurposing what you can immediately rather than keeping it for years because you are going to get to it someday. Do it today, and if not, then it is best to make an alternative plan.

My favorite things to repurpose are items for my closet, and I have garnered so many ideas over the years. Here are my three favorites:

>> **Ice cube trays:** If your ice cube tray is leaking or you don't need it anymore, it can be used to store small jewelry or pins that you always need for quick fixes.

>> **S-hooks or shower curtain rings:** These are great for hanging belts, purses, hats, and umbrellas. Seriously, I love a good S-hook.

>> **Anything acrylic:** If you can see through it, I love it already. Acrylic dividers and boxes are the best, and you can often use them for a multitude of things.

If there are no creative uses for your clutter, can you recycle it? As a general rule, if there is some plastic, tin, or glass and it is relatively clean, you should be able to recycle it. If not, you should be able to recycle some parts of it.

Here is a quick but not exhaustive list of recycling information to ensure you are taking every last step before something has to end up in the landfill:

>> **Plastics/bottles:** From food items to storage bins

>> **Paper and cardboard:** Includes snack and cereal boxes

>> **Paperwork:** Phone books, magazines, mail, office paper, and newspaper

>> **Metals:** Tins, aluminum, and steel cans

>> **Glass:** Food storage and bottles

Last Resort — The Landfill

Now, I don't like sending things to the dump. If at all possible, try to at least recycle. It's amazing what can be recycled today.

If, however, you need to get rid of an item that can't be donated, sold, exchanged, repurposed, or even recycled, you have no other choice but to simply throw it away.

Be sure to reflect on what you are taking to the landfill or throwing in a dumpster. Could you have avoided buying that item in the first place?

REMEMBER

Chapter **19**

Ten Tips for Organizing What's Left

I tried to be as exhaustive as possible with this book, but the reality is that you and I are different. Everyone who reads this book will have different hobbies, careers, habits, and decluttering mindsets. I may have only touched upon a small portion for some of you, and for others I may have covered way too much. The great thing about this book is that you can jump to whatever section you need.

I focus mostly on decluttering rather than organizing because they are two different topics; however, I feel it is important to mention organizing at least at the end since I am a professional organizer and it's my true passion. I have helped hundreds of individual and corporate clients declutter and get more organized. I know they go hand in hand, and the first step is removing the clutter and then making an organizing plan that fits your current lifestyle and can also be adapted when your lifestyle changes.

It sounds straightforward, but I understand the challenges around organizing and how overwhelming it can be to even think about it. The good news is that you can get started just as quickly as you did with decluttering, with ten minutes a day.

These top ten tips are general, and some of this information may be repeated in previous chapters around decluttering. If you implement these tips into your daily life, I know you can live a happier and stress-free life.

Put Things in Proper Perspective

The gradual or instant accumulation of clutter can be stressful and cause daily stress and challenges. However, there are many steps you can take to mitigate this issue. First, you have to get rid of the physical and mental clutter, and then you need to adopt different practices, habits, and mindsets to keep yourself decluttered. It's important to not let the clutter infringe on your clarity and ability to achieve your goals.

REMEMBER

But what I really want to stress about decluttering is that it only helps if you buy less and focus on constantly being on top of the physical and mental clutter. Just telling you to buy less stuff or to get rid of that t-shirt you've had since fifth grade that you are emotionally attached to won't automatically solve your problems. I can give you advice, but you need to change your perspective. It's like going on a diet. If you only temporarily eat better and cut out bad food, the minute you start bingeing again, the weight will come back.

What possessions are essential, and what adds value to your life? What possessions are in the way of you achieving your real goals and desires?

For organizing the items you want to keep, you also need to have a healthy perspective and prioritize items based on your lifestyle. This means getting really clear on what your current lifestyle is — not someone else's, and definitely not what you see in magazines. I encourage you to reflect back on the second chapter where I ask you to look at your decluttering goals and how they relate to your life goals. The same principles apply to organizing.

Understand what is important to you and your family in terms of where your time is spent and where you know you are losing time and efficiency. Then, make it a priority to improve those areas of your space.

Organize for You, Not Instagram

My organizing approach gets down to what is really important in life. Look at your main activities. What do you spend time doing at work and at home? Adapt your organizing systems and routines to your lifestyle.

I also encourage you to organize because it makes you more efficient. I struggle when people ask me for before-and-after pictures because I find that sometimes the after pictures don't look perfect but are the most efficient organizing solutions.

I disagree with articles and photos where everything has to look ultra-organized. When you have a busy life to sustain, this may be impossible and only cause you more stress. Of course, you may want to have things in nice boxes and match your décor and design, but I encourage you to make it functional first and then you can focus on the pretty.

Tailor Your Organizing to Your Clutter Personality

In the first chapter of this book, one of the things I talk about is your clutter personality. Understanding what your clutter personality is can help you overcome the clutter hurdles associated with it. Remember that it is common to have multiple clutter personalities. The personalities include the following:

>> The Emotional Clutterbug

>> The "Just-in-Case" Clutterbug

>> The "I'm Not a Clutterbug" Clutterbug

>> The "I'll Do It Later" Clutterbug

>> The "I Can't Decide" Clutterbug

>> The "Techie" Clutterbug

>> The Knowledge Clutterbug

>> The Collector Clutterbug

>> The "I Can Use It Someday" Clutterbug

I bring this up again because one or more of these probably describes your organizing personality as well. When you think about organizing, do you get overwhelmed, procrastinate for another day, or feel like you don't know where to start or can't decide how to organize? First, identify what clutter personality you are and then relate this to how you further organize your remaining items. Get real with yourself about why your organizing personality has been stopping you from getting organized and address this issue head on.

TIP

And here are some tips that can apply to any clutterbug:

>> **Commit to regularly evaluating your sentimental items.** If you own a box of concert shirts that are tucked away but you never look at them, then why keep them? After regularly committing to evaluating your sentimental items, you may be ready to part with them.

>> **Repurpose sentimental items.** Your could frame your favorite concert shirts so that they can be visible all the time, and discard the rest. This can bring you more joy and reduced clutter!

>> **Keep only a small dedicated space for sentimental items.** Have a space in your home that is precious real estate and dedicate this space to your sentimental items. This will help you be more conscious of what resides there.

>> **Envision the joy of being able to actually enjoy the true sentimental items you do keep.** Enough said!

Set Aside Time to Declutter AND Organize

Time. Our most valuable asset. I love time and want more of it. You can have more time if you set up organizing systems that fit your current lifestyle.

As I mention several times throughout the book, when you start decluttering, you may need to set a specific time for a few days, weeks, or months to focus on your decluttering goals. Even if it is ten minutes, every day makes a difference.

The same goes for organizing. Once your space is ready to be organized, start scheduling time to stay organized. Put in calendar invites at the beginning or end of your days, enlist your family to be involved, and commit to making organizing time part of your routine.

And as always, use a time cube to help! See Figure 19-1. I talk about using a time cube in several chapters, including Chapter 2, where I discuss the small challenges you can do to get you started decluttering. You can use the time cube in the same way for organizing. Set the timer for 15 minutes and devote that time to nothing but organizing.

FIGURE 19-1:
Time cube
organizing.

Image courtesy of author

Use Boxes, Baskets, and Other Containers

I am advocate of keeping boxes, bins, or cans labeled "Donate," to help encourage daily decluttering. I am also an advocate of keeping labeled bins, baskets, or boxes of the items you do keep to help them stay organized and in good condition.

Keep your organizing routines and the system of bins you use or adapt when needed, and you will soon find you are organizing automatically. Just like your decluttering mentality, organizing is also a mentality.

REMEMBER

Conduct Organizing Challenges

Just as I have suggested decluttering challenges with the people living in your house, you can also have organizing challenges. Or, just like donating something every day, which means that by the end of the year you will have donated 365 items, you can organize something every day.

TIP

Humans are competitive and usually do things more easily if they are a bit fun or if there is a challenge attached to them. Here are a few tips:

>> **Make organizing fun.** Use music, friends, champagne, or whatever it takes. Labels, boxes, putting up shelves, and creating organizing spots is always more fun with friends and family. Plus, it will definitely motivate them to get more organized too.

>> **Create organizing games.** Create small challenges or judging competitions with your household. For example, do a 30-minute bedroom organizing game and pick a winner based on whose room is the most organized. Or do weekly challenges of who can keep their organized systems the longest. It is surprising how simple tricks can help even the most unorganized household turn competitive around this often-mundane task.

>> **Make a 15-day organizing task list.** Each day focus on organizing a different space in your home and stick to the schedule. For example, day 1 organize the junk drawers, day 2 organize your mudroom, day 3 clean out kitchen utensils. The fun is that the tasks can switch spaces every day, making it more exciting than only organizing your kitchen for days. Switch it up.

Hold Yourself Accountable to Staying Organized

Commitment is key to staying organized and clutter-free, as is making sure that your friends and family are also aware of your goals and mindset. Here are two tips to help you hold yourself accountable:

>> **Find an accountability partner.** Hopefully, those living directly with you will help and be involved, but also look at how others can help you achieve your goals! Many people want to get more organized but often don't know where to start and would welcome the support.

>> **Plan an event or party to showcase your newly organized space.** It is amazing what happens when the pressure is on! Let friends know you're having a party to showcase your newly organized closet, and see how motivated you become to get it done.

Be Kind to Your Items

After you've finished decluttering everything that doesn't serve a purpose, the least you can do for your remaining items is treat them with the utmost respect. Organize not only for efficiency but also for the value you see in the stuff you keep in your spaces.

Giving your stuff a spot in your precious real estate of your home, office, or mind should be a privilege. Make sure your stuff has the proper shelves, boxes, and protection and display it when possible.

After decluttering, what you keep needs to be front and center in your space because it likely (hopefully) serves an important purpose.

Focus Your Attention on Organizing Traps

In Chapter 2, I bring up the most common clutter traps that we often forget about. I reiterate them in the following sections because these are often the most disorganized spaces in our homes.

Entryways and mudrooms

These areas can be major clutter traps that we always seem to forget about. The entryway is usually the spot where we enter the house and then typically leave items without giving them a proper home. It's an easy place to also stow-and-go when you're in a hurry and racing to the next meeting or appointment. The key to keeping your entryway and mudrooms clutter-free is to ensure that everything and everyone has a designated space. By "everyone," I don't mean you have to physically have a place for a human to reside but a spot for each person's essential entryway stuff, such as hooks for backpacks and jackets, dishes for keys, bins for hats, and so on. It's important to determine what is needed and then create specific spots for those items.

Paper

Manage your paper trails because they can often become one of the biggest clutter traps!

If you do not use digital organization and do have lots of paper, make sure you have some kind of drawer or basket to put it in. Then when you're ready, deal with it swiftly.

Get rid of flyers and junk mail first and fast. Tear out pieces of things you want to read or catalog items if you need them to avoid keeping what you don't need. Bills, time-sensitive things, correspondence, invitations, and so forth should be dealt with and then immediately discarded. Take a photo of the invite or add dates to your calendar if you want to get seriously organized. I try to focus on the bills first because you usually want to maintain good relationships with the folks who send these, and you want your services to continue, such as electricity.

When you're done sorting and dealing with the important items, you can move on to the leisure catalogs and items you put aside. Keep in mind that the more catalogs you get, the more stuff you want to get. Same goes for certain types of magazines that are known to make us want to consume the newest gadgets and trends. Alas, I enjoy reading about my passions just as much as you do; just be aware of the potential clutter they can tempt you to buy.

Junk drawers

You probably know by now that I don't believe in junk drawers. I believe in what I call an "essentials drawer" for the items that you really need. But simply calling it a junk drawer is something I don't agree with because then you are more likely to fill it with junk. Get rid of your junk drawer once and for all.

Anything that can't close

If your closet drawer is too full and it can't close, this is a pretty clear sign that it is a clutter trap and you need to deal with it. If you can't close your desk drawer because it is overflowing, then declutter and reorganize it.

Boxes that aren't see-through

It's important to label any boxes that are not see-through. I love see-through boxes because you can see exactly what is inside them, minimizing the potential for clutter to build up. Labels are the next best thing if you have a bunch of boxes and need to know what is inside.

Anything behind closed doors

Not only is a door you can't close a problem, but anything you keep hidden behind even doors that do close properly is probably clutter.

There is also unnecessary memory clutter. I can't stress this enough in this book, but your home is not a museum, and therefore it is not meant to display or house everything that once created a memory for you. I talk a bit about the sentimental saver in Chapter 1 and more on this in Chapter 11. Some people even keep something they don't like or use because someone gave it to them, making them feel guilty to let it go because it cost so much or is rare. However, it's completely useless taking up valuable real estate in your home. And if something really is valuable, then you can donate or sell it and make someone else happy!

Items from your life are sometimes hard to part with, while others don't have value. The key card from the first vacation with your husband has no meaning to anyone else. But the rule of thumb should be that if it serves no purpose, it has to go.

Don't Accumulate in the Future

My hope is that after decluttering and reading this book, you will want to be more careful about the clutter that you could be letting back into your life. I love organizing, but I never want to organize anything that should not be in my space in the first place, so I really try to stick to these tips that I mention in the very first chapter:

» **Schedule shopping trips.** This helps you avoid overbuying.

» **Know what you have.** You should be able to keep some sort of inventory of items that you know always end up being clutter. A list, app, or photos can help with your inventory tracking.

» **Envision the rewards of not only how much time you will save in your space, but also how much better you will feel with the carefully selected items that remain.** A clear space leads to a clear mind!

Index

Numbers

A

B

K

Keeper website, 223

kids. *See* children

Kids Labels websites, 161

Kijji, 274

kitchen. *See also* linens

  analyzing needs in, 110–114

  basic tips in, 106–107

  cooking utensils in, 114–116

  daily decluttering of, 105–106

  dishes and cutlery in, 117–121

  evaluating space in, 107–109

  excess items in, 106

  junk drawers in, 122–124

  pantries, 121–122

  taking inventory in, 110–114

knowledge clutter

  definition of, 17

  sharing and, 17

  sources, 15, 16

  stress from, 27–29

Knowledge Clutterbug, 281

L

labeling

  apps for, 268

  bags, 164

  boxes for donating, 273

  with computers, 264–265

  dangerous items, 269–270

  decluttering boxes, 54–55, 79–80

  documents, 205

  engraving, 266–267

  food items, 269

  handwritten, 266, 267

  importance of, 49–50

  items with personal information, 270

  jewelry, 269

  of linens, 138

  making labels, 262–263

  money, 269

  organizing by, 160–161

  overview of, 261–262

  with photos, 268

  pre-written, 267

  of sentimental box, 12

  storage containers, 267

  teaching kids to, 161

  tools in garage, 175

  updating existing labels, 261

  websites for, 161

landscaping, outsourcing, 179

LastPass website, 223

laundry. *See also* linens

  categorizing items related to, 141–143

  clutter from, 126, 129

  conservation and, 147

  detergent, 144

  organizing area for, 141

  schedule for, 102, 147

  space-saving tips for, 145–147

  time-saving tips for, 144–145

lawn equipment, 179

libraries, 157

life goals

  achieving, 9

  decluttering and, 37–38

lifestyle

  adapting system of organizing to, 280–281

  evaluating, 38–41

  goals, 38–41

  items reflecting, 164

  mindset, 26–27

  prioritizing items based on, 280

linens

  determining needs for, 136–137

  donating, 140–141

  folding, 139–140

  minimal amount of, 131

  organizing, 138–139

  sleep and, 135

lists, 58–59, 60, 63

lockers, 170

lost items

  new purchases to replace, 24

  wasted time and, 9, 58

LUX Luxury Shops website, 275

LXR and Co website, 275

M

Mabel's Labels website, 161, 267
magazines, 198–199
magnetic strips, 172
makeup, 182
manuals, 217
mapping process
  to find blockages, 41–42, 43
  to find improvements, 43
  simplicity in, 42
marketing tactics, 151–152
media
  detoxing from, 29
  information overload from, 28–29
  negative, avoiding, 29
medicine cabinet, 92–93, 97, 116
memory sticks, 222
mental clutter
  affecting productivity, 255
  attending to, 2
  definition of, 1, 27–28
  digital devices and, 227
  freelancing and, 254
  health impacted by, 255
  from sentimental items, 11, 12
  social media and, 236
metals, repurposing, 278
mindset
  benefits of generous, 161–162
  clutter style reveals, 19
  determining, 37–44
  on donating, 154
  on email, 233–234
  focus, 54
  of kids, changing
    consumerism, 152–153
    decluttering as priority, 156
    donating, 156–157
    future benefits, 161–162
    generosity, 157
    hand-me-downs, 158–159
    making decluttering fun, 154–155
    overview of, 152
    recycling, 154
    repurposing items, 157–158
    setting example, 153–154
    sustainability, 162
  on organizing, 280
  on printing, 219
  proactive versus reactive, 52
  when decluttering, 22
minimalism
  in bedroom, 126–127, 131
  benefits of, 23
  committing to, 4, 10
  definition of, 23
  with laundry, 102, 147
  with linens, 131, 136–137
  time management and, 23
money, labeling, 269
mops, 143
motorcycles, 177–178
motorized equipment,
    176–179
movies, 33
mudrooms, 48, 147–149
multitasking, 27–28
music, 33, 64, 228
muting, in social media, 237

N

National Geographic, 16
NEAT app, 225, 226
Netflix, 54
90-day plan, 38–39
notifications, 239

O

Obsessive-Compulsive Disorder (OCD), 10
office space
  calendars and, 210–212
  digital, 212
  files in, 204–208
  freelance lifestyle and, 254
  overview of, 203–204
  sentimental items in, 205
  shared, 212–213
  supplies for, 208–209

retail therapy. *See also* shopping; unnecessary purchases
  avoiding, 41, 60–64, 70
  impulse buying in, 21, 22
  low self-esteem and, 19
reward system, 14–15, 70
routines. *See* habits; processes

S

safety
  with beauty products, 94–96
  with floors, 147
  with food, 25, 107–108
  with medication, 92–93, 97, 116
  with sensitive information, 16
safety equipment, 185
Salvation Army, 272
sand toys, 179
scanning
  apps for, 220
  overview of, 218–219
scarcity mentality
  defeating, 57–58
  examples of, 12–13, 14, 17, 18
  hoarding and, 17–18, 19
scarves, 84–85
seasonal items
  clothing, cleaning, 166
  in garages, 166–168
  selling, 165
  storing, 165, 168
self-esteem, 19
self-sabotage, 11
selling, 79
  by consignment, 274–276
  decluttering and, 274–276
  vs. donating, 258
  seasonal items, 165
sentimental items
  accumulating, 11–12
  dealing with, 12, 18, 19, 57
  disposing of, 190
  evaluating, 282
  finding location for, 191–192
  for kids, 161
  limiting, 12

  in office space, 205
  parting with, 190–191
  practical versus, 44–45
  repurposing, 282
  selecting, 189–190
  storage box for, 11–12
  in storage spaces, 189–192
7 Habits of Highly Effective People (Covey), 52
sharing, 17, 20
  documents, 220, 222
  email address, 232
  office space, 212–213
shelves, 76, 77–78
shoe organizers, 172
shopping. *See also* retail therapy; unnecessary purchases
  analyzing needs when, 41, 64, 70, 99–100
  bathroom clutter and, 89–90
  for furniture, 130–131
  online, 61–62
  payment methods and, 62–63
  research before, 61–62
  scheduled, 60, 61, 62
  Snupps app for, 58–60
  as therapy, 10, 14–15
  unnecessary, 60–64
shower curtains, 103
shredding paper, 217
Skype, 33
sleep
  bedside tables and, 126–127
  electronic items and, 129–130
  importance of, 133
  linens and, 135
Sleep Revolution, The (Huffington), 133
slides, 242–243
small spaces, 77
small tools, 182
snacks, 182
snow equipment, 176–178
Snupps app, 58–59, 60, 75, 268
social media, 28–29, 54
  automating and outsourcing, 238–239
  blocking in, 237
  maintaining profiles, 237–238
  managing, 236–239
  mental clutter and, 236

muting in, 237

time management and, 236–237

unfollowing in, 237

someday stash, 57, 58

spam emails, 232

spoilage, 25, 107–108

sporting equipment, 169–170, 179

spring, organizing items used in, 166–167

stacking, 10, 16

Stewart, Martha, 139

storage containers. *See* boxes

storage devices, photos on, 244–248

storage facilities, 10, 25

storage spaces

books in, 193–194, 198–199

determining what to keep in, 187

electronic and audio books, 194–195

electronic items, 196–197

functional, 164

furniture, 195–196

organizing, 184–187, 287

overview of, 183–184

packing material in, 188–189

paper in, 197–199

safety in, 185

sentimental items in, 189–192

storing

bicycles, 169

in cloud and internal drives, 221–222

items in garage, 172

motorcycles, 177

passwords, 223

receipts, 225–226

seasonal items, 165, 168

toys, 159–161

stress

caused by clutter, 19, 20, 21, 25

decluttering and, 1, 14–15, 53

disorganization and, 11

effect of clutter on, 9, 10, 13

multitasking and, 27–28

reducing, 20–21

subconscious, 13–14

studio apartments, 125–126

stuffed animals, 159

style of clutter

collector, 17

determining, 1, 10–11, 18

digital, 15–17

emotional, 11–12, 45

knowledge, 15–17

scarcity mentality, 12–13

technology, 15

understanding, 18

supplies, 141–143

sustainability, 162

syncing digital files on cloud, 221

systems. *See* habits; processes

T

tablet, organizing, 240

tackle boxes, 181–182

targeted marketing, 61, 90

taxes

keeping receipts for, 224

organizing files regarding, 205–206

overview of, 217

"Techie" Clutterbug, 281

technology clutter

in bedroom, 127

examples of, 15

sleep and, 129–130, 133

textbooks, 15

ThinkNatalia website, 238

thrift stores, 272–273

time cube

to increase focus, 28, 54–55

when identifying needs, 44

when identifying trash, 46–47

time management

calendars and, 210

clutter and, 21, 32

decluttering and, 54, 255

digital devices and, 239

laundry and, 144–145

minimalism and, 23

organization and, 43

phones and, 239

social media and, 236–237

About the Author

Jane Stoller is a Swiss-Canadian life-biz organizer, speaker, author, and university instructor whose passion is in decluttering spaces and organizing business processes. Jane wrote her first book, *Organizing for Your Lifestyle,* in 2016 to help friends get more organized. It ultimately gained international attention, and this allowed Jane to turn her passion into a profitable business, Organized Jane. Stoller travels all around the world, working with individuals looking to revamp one space, large corporations needing a complete business overhaul, and entrepreneurs wanting to organize their businesses to gain more time, money, and freedom.

"My goal is not to turn someone's home into a magazine-perfect image; it is not sustainable," says Stoller. "I work around a client's specific lifestyle, or an aspect of their life they want to focus on, and develop a custom organization system from there. The end result? Reduced stress, increased productivity, and happiness."

When Stoller sets down her pen and paper, she puts on her teaching hat. Stoller lectures at Vancouver Island University in Canada for part of the year, helping students learn management skills.

Prior to launching her organizing business, Stoller worked for the largest cement company in the world, which allowed her to live all over Canada and Europe. Jane had an invaluable experience, but she decided to make a nerve-wracking jump to entrepreneurship after realizing she wanted to live life to its fullest and follow her passion for organizing.

Stoller is passionate about sharing her knowledge through her various social media platforms, books, international speaking events, teaching, and business coaching.

In her spare time, Stoller enjoys spending time with family, and staying active via skiing as she currently resides in Whistler, British Columbia, Canada, and has a secondary home in Exuma, Bahamas.

Dedication

I dedicate this book to my family. My parents who have been a constant support and have watched my organizing and decluttering habits starting with when I would organize my pet cats, stuffed animals, and children's books. My parents have dealt with my organizing demands and inspiration and continue to this day. I also dedicate this book to the Handleys, who provided the needed research about what decluttering means for busy families with kids. Because I didn't have kids when writing this book, it was important I provided real content and advice. I could not have written this book without their support.

Author's Acknowledgments

Special thanks to my team, including Charlotte Silverstein, for providing consistent and excellent public relations support and helping me market my business and this book! Thank you to Riley Webster for being my cheerleader when writing this book and keeping me on track with my business content, especially when I was busy writing. Thank you for also being part of the Dummies team as a technical editor. No one knows my organizing tips and process as much as Riley, as she is now truly an expert on the topic. Thank you to Miranda for keeping my brand graphically on track and for being the genius behind my branding strategy. As well, thank you to everyone who follows and engages with me on all my social platforms, especially Instagram and YouTube. I work hard every day to add value for my followers in hopes of providing inspiration to get and stay more decluttered and organized.

Publisher's Acknowledgments

Executive Editor: Steven Hayes

Editorial Project Manager and Development Editor: Christina N. Guthrie

Copy Editor: Christine Pingleton

Technical Editor: Riley Webster

Production Editor: Siddique Shaik

Cover Photos: © Hero Images/Getty Images

PERSONAL ENRICHMENT

Staying Sharp
9781119187790
USA $26.00
CAN $31.99
UK £19.99

Facebook
9781119179030
USA $21.99
CAN $25.99
UK £16.99

Guitar
9781119293354
USA $24.99
CAN $29.99
UK £17.99

Investing
9781119293347
USA $22.99
CAN $27.99
UK £16.99

Beekeeping
9781119310068
USA $22.99
CAN $27.99
UK £16.99

Digital Photography
9781119235606
USA $24.99
CAN $29.99
UK £17.99

Meditation
9781119251163
USA $24.99
CAN $29.99
UK £17.99

Pregnancy
9781119235491
USA $26.99
CAN $31.99
UK £19.99

Samsung Galaxy S7
9781119279952
USA $24.99
CAN $29.99
UK £17.99

iPhone
9781119283133
USA $24.99
CAN $29.99
UK £17.99

Crocheting
9781119287117
USA $24.99
CAN $29.99
UK £16.99

Nutrition
9781119130246
USA $22.99
CAN $27.99
UK £16.99

PROFESSIONAL DEVELOPMENT

Windows 10
9781119311041
USA $24.99
CAN $29.99
UK £17.99

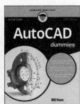
AutoCAD
9781119255796
USA $39.99
CAN $47.99
UK £27.99

Excel 2016
9781119293439
USA $26.99
CAN $31.99
UK £19.99

QuickBooks 2017
9781119281467
USA $26.99
CAN $31.99
UK £19.99

macOS Sierra
9781119280651
USA $29.99
CAN $35.99
UK £21.99

LinkedIn
9781119251132
USA $24.99
CAN $29.99
UK £17.99

Windows 10
9781119310563
USA $34.00
CAN $41.99
UK £24.99

SharePoint 2016
9781119181705
USA $29.99
CAN $35.99
UK £21.99

Fundamental Analysis
9781119263593
USA $26.99
CAN $31.99
UK £19.99

Networking
9781119257769
USA $29.99
CAN $35.99
UK £21.99

Office 2016
9781119293477
USA $26.99
CAN $31.99
UK £19.99

Office 365
9781119265313
USA $24.99
CAN $29.99
UK £17.99

Salesforce.com
9781119239314
USA $29.99
CAN $35.99
UK £21.99

Coding
9781119293323
USA $29.99
CAN $35.99
UK £21.99

dummies.com

dummies®
A Wiley Brand